THE SCIENCE OF FENCING

William M. Gaugler

THE SCIENCE OF FENCING

A COMPREHENSIVE TRAINING MANUAL FOR
MASTER AND STUDENT; INCLUDING LESSON
PLANS FOR FOIL, SABRE AND ÉPÉE INSTRUCTION

WILLIAM M. GAUGLER

MAESTRO DI SCHERMA
ACCADEMIA NAZIONALE DI SCHERMA, NAPLES, ITALY
HONORARY MEMBER, ASSOCIAZIONE ITALIANA MAESTRI DI SCHERMA

A LANCE C. LOBO BOOK

LAUREATE PRESS
BANGOR, MAINE

Laureate Press – Telephone 800-946-2727

Manufactured in the United States of America.

Italian Edition – *La Scienza della Scherma: secondo la "scuola italiana"*

German Edition – *Fechten für Anfänger und Fortgeschrittene*
© 1983 by Nymphenburger Verlagshandlung
in F. A. Herbig Verlagsbuchhandlung GmbH, Munich

∞ The paper used in this book meets the minimum requirements of the American
National Standard for Information Services – Permanence of Paper for Printed
Library Materials, ANSI Z39.48-1984.

2 4 6 8 10 9 7 5 3
First Printing May 1997
Second Printing May 1999

Library of Congress Catalog Card Number: 96-80248

Library of Congress Cataloging in Publication Data
Gaugler, William M. 1931–.
   The Science of Fencing: A Comprehensive Training Manual for Master and Student;
   Including Lesson Plans for Foil, Sabre and Épée Instruction
      p. cm.
   "A Lance C. Lobo Book"
   Includes glossary and bibliographical references.
   ISBN 1-884528-05-8 (alk. paper) $24.95
1. Fencing. I. Title.
GV1147   96-80248
786.8'6—dc20   CIP

To my masters,
Amilcare Angelini
Umberto Di Paola
Aldo Nadi
Giorgio Pessina
and
Ettore Spezza

CONTENTS

PART III – THE ÉPÉE

ILLUSTRATIONS

PICTURE CREDITS

W. Gaugler: Cover and Plates I-XVI, I-9, 23-34, 56-65, 113-116, 125
B. Radde: 10-22, 35-55, 66-112, 117-124, 126-134

FOREWORD

This work of Professor Gaugler is not only a technical manual, but also an acknowledgment of a school that has survived the test of time and is still valid today.

I am therefore honored to present this book, which the author, in his love for fencing, offers to those who wish to learn a sport that is also a science and an art.

The volume reflects in itself the fact that, in spite of the evolution in methods of instruction, the basic elements of fencing are substantially immutable.

This book is directed to all those who wish to take the "courtly" weapon in hand, with the intention of arousing their enthusiasm for fencing, and to all those who desire professional guidance in learning to fence and in fencing pedagogy.

Maestro Niccolò Perno
Past President, *Associazione Italiana Maestri di Scherma*
and *Académie d'Armes Internationale*

INTRODUCTION

With German, English, and Italian editions in print, my treatise on fencing has become the most widely-read work of its kind in the world. In this
revised English, and in the Italian edition, I have amplified various observations and added sample lessons for each of the weapons. The lessons
were created by outstanding fencing masters of the past, and are included
as a guide to the instructor for the development of his own lessons.

As indicated in the preface of the earlier editions, the function of this
volume is to provide the teacher and student with a complete text on the
science of fencing. Both the method of instruction and organization of
material are based on the system of education employed at the *Scuola
Magistrale Militare di Scherma* in Rome. And since the principles governing fencing are universal, the pedagogical method described in this book
is applicable to all fencing instruction, regardless of national school, or
type of weapon grip.

Actions are presented in the exact order in which they should appear
in the lesson. Each item is numbered for easy reference, with the same
number used again in the tables that follow the section on foil.

Because foil technique forms the basis for sabre and épée instruction,
it must be taught first. I strongly recommend using the Italian foil and
épée because they are especially well suited for the development of tight
point control and sensitive touch. Crossbar and wrist strap reduce strain
on the hand, and make disarmament virtually impossible.

English fencing terminology, like German, draws heavily on foreign
words. In the German editions of this work I sought to translate as many
Italian terms into German as possible, and I have followed this same practice in the English editions, substituting English for French or Italian words.
Consequently, I employ numbers in English for the four Italian foil and
épée invitations, engagements, and parries. The few remaining Italian terms
such as *inquartata* and *passata sotto* are left in their original form since they
are used universally; the words *appuntata* and *imbroccata*, having no English equivalents, also remain in the Italian. In the case of "flanconade," I
have deliberately adopted the eighteenth-century English spelling to distinguish it from the French.

To facilitate matters, I have included the French equivalents to the
Italian numbers for invitations, engagements, and parries in the section

on invitations. The Italian system of four numbers, as opposed to the French system of eight, is by far the easier for the student to comprehend, and finds its parallel in the first four invitations, engagements, and parries in sabre.

It should be observed that the majority of Italian masters, like their French colleagues, instruct students to execute the placements of the weapon with the hand in supination, that is to say, with the palm turned upward. The Italian numbers of first, second, third, and fourth in foil and épée therefore correspond to French high *septime*, *octave*, *sixte*, and *quarte*. Positions of the weapon with the hand in pronation, or palm rotated downward, have been generally abandoned by both schools.

I have translated the Italian *circolazione* and German *kreisstoß* as "deceive." This term is an exact translation of the French *tromper*, and is commonly used in English fencing terminology to describe a circular thrust in a compound action. But the same movement is sometimes called a counter-disengagement. I prefer to reserve the term "counter-disengagement" for a circular thrust performed as a simple action in time. This is, in fact, the original meaning of the word *controcavazione* or "counter-disengagement." The seventeenth-century Venetian master, Nicoletto Giganti, for example, tells us that the counter-disengagement is employed in opposition to the adversary's disengagement.

For the reader familiar with the French system of the military masters school at Joinville-le-Pont, similarities in method between the Italian and French schools are striking. Principal differences lie in tactical approach, and may be found in the Italian predilection for actions on the blade, and emphasis on offense and counteroffense.

I have sought in this work to preserve in its entirety the pedagogical method of the Italian school. As is well known, the French, German, and Hungarian schools developed from the Italian, so that its system provides an historical basis for understanding the other three. Some of the material contained in this book has never appeared in print outside Italy, for instance, the tables of fencing actions and counteractions. These valuable instructional aids have been in use since the late nineteenth century, yet are known only to Italian professionals. Similarly, there are observations following many of the fencing actions that are now in print for the first time; these remarks, concerning the refinement of an action, or its tactical application, were passed on verbally from one generation of Italian fencing teachers to another. Such comments represent the practical advice that Maestri Carlo Pessina, Eugenio Pini, Beppe Nadi, Antonino Pomponio, Nedo Nadi, Aldo Nadi, Giorgio Pessina, and Umberto Di Paola offered their students during the course of the lesson.

While my text follows essentially the pedagogical method of the southern Italian school, that is to say, the *Scuola Magistrale Militare di Scherma*, which was founded in 1884 by the Neapolitan master, Masaniello Parise, I have for logical and practical reasons introduced some elements from the northern and central Italian schools. For example, to avoid ambiguity I define a simple attack as an offensive action consisting of a single blade movement, rather than an offensive action not intended to elude a parry. The straight thrust, disengagement, and glide are classified as simple attacks because they are executed with one blade motion; but the simple beat and straight thrust is grouped with the compound attacks because it requires two blade movements.

Like the nineteenth-century Florentine master, Ferdinando Masiello, I direct the glide in first to the inside low line, and the glide in fourth to the inside high line. The transport from first to third and glide, and the flanconade in fourth are, naturally, still in the repertoire of actions; the first can be found among the actions on the blade, and the second, under the simple attacks.

I also include in my lessons compound attacks consisting of triple feints. Parise states in his text that such actions are especially susceptible to the arrest. His caution is, of course, perfectly justified, since even one feint can expose the attacker to the arrest. But as a pedagogical device, exercises with triple feints can be useful. Eugenio Pini and Aldo Nadi – both of whom were duelists – employed triple feints to develop point control. One would have had to see Aldo Nadi fencing to appreciate fully the degree of precision he attained with triple feints: his sword arm was extended and immobile; blade movement was controlled by the fingers alone, and the point of the weapon penetrated steadily forward in tiny, geometrically-perfect half-circular motions.

It is to the cumulative knowledge of more than four hundred years of fencing experience that the Italian school owes its success. From the time of Achille Marozzo's publication *Opera nova* (1536) to the present, the technical approach of the Italian school has remained substantially unchanged. All fencing actions in use today were already known by the end of the sixteenth century and are mentioned in the works of Salvator Fabris (1606), Nicoletto Giganti (1606), and Ridolfo Capo Ferro (1610); the only contributions since that time have been in the area of pedagogy. Teaching method has been refined, and the materials of fencing reorganized periodically to simplify instruction. In our own century the most telling proof of the efficiency of the Italian pedagogical system is the many gold medals that Italian fencers have won in the World Championships and Olympic Games. The outstanding example is Nedo Nadi who received five gold medals in the Olympic Games at Antwerp in 1920. Ten years after his Olympic victories, at the age of thirty-six, he won the Professional Épée Championship of the World, and the following year, in a sabre match that received world-wide attention, he defeated the current European and future Olympic Sabre Champion, György Piller, 16 to 12.

Nedo Nadi's brother, Aldo, in his treatise, *On Fencing*, (Laureate Press, 1994), noted that Nedo's principal mode of attack in foil, especially in his earlier years, was the simple beat in fourth and straight thrust with a jump lunge. Aldo Nadi writes:

> [Nedo's] defense was confined almost entirely to the double counter-of-quarte.... Once he had started the first counter, his blade went on spinning with tremendous rapidity and power until the incoming attack was smashed. If necessary, he made three or four counters in succession, and any adversary who tried to catch up with them was only sealing his own doom. For as soon as his blade was found, the riposte followed with lightning speed.... He hardly ever broke the line, and seldom made a counter-of-sixte.

Aldo Nadi, describing his own tactical approach, in his book, *The Living Sword: A Fencer's Autobiography* (Laureate Press, 1995), comments:

> Above all, I tried to rely to the maximum upon exploitation of all my opponent's mistakes.... I deliberately avoided each of my opponents' weaknesses, trying to score, instead, in the lines best protected, against and through their favorite, most effective parries. Furthermore, I insisted on launching my attacks as far from the target as feasible....

At the time of his retirement from competitive fencing, Aldo Nadi had been unbeaten for a decade in all three weapons, and had defeated the strongest fencers of his generation, including fourteen French champions.

Unlike most trainers of athletes, the fencing master – even in his later years – is capable of performing technical feats at a level equal to his best pupil; in other words, despite advancing age, timing, control of fencing measure, and precision and speed of the hand remain intact. For this reason it is not unusual to see fencing teachers in their seventies and eighties still engaged in preparing world-class competitors. The longevity of fencers is, in fact, proverbial: Agesilao Greco, whose competitive career began in Florence in 1887, was still active in 1934 when he demonstrated his overwhelming superiority in a sabre match in Rome with the Hungarian champion, Endre Kabos, a man some forty years his junior.

Interesting, too, is the fact that Luigi Barbasetti, Carlo Pessina, Agesilao Greco, Nedo and Aldo Nadi, Oreste Puliti, Gustavo Marzi, Ugo Pignotti, Giulio Gaudini, Renzo Nostini, Edoardo Mangiarotti, and Antonio Spallino all were skilled in the use of more than one weapon. Such versatility can be explained by the fact that the classical Italian school stresses the technical and tactical elements common to the three arms. This makes the transfer from one weapon to the other relatively simple. By adding cutting actions to the point thrusts in foil, sabre technique is developed; and by including the advanced target and emphasizing renewed attacks and counterattacks, épée technique is created.

Through correct application of theory, the experienced fencer is able to oppose each of his adversary's actions with its appropriate counteraction or contrary. There is neither a secret thrust nor a universal parry. Every attack can be parried, and every parry can be eluded with an attack; for example, the feint direct and disengagement may be countered with two simple parries, and two simple parries can be eluded with the double feint direct and disengagement; the disengagement in time may be opposed with the parry and riposte in countertime, and the parry and riposte in countertime can be countered with the feint in time.

It is the proper use of counteractions that leads to success on the competitive fencing strip. Whether or not an opponent is orthodox or unorthodox, or has some knowledge or no knowledge of fencing theory, is immaterial, every one of his offensive, defensive, and counteroffensive actions can be met with a countermovement.

At what age should fencing instruction begin? In my opinion, ideally between the ages of ten and twelve. At that stage of development the young person is sufficiently mature, both mentally and physically, to undergo the rigorous discipline serious fencing requires. There is no upper age limit for learning to fence, but the prerequisites are good health and a long history of uninterrupted physical exercise.

I have deliberately omitted discussion of electrical fencing because it is subject to constant technological change. In any case, a trained swordsman can always modify his method of fencing to suit the kind of weapon he has in hand. Beppe Nadi once remarked that a skilled fencer should be able to fence with even a broomstick.

Only after the student has acquired a sound foundation in foil technique should he be permitted to begin sabre lessons. As a rule, foil preparation alone necessitates a minimum of two to three years of intense work, while the fundamentals of sabre generally require an additional year or two of study.

We know that the prototype for the sabre existed in Europe already in classical antiquity; for instance, representations of an edged weapon with a curved blade and ornamental elements forming a partial knuckle guard appear in the late Etruscan tomb of the Volumni near Perugia. During the Middle Ages varieties of broadswords, designed principally for cutting, were employed throughout Europe. But by the sixteenth and seventeenth centuries the rapier replaced the broadsword as a side arm, and emphasis shifted to use of the point rather than the cut. However, mounted troops still required a cutting weapon, and the sabre, based on eastern models, filled this need. It was then that the Germans developed a system of sabre play for a practice cutting arm known as the *dusack*. In some other European countries, including England, single-stick fencing became a popular form of mock sabre play. In its most sophisticated form, this kind of practice sabre fencing consisted of circular blows or cuts, as well as parries corresponding to modern sabre first, second, third, fourth, and fifth.

But the development of modern sabre play, with a light, narrow-bladed weapon, can be traced to the nineteenth-century Milanese fencing master, Giuseppe Radaelli. In 1869, after distinguished military service and a successful career as a fencing master, Radaelli was officially appointed director of the newly-created *Scuola Magistrale Militare di Scherma* at Milan. He remained in charge of this institution until his death in 1882. Numbered among his disciples were some of the most illustrious teachers of the next generation, such as Luigi Barbasetti, Salvatore Pecoraro, and Carlo Pessina.

In the opening pages of his book, *Istruzione per la scherma di sciabola e di spada* (1876), Radaelli states that the fundamental principle of his sabre technique is that the arm should be held in a firm and balanced manner, with principal movement effected by the forearm, so that cuts and parries can be dextrous and rapid, and the cutting edge properly directed. In his discussion of exercises with circular cuts he observes:

> The articulation of the elbow must be the principal pivot for the rotational movement of the arm and sabre in every circular cut. The body must always assist the movement of the steel to acquire the necessary elasticity and to learn to stretch forward, direct, fix the cut, and withdraw on guard with maximum balance and ease.

The question of where movement should be centered in the execution of a cut was, however, already raised centuries earlier. Salvator Fabris, in his publication, *Sienza [sic] e pratica d'arme* (1606), states that there are three ways to deliver a cut, the first is from the shoulder, the second, from the elbow, and the third, from the wrist. Of these, he prefers the third, that is, from the wrist, since this results in the tightest and most rapid cutting action, and provides the best protection during its execution. But Fabris was speaking of the rapier. Like many of his contemporaries, he preferred the point to the cut, for he writes: "…in all respects… wounding with the point is the more advantageous, and also the more mortal, [for] with the… point one wounds from greater distance, and with more speed.…" Radaelli, on the other hand, was concerned exclusively with military use of the sabre; there, the cut played a principal role. As a teacher of mounted troops he sought to develop a sabre technique that would result in precise, rapid, and damaging actions. He probably reasoned that blows delivered from the wrist lacked the force necessary to inflict serious injury on the enemy.

In 1882 the Italian Ministry of War, prompted by political pressure from southern Italian fencing masters, announced a national competition for the selection of a single textbook to be used by all military fencing teachers and their students. Underlying the matter was a long-standing rivalry between northern and southern Italian fencing masters. The nationalism and anti-foreign sentiments fostered by the unification of Italy provided a pretext for the attack: the southerners, as custodians of a "pure" Italian system of swordplay, accused their northern antagonists of teaching a method of foil fencing that was corrupted by foreign influence. They singled out for condemnation the pedagogical systems of Alberto Marchionni, Luigi Zangheri, Cesare Enrichetti, and Giuseppe Radaelli.

Among the treatises submitted to the commission charged with selecting a text was Radaelli's volume, which originally had been written by order of the Ministry of War. After lengthy deliberation, the commission members decided that the choice lay between two works, Radaelli's manual and a manuscript written by the young Neapolitan master, Masaniello Parise. It should be noted that at the time of the competition, Parise was aide to the Director of the *Accademia Nazionale di Scherma di Napoli*, *Maestro di Sala* of the *Accademia*, and *Primo Maestro* of the *Società di Scherma Napolitana*; in other words, he was a leading exponent of the southern school, and, as such, was an enemy of the Radaellians.

During the comparison of the texts, Parise's supporters on the commission attacked the Radaellian foil and sabre systems mercilessly. In sabre they condemned the use of the elbow, and accused the Radaellians of gripping the weapon with too much strength, delivering cuts with the force of a hammer, and encouraging use of the counterattack instead of the parry riposte. This last criticism was a direct reference to Radaelli's well-known dictum that the parry does not exist *(la parata non esiste)*.

What he meant, of course, was that if the attack is properly executed, it cannot be parried.

After the votes were counted, Parise was declared winner of the competition, and arrangements were made to publish his treatise at state expense. In addition, he was named head of the new *Scuola Magistrale Militare di Scherma* which was to be located in Rome. The Radaellian military fencing school at Milan was closed, and all military fencing masters were ordered to report to the new school in Rome for instruction by Parise. The bitterness this caused is clearly evident in publications such as Ferdinando Masiello's, *La scherma italiana di spada e di sciabola* (1887). He observes angrily that the only thing accomplished by the competition was that it united the graduates of the Enrichetti-Radaelli school, and placed upon them the obligation to reaffirm practically and scientifically the excellence of their system; and he concluded that there was no possibility of a reconciliation between the Radaellians and the false southern school (*falsa scuola meridionale*).

But despite the outrage among the Radaellians there was posthumous vindication for the Milanese master: Parise's earliest assistants, and his successors as directors of the *Scuola Magistrale Militare di Scherma* after his untimely death in 1910, were two of Radaelli's disciples, Salvatore Pecoraro and Carlo Pessina. In fact, the very year of Parise's death Pecoraro and Pessina published their sabre treatise, *La scherma di sciabola*, which became the new, official text for sabre instruction at the *Scuola Magistrale Militare di Scherma*, and it was purely Radaellian. For example, the authors observe that the aim of the exercises with circular cuts is to help the student acquire looseness and elasticity in handling the sabre, and to teach him to grip it in a firm and balanced manner so that he can direct the cutting edge of the blade with precision, and strike with force and speed. Moreover, they state that in the execution of circular cuts, the elbow must serve as the center of rotation, with minimal help from the wrist. And they add that the movement of the steel should be reinforced by a forward inclination of the body.

Luigi Barbasetti, a follower of Radaelli, also taught at the *Scuola Magistrale Militare di Scherma* in Rome. In his treatise, *The Art of the Sabre and the Épée* (1936), he says of the circular cut: "This movement must be executed by the forearm, using the elbow as a pivot. There should be as little bending as possible of the wrist." In 1894 Barbasetti left Italy to establish his own fencing academy in Vienna, where his pedagogical skill soon led to his appointment as fencing master of the Austro-Hungarian Military School at Wiener-Neustadt. Moreover, in 1896 Italo Santelli, a graduate of the *Scuola Magistrale Militare di Scherma* at Rome, and Carlo

Pessina's prize pupil, was invited to teach in Budapest. With Barbasetti in Austria, and Santelli in Hungary, the Italian influence became paramount in the Austro-Hungarian Empire. Indeed, in Hungary elements of the Radaellian sabre method persisted well into the second half of the twentieth century. István Lukovich, for instance, in his book, Vívás (1975), writes: "Although the sabre as practiced today does not move only from the elbow, this joint maintains a central role in manipulating the blade, acting much like a control tower."

Finally, it should be noted that Giorgio Pessina and Ugo Pignotti in La sciabola (1972), the most recently published Italian textbook on sabre instruction, still recommend that circular cuts be based on the articulation of the elbow, with slight assistance from the wrist.

The English term "épée" is derived from the French word for sword. In the sixteenth century the French wrote éspée, which was close to its Italian and Spanish cousins, spada and espada. Although originally generic, the term éspée came to mean specifically the rapier, that is, the slender-bladed weapon used during the sixteenth and seventeenth centuries for both thrusting and cutting. The more progressive fencing masters of those time periods, however, tended to place primary emphasis on the thrust. For example, Giacomo di Grassi in his book, Ragione di addoprar sicuramente l'arme si da offesa, come da difesa (1570), observes: "Without a doubt, the point must be preferred to the cut, for it wounds in less time, and in wounding in less time, does greater damage."

In fencing schools, practice swords were in common use. Surviving examples resemble a rapier with a heavy foil-like blade. Camillo Palladini in his manuscript, Discorso sopra l'arte della scherma (written after 1553), speaks of the spada da gioco, Angelo Viggiani in his treatise, Lo schermo (1575), mentions real swords, spade da filo, and practice swords, spade da marra, and Shakespeare in his play, Hamlet (Act V, Sc. II, 265-80), uses the word "foils." By the late seventeenth century Francesco Marcelli in his book, Regole della scherma (1686), speaks of both the practice rapier or smarra and the foil or fioretto. And in the following two centuries the term smarra was used for the heavy foil employed by the student in the lesson, while the fioretto was the light foil he used in the assault. We know also that the fencing master employed only the light foil while giving lessons in order to reduce hand fatigue.

Fencing exercise during the early nineteenth century was conducted in the sala di scherma, or fencing room, with foils only; the dueling sword was not permitted in the academy. This naturally created a gap between what one learned in school and what was needed on the terrain. But the distance between fencing practice in the *sala di scherma* and swordplay on the dueling ground was, nonetheless, never very great in Italy. In France, however, there was a marked difference between the academic approach to fencing in the schools and swordplay with dueling weapons on the terrain; and for this reason some fencing masters allowed the dueling sword or épée to be brought into the *salle d'armes* for exercise. But the more conservative French teachers condemned such a practice, declaring that the introduction of the épée into the *salle d'armes* was the prostitution of fencing.

And when French fencers, trained in the academic manner, first confronted Italian adversaries, during the final years of the nineteenth century, they found themselves at a disadvantage because the Italian method of swordplay was still deeply rooted in dueling practice. Parise, in the fifth edition of his treatise (1904), added a section on the épée. In this he quotes the French master, Charles Laurent, as reporting to the *Société d'Encouragement de l'Escrime:*

> In the *salle* or on the terrain, the Italian fencer is served by an identical arm, the handle and the guard are the same, only the blade is a little stronger on the dueling sword. Habituated to handling the same weapon which has served him in the same fashion, the Italian fencer has nothing other to do on the terrain than that which he has learned to do in the *salle d'armes.*

Parise also quotes Maurice Maindron who writes:

> The modern Neapolitan system of fencing is based on the old principles of fencing with the long rapier, but it proscribes all useless movement of the body, in the same way as parries with the left hand. In summary, it is simpler than the French system, and though less brilliant in foil play, it is perhaps best suited to the épée.

Parise's addition of the épée to his work on foil and sabre is followed by Italian publications dedicated exclusively to épée instruction. The earliest of these are Aurelio Greco's *La spada e la sua applicazione* (1907), and Agesilao Greco's *La spada e la sua disciplina d'arte* (1912). The Greco brothers were, in fact, Italy's earliest and greatest exponents of épée fencing. Agesilao, the older of the two, was trained by Parise, and a graduate of the *Scuola Magistrale Militare di Scherma*; he, in turn, taught his younger brother, Aurelio. In a benefit program for the ailing French master, Alphonse Kirschoffer, held at the Nouveau Cirque in Paris on 12 January 1911 be-

fore a crowd of eight thousand spectators, Agesilao Greco, in the principal encounter of the evening, soundly defeated the French épée champion Jean Joseph-Renaud, scoring with attacks repeatedly to the chest,
and terminating the assault with a riposte in countertime to the chest.

In the introduction to his book, Aurelio Greco observes that there
are significant differences between foil and épée fencing. He says that foil
play is entirely conventional, with a limited target. Foil fencing, he continues, consists of complicated actions, which are possible only with that
weapon. Moreover, mastery of these actions requires long study. In contrast, he remarks, épée play excludes all that is superfluous, inefficacious,
and not absolutely essential for a practical result. The principle of épée
fencing, he notes, is simple: to touch and not be touched. And he con-
cludes that while some foil actions are possible in épée fencing, the épée
fencer should, for the most part, direct his thrusts to the arm and face, so
that he can take his opponent out of combat, and eliminate the risk of a
double hit.

Now, the Italian dueling sword of the late nineteenth century did not
provide sufficient protection for the armed hand, especially for the back
of the hand; in appearance, it was simply another version of the so-called
Neapolitan foil. To improve the weapon the Greco brothers designed an
épée with a large, offset bell guard that shielded the entire hand, and with
a crossbar that extended inside the bell guard from one side to the other.
This new dueling sword became the modern Italian épée.

Despite the success in competition of Agesilao and Aurelio Greco,
the épée continued to be regarded with distrust by many Italian fencing
masters. Beppe Nadi, for instance, threatened to boot out of his academy
in Livorno anyone who entered with an épée in hand, yet his sons, Nedo
and Aldo, were two of the strongest épée fencers of their generation. For
Beppe, Nedo, and Aldo the foil was the queen of arms. Still, Nedo, at the
age of fifteen, having practiced épée in secret, won the Franz-Josef Trophy
at Vienna in a tournament that attracted many of the finest épée fencers
of the time. When his father learned of Nedo's triumph, he announced
proudly that his son's victory simply confirmed what he had always be-
lieved, that a skillful foil fencer could pick up an épée and use it effectively against any épée specialist. Later, in the Olympic Games of 1920,
Nedo, and his younger brother, Aldo, led the Italian team to victory in
the épée event. Between 1925 and his retirement from competitive fencing in 1935, Aldo defeated every world-class épée fencer who dared chal-
lenge him, while his brother, Nedo, in 1930, won the Professional Épée
Championship of the World with the remarkable record in the final of
nine victories, no defeats, and having received only five hits.

Aldo Nadi once remarked that any well-trained foilsman could easily and quickly be transformed into an effective épée fencer. Naturally, he meant that with a foundation in foil it was relatively simple to make the necessary modifications in target area, fencing time, and choice of actions to score with the triangular arm. For him the épée lesson was in essence an improvisation on the foil lesson. The order of actions within the framework of the lesson was similar, but emphasis differed, and the range of fencing actions was more restricted.

Although Maestro Nadi intended to write companion volumes on sabre and épée to his book on foil, teaching responsibilities and, ultimately, death prevented him from accomplishing this. It is therefore my hope that in the present work I have not only provided the reader with an accurate and complete description of the pedagogical method of the *Scuola Magistrale Militare di Scherma*, but that I have also managed to preserve in my text certain of the key elements of Maestro Nadi's sabre and épée instruction.

For the purpose of identity, the fencers in many of the illustrations for this book posed without masks; but it is imperative that a mask, as well as protective equipment for the entire body, always be worn during the lesson and free fencing.

Fencing is a sport in which both sexes can participate on equal footing because success depends on skill rather than physical strength. In the past, women fenced foil exclusively, but in recent years they have shown an increasing interest in sabre and épée as well. Since Italian sabre technique and épée technique closely resemble foil technique, they are ideally suited for fencers already trained in foil, as is commonly the case with women fencers. The simplicity, precision, efficiency, and elegance of the Italian system should make it especially appealing to foil teachers engaging in sabre and épée instruction for the first time. For the sake of brevity, and not through discourtesy, I have written "he" throughout the text, instead of "he or she," which is, when repeated frequently, a burdensome locution.

Before concluding, I should like to take this opportunity to thank Master at Arms Ralph Sahm and Mr. Neil Honeychurch for posing in the illustrations, Prof. Bruce Radde for his assistance with the photography, Mr. Wolf Dieffenbach and Dr. Franco Luxardo for their critical examination of the text and helpful suggestions, and Maestri Umberto Di Paola, Niccolò Perno, Enzo Musumeci Greco, Pierre Lacaze, Ing. Renzo Nostini, and my publisher, Mr. Lance Lobo, for their encouragement and support.

PRELIMINARY MATTERS

SELECTING A TEACHER

Although a book such as this is an important aid to fencing instruction, it is no substitute for a fencing master. He is absolutely essential, since, in the course of the lesson, he takes the place of the adversary. In this respect he is unique among teachers or coaches of athletes, who generally give instruction from the sidelines, for he is an active participant, whose timing, speed, control of fencing measure, precision of blade work, and tactical knowledge must exceed that of his most accomplished student.

Now, while there are many dedicated amateurs teaching fencing in this country, there are, in fact, few certified professionals; therefore, the pupil who intends to go beyond recreational fencing must be extremely selective in finding a master. There are questions to be asked, and observations to be made.

How much formal education in fencing pedagogy does the teacher have? Where did he acquire his diploma? Is he a master, provost, or instructor? Are any of his students nationally ranked?

Does the teacher stress the importance of fencing safety? Does he begin fencing instruction with the foil? Are his initial lessons devoted to developing a sound guard position and an efficient lunge? In the guard position does he insist on keeping the left arm elevated, elbow a little higher than the shoulder? And in the lunge does he demand full extension of the sword arm before moving the right foot, and a completely straightened left leg, knee locked, with the left foot pressed flat against the floor?

Do the master's lessons move progressively from simple to complex actions? Are his first two offensive movements the straight thrust and the disengagement? Are his blade motions tight? Does he also require that his pupil's movements be kept as small as possible? Does he delay introducing actions in time and mobility until his student has mastered all actions from immobility? And does he prohibit free fencing until his pupil is capable of executing all of the actions he has been taught in the lessons?

Except for the first three questions, which require more than a simple "yes" or "no," all the other questions must be answered in the affirmative.

FENCING EQUIPMENT

In comparison with a number of sports, the cost of equipment for the beginning fencer, who employs standard rather than electrical weapons, is comparatively modest. He will need an Italian foil with several spare blades, a mask, fencing glove, wrist strap, elasticized bandage, fencing shoes, and a close-fitting fencing uniform consisting of a jacket, knickers, underarm protector, and long socks. In this regard the appendix provides names of some sources for fencing equipment in the United States.

BEFORE THE FIRST LESSON

Before taking the first fencing lessons it is helpful for the student to be familiar with Chapters One through Five of this text. These indicate, in proper sequential order, what he ought to learn initially.

And it should be noted that exercise during the month or so preceding the first fencing lesson is vital, and must include running to build endurance, and squatting to strengthen the leg muscles.

DURING THE FIRST LESSON

The continuity of the lesson is important, so that no matter how curious the pupil may be, he should refrain from asking questions. The answers he seeks will probably be in the text; and if this is not the case, he can always ask the master before the next lesson.

During the lesson every movement must be performed slowly at first, so that the muscles can warm up gradually. The body should be kept as relaxed as possible, and the mind completely focused on the teacher's commands. There is, of course, nothing natural about the body positions used in fencing; the guard alone requires weeks of training before it begins to feel comfortable, while the lunge necessitates months of practice until its complex coordinations can be mastered.

AFTER THE FIRST LESSON

Since the body movements in fencing differ from those encountered in other sports, even an exceptionally well-conditioned athlete will generally suffer sore leg muscles after the first fencing lesson. With each successive lesson the flexed position of the legs should become more natural, and the physical discomfort will gradually diminish. In this respect, the more lessons one takes, the more comfortable the guard position becomes.

SUBSEQUENT LESSONS

In the lessons that follow, great importance should be placed on the development of a mechanically perfect and rapid straight thrust, for this is the fundamental offensive and counteroffensive action in fencing. All attacks, ripostes, and counterattacks in foil and épée terminate with this movement. In other words, even in indirect offensive actions, such as the disengagement and the cut-over, the point, in its final phase of entry, follows a straight line to the target. With this in mind, it is obvious that correct execution of the straight thrust is essential.

NUMBER OF LESSONS PER WEEK

In the nineteenth and early twentieth centuries it was traditional for serious fencers to take at least three lessons a week. An exceptional swordsman like Nedo Nadi took daily technical lessons, and then, after his work on the plastron, fenced a number of carefully chosen opponents, each selected on the basis of special problems he presented, for example, having a tendency to counterattack, or being left-handed.

In the case of a beginner, a minimum of two, and a maximum of three, lessons a week are recommended for the first few months. Then, when he attains the necessary level of endurance, and can perform basic fencing actions with relative ease, the number of lessons per week can be increased. But above all, no phase of the instruction should be hurried, for each element of the foundation must be firmly in place before the novice is permitted to engage in combat.

PART I

THE FOIL

CHAPTER 1

ESSENTIAL ELEMENTS

1. PARTS OF THE FOIL

The foil is divided into two principal parts: the guard and the blade.

The guard is composed of six elements: bell guard, cushion, crossbar, arches, grip and pommel (Fig. 1).

1) The bell guard is a circular metal shield, less than 12 centimeters in diameter, with a rectangular opening for the tang and ricasso.
2) The cushion is a leather, fabric, or rubber pad, perforated at the center, and fitted behind the bell guard.
3) The crossbar is a metal rod, equal in length to the diameter of the bell guard, with a hole in the center for the tang.
4) The arches are metal supports that unite the crossbar with the bell guard.
5) The grip is a hollow wooden or plastic handle through which the tang passes.
6) The pommel is a cylindrical metal counterbalance that receives the threaded end of the tang.

Figure 1. Parts of the foil.

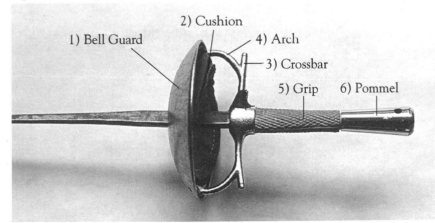

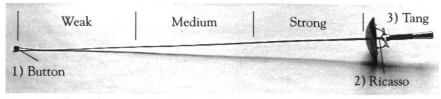

Figure 2. *Three Elements of the blade and its divisions.*

The blade consists of three elements: button, ricasso, and tang (Fig. 2).

1) The button is an enlargement at the point of the blade.
2) The ricasso is a portion of the blade between the bell guard and the crossbar.
3) The tang is a part of the blade that passes through the grip and screws into the pommel.

The blade is made of tempered steel. It is rectangular in cross section, and must not exceed 90 centimeters in length from the convex side of the bell guard to the button.

To distinguish the different degrees of strength, the blade is divided into three equal sections: strong, medium, and weak. The strong is the third closest to the bell guard, the medium is the middle third, and the weak is the third nearest the point.

Observation: In general, it may be said that the first half of the blade, from the bell guard to the center, is used for defense, while the second half of the blade, from the center to the point, is employed for offense.

2. BALANCE, WEIGHT, AND LENGTH OF THE FOIL

The foil is correctly balanced when its center of gravity is at the strong of the blade, approximately four fingers from the bell guard.

A weapon can be tested by placing it on the hand, little finger against the bell guard, and then rotating the hand so that it is perpendicular to the floor, with the blade resting on the index finger alone. If the weight is properly distributed, the foil will remain poised on the index finger.

By regulation, the foil must be under 500 grams in weight, and must not exceed 110 centimeters in length, measuring from the tip of the blade to the end of the pommel.

3. Holding the Foil

The Italian foil is gripped by placing the index and middle fingers be-tween the ricasso and left arch, with the first phalanx of the index finger flexed under the ricasso, fingernail touching the cushion, and the first pha-lanx of the middle finger resting between the ricasso and crossbar; the thumb is extended over the crossbar and along the ricasso where it is set in opposition to the index finger; the ring and little fingers are curled around the grip, holding it firmly in the hollow of the hand, with the pommel centered at the wrist (Fig. 3).

Observation: The hold on the weapon can be further secured through use of a wrist strap. This is worn over the fencing glove, and presses the pom-mel against the wrist. The strap should be drawn as tight as possible with the pommel inserted under it. To prevent cutting blood circulation, an elastic bandage must be worn under the glove and strap. The strap should be fastened near the hand, with the buckle facing outward in the center of the wrist. If the grip is of proper length, the end of the pommel will project slightly beyond the strap.

Figure 3. Holding the foil.

4. Hand Positions

In foil fencing there are six hand positions. Four of these are designated principal positions, and two, intermediate positions. The principal positions are first, second, third, and fourth; and the intermediate positions, second in third, and third in fourth.

With the weapon in hand, the positions are obtained by rotating the hand one quarter turn for the principal positions, and one eighth turn for the intermediate positions. In first position the back of the hand faces left, crossbar vertical (Fig. 4); in second position the back of the hand faces up, crossbar horizontal (Fig. 5); in third position the back of the hand faces right, crossbar vertical (Fig. 6); in fourth position the back of the hand faces down, crossbar horizontal (Fig. 7); in second in third position the back of the hand faces obliquely up toward the right, crossbar diagonal (Fig. 8); and in third in fourth position the back of the hand faces obliquely down toward the right, crossbar diagonal (Fig. 9).

Observation: All positions in the text are described from the point of view of a right-handed fencer; for the left-handed swordsman they are merely reversed.

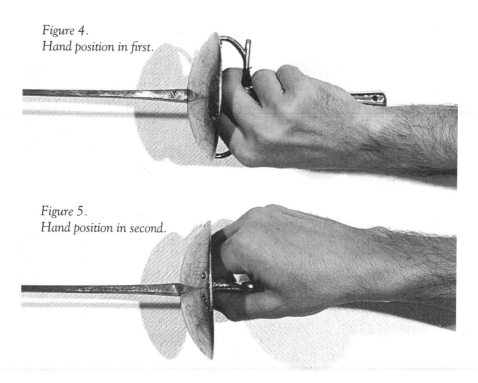

Figure 4.
Hand position in first.

Figure 5.
Hand position in second.

Figure 6.
Hand position in third.

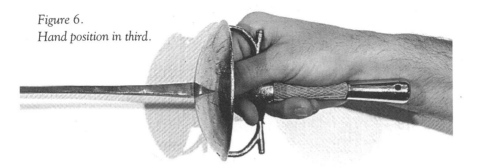

Figure 7.
Hand position in forth.

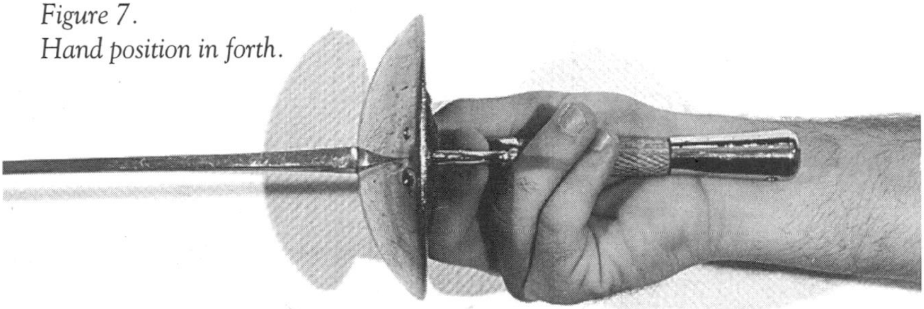

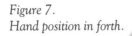

Figure 8.
Hand position in
second in third.

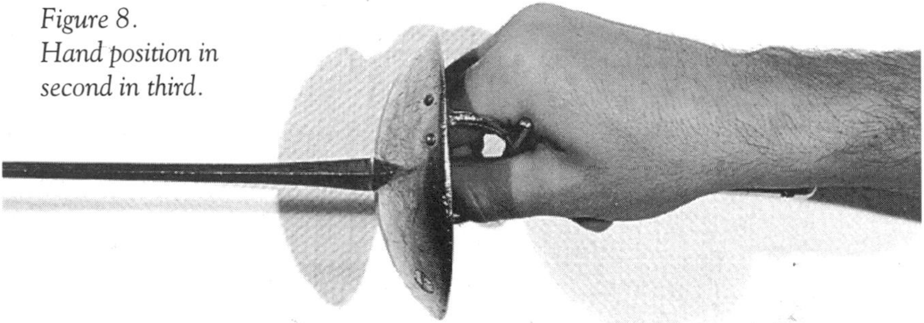

Figure 9.
Hand position in
third in fourth.

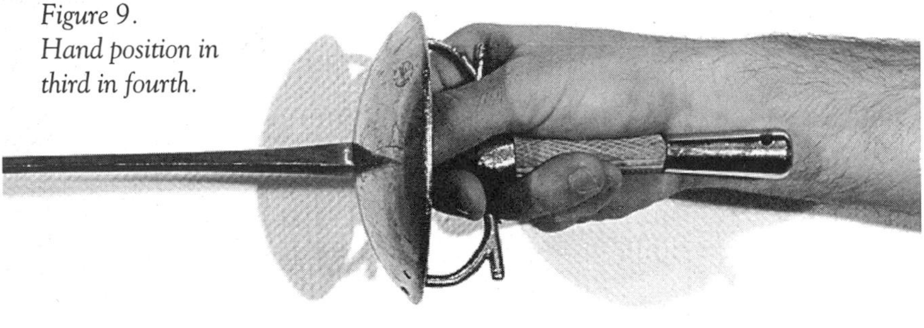

CHAPTER 2

THE GUARD AND THE LUNGE

5. FIRST POSITION

The posture assumed by the fencer with his body and weapon before the salute and during periods of rest is called first position.

In first position the body is held erect, head up, eyes fixed on the adversary, shoulders down and level, legs together, feet at right angles, heels touching, and right toe pointing at the opponent; the armed right hand is placed against the body, a little below the belt, with the blade directed diagonally toward the ground, as though ready to be drawn from its sheath, while the left hand rests on the hip, fingers in front, and thumb behind (Fig. 10).

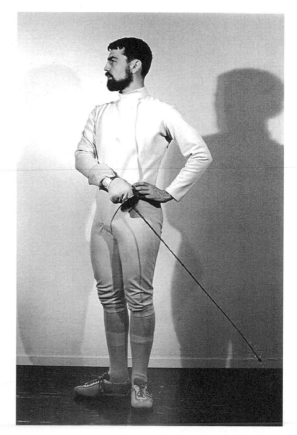

Figure 10. First position.

6. Weapon in Line

The weapon is in line when it forms, with the extended right arm, a straight line parallel with the floor.

From first position the foil is brought into line with a circular sweep of the blade from low to high, hand carried past the left temple, and arm extending progressively as it descends. At shoulder level the movement is completed, with the arm fully extended, hand in fourth position, and tip of the weapon pointing at the opponent's chest.

7. The Salute

The salute is a traditional act of courtesy directed to the adversary and spectators, and must always be observed at the beginning and end of the lesson and combat.

From first position the foil is brought in line with a circular movement from low to high (Fig. 11). The arm, bending at the elbow, is then drawn back toward the body until the forearm and blade form a vertical line, bell guard level with the chin, and blade in front of the right eye (Fig. 12). Now the arm is extended and the weapon carried into line again, hand in fourth position (Fig. 13); this constitutes the salute to the opponent. Next, the observers on the left are saluted: the arm is bent back (Fig. 14), and extended again, though not fully, with the hand in third in fourth position (Fig. 15). Finally, the viewers on the right are saluted: the arm is drawn back once more (Fig. 16), and then extended, elbow slightly flexed, hand rotated into second in third position (Fig. 17).

Figure 11.
First movement of the salute.

Figure 12.
Second movement of the salute.

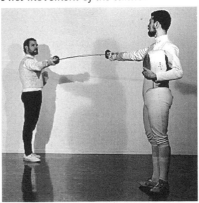

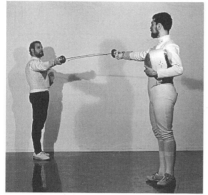

Figure 13.
Third movement of the salute.

Figure 14.
Fourth movement of the salute.

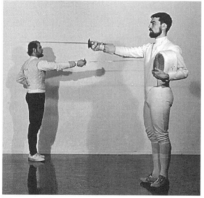

Figure 15.
Fifth movement of the salute.

Figure 16.
Sixth movement of the salute.

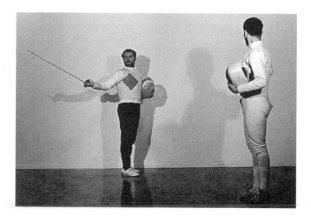

Figure 17. Seventh
movement of the salute.

The various movements of the salute should be performed smoothly, in a flowing and relaxed manner, with each motion of the blade followed by the eyes.

Observation: The salute is executed with the mask off. At the end of the lesson or fencing bout, the master and pupil, or competing fencers, shake hands.

8. THE LINE OF DIRECTION

The imaginary line connecting two fencers, beginning at the left heel of one, passing through the axis of his right foot, and continuing until it encounters the same points in his adversary's feet, is called the line of direction. This is the normal route the feet must travel in the lesson, in exercise, and in combat (Fig. 18).

Figure 18. The line of direction.

9. THE GUARD

The position taken by the fencer with his body and weapon to be ready for the offense, defense, or counteroffense is called the guard (Fig. 19).

From first position the guard is assumed in two movements:

1) The foil is carried into line with a circular motion from low to high; simultaneously, the left arm, following a similar movement, but in the opposite direction, is extended to the rear, thus forming, with the right arm and weapon, a straight line parallel with the floor (Fig. 20).

Figure 19. The guard.

Figure 20.
First movement of the guard.

Figure 21.
Second movement of the guard.

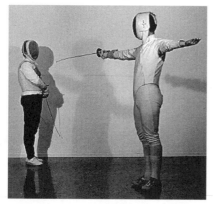 

2) The right foot is advanced approximately one and one half shoe lengths, and the legs bent, right knee over the center of the right foot, left knee perpendicular to the left toe, feet at right angles, and heels in line; contemporaneously, the arms are shifted into position: the right arm is drawn slightly back, right hand in fourth position, and at chest level, point of the foil directed to the opponent's collarbone; the left arm is flexed upward, elbow a little higher than the shoulder, and left hand bent forward at the wrist, thumb out, and fingers together (Fig. 21).

In the completed guard the weight of the body should be distributed equally between the legs, with the torso profiled, and inclining slightly forward, head up and turned to the right, eyes on the adversary, shoulders down, right arm well extended and relaxed, elbow in line with the flank, hand in central position on the line of offense, midway between invitations in third and fourth, and forearm and weapon forming an unbroken line. For the line of offense and invitations in third and fourth see below and pages 22 and 23.

Observation: With the command "On!" the student places his weapon in line, and with the order "Guard!" he assumes the guard position.

10. THE LINE OF OFFENSE

The weapon is considered in the line of offense when its point, with the arm naturally extended, menaces some part of the adversary's valid target.

11. THE LUNGE

The lunge is the position the fencer assumes with his body at the end of an offensive action executed from the guard (Fig. 22). The passage from guard to lunge must be effected in a single movement.

During the development of the lunge it is essential that absolute precedence be given to the point of the weapon, with foot motion delayed until the sword arm reaches full extension. In sequential order, the right arm is extended smoothly, right hand rising to shoulder height, shoulder relaxed, and trunk leaning progressively forward; as the foil arm achieves

Figure 22. The lunge.

complete extension, and without interrupting the flow of movement, the right foot is lifted, toe first, and carried forward, almost grazing or shaving the floor surface as it travels along the line of direction; simultaneously, the left leg is straightened vigorously, knee locking, left foot pressed flat against the ground, and left arm thrown forcefully back to a horizontal position, with the palm of the hand facing up, thumb out, and fingers together; the right foot, as it reaches its destination, lands, heel first.

In the completed lunge both arms must be extended, forming a line parallel with the floor; the torso should be inclined forward and in profile, head up, shoulders level and relaxed, and plane of the hips horizontal. The right knee must project over the instep, right thigh parallel with the ground, and left leg stretched full length, with the knee locked, and left foot flat on the floor.

The prerequisites for an efficient lunge are speed, violence, length, balance, and coordination. Speed is necessary to surprise the adversary; violence, to maintain the direction of the thrust even if it is opposed by a weak parry; length, to strike from as far away as possible with minimum risk; balance, to sustain the force of a parry and return safely on guard; and coordination, to combine the various elements of the lunge into a single, harmonious, flowing movement.

Observation: The speed of the attack is dependent upon the efficiency of the lunge; properly executed, the lunge is an explosive movement that propels the body forward.

During the lunging motion special care should be taken that the right foot does not overshoot its mark, that the left knee locks firmly, and that the left foot remains flat against the ground. The left foot must serve as a brake; it should not be permitted to roll over.

The role of the left arm in the lunge is also significant; it gives impetus to the thrust. Timing is critical: the left hand must be thrown down halfway through the development of the lunge. It should travel straight back to form a horizontal line directly above the left leg. If the left arm drifts to the right or left of the line of direction, the point of the weapon is likewise apt to move off its course.

12. THE RETURN ON GUARD

The recovery from the lunge back to the guard position is called the return on guard.

In the recovery, the right foot pushes away from the floor, the left knee bends, and the left leg contracts, shifting the weight of the body backwards; the right foot returns to its original position, touching ground, heel first, one and one half shoe lengths from the left foot; contemporaneously, the left arm returns to its flexed position on guard.

13. THE ADVANCE

The advance is a step forward to decrease measure between oneself and the adversary. This movement is also referred to as gaining ground.

From the guard position the advance is executed in two motions:

1) The right foot, toe first, is raised slightly off the floor, and carried, one shoe's length forward, along the line of direction, and set down, heel first.

2) The left foot is brought quickly forward the same distance, and placed on the ground, ball of the foot first.

During the advance the trunk should remain balanced and in profile, with the legs bent, and feet barely leaving the surface of the fencing strip. At the conclusion of the step forward both feet must be spaced in the guard position just as they were before the advance was made.

Observation: It must be noted that the step forward should generally be unhurried, so that the antagonist is not alerted to the fact that distance is being closed.

14. THE RETREAT

The retreat is a step backward to increase measure between oneself and the opponent. This motion is also called breaking ground.

From the guard position the retreat is performed in two movements:

1) The left foot is carried backward, as far as necessary, along the line of direction, and set down, ball of the foot first.

2) The left knee is bent, and the right foot moved rapidly backward, and placed on the ground, heel first.

Throughout the retreat the torso should remain balanced and in profile, with the legs flexed, and feet almost gliding over the surface of the floor. At the completion of the step backward both feet must be spaced in the guard position.

15. THE JUMP BACKWARD

The jump backward is a movement in which the right foot is brought backward beyond the left foot. Its function is to increase measure, and it can be executed from either the guard position or lunge. In sequence, the right foot is sent backward past the left foot; the left foot is then shifted a distance behind the right foot, so that at the completion of the movement both feet are again in the guard position.

16. THE APPEL

The appel is a foot stamp that may be employed to give impetus to the thrust in a renewed attack, or to accent the feint. It can also be used in the lesson as an instructional device to retard the impulse to lunge early. By adding an appel to the feint, the student is forced to delay the lunge until his sword arm is fully extended for the final motion of the attack.

To effect the appel the right foot is raised about two centimeters from the floor, and then brought down sharply, heel first. Correctly timed, the sound of the appel will coincide with the completion of the feint, thus giving the feint a greater sense of realism.

17. FENCING MEASURE

Fencing measure is the distance that separates two fencers placed on guard. There are three measures: out of distance, correct distance, and close distance.

1) From out of distance the adversary's chest can be touched by taking a step forward and lunging.

2) From correct distance the opponent's chest can be hit by lunging.

3) From close distance the adversary's chest can be reached without lunging.

When two fencers are on guard facing one another with weapons in line, they are out of distance if the tips of their foils are at the point where the medium is distinguished from the weak of the blade; they are at correct distance if the points of their weapons extend four fingers beyond the bell guard; and they are at close distance if the tips of their foils can reach the chest.

18. THE ADVANCE LUNGE

When a lunge is preceded by a step forward the combination of foot motions is designated an advance lunge. The function of the advance lunge is to close distance.

From the guard position the advance lunge consists of three movements: 1) advance of the right foot, 2) advance of the left foot, and 3) lunge.

Properly executed, the step forward and lunge fuse into a smooth, uninterrupted flow of motion which carries the point of the weapon forward at a constant rate of acceleration.

Observation: During the advance the legs should remain flexed, with the body moving forward in a low position. The tendency to rise with the step forward must be kept in check.

19. THE JUMP LUNGE

When a jump forward is combined with a lunge the resulting movement is termed a jump lunge. The purpose of the jump lunge, like that of the advance lunge, is to gain distance.

In its execution the jump should be small, with the feet close to the surface of the floor, the ground serving as a springboard for the lunge. If the jump is performed correctly, the legs stay flexed, and the feet evenly spaced throughout the motion. The landing is accomplished on the balls of the feet, which on touching the fencing strip immediately trigger the lunge.

Again, in the jump lunge, as in the advance lunge, the combination of foot movements must blend into a harmonious flow of motion.

20. GAINING ON THE LUNGE

Another method for closing distance is gaining on the lunge. This is accomplished by drawing the left foot forward until the left heel touches the
right heel and then lunging. The ground covered in this way may be equal
to, or even greater, than that obtained by means of the advance lunge.

21. THE RUNNING ATTACK

The running attack is a rapid advance with the left foot passing the right.

To execute the movement from the guard position, the right arm is
extended completely, torso profiled and inclining forward, weight shifting
to the right foot, heel lifting, and right knee bent; the left arm is straightened out behind, and the left foot brought forward, left knee flexed; the
right leg is extended vigorously, right knee locking, and right foot pushing
off the ground.

In the final phase of the motion both feet are elevated above the floor,
the left knee projects forward, and the body and right leg stretch out in an
almost horizontal position.

Observation: Only when the student has mastered the lunge should he be
permitted to execute the running attack. This movement must never become a substitute for the lunge; rather, it should be treated as a surprise
action to be used on rare occasions.

CHAPTER 3

PLACEMENT OF THE WEAPON

22. PLACEMENT OF THE WEAPON

Placement of the weapon refers to the position the fencer on guard adopts with his armed hand in relation to his adversary. There are three such positions, and they are designated: invitation, engagement, and blade in line.

1) In the position of invitation, the foil is placed so that a portion of the target is exposed.

2) In the position of engagement, blade contact is made, and the opposing steel dominated and deviated from the line of offense.

3) In the position with the blade in line, the arm is naturally extended, and the point directed to the opponent's chest.

Observation: In a general sense, both the position of engagement and the position with the blade in line constitute invitations. With the opposing steel engaged the adversary is invited to disengage; with the blade in line he is invited to perform an action on the blade.

23. THE FOIL TARGET

The foil target is restricted to the torso; it extends in front from the upper limit of the collar out to the arm seams and down to the lines of the groin, and in back from the upper limit of the collar out to the arm seams and down to a horizontal line that passes across the top of the hip bones.

To describe the lines of attack the adversary's body is divided into four quarters: 1) inside, 2) outside, 3) high, and 4) low.

With the opponent in the correct guard position, all assaults will pass to the right or left of his sword arm, and above or below it. An attack to the right of the arm is said to enter the outside line; to the left of the arm, the inside line; above the arm, the high line; and below the arm, the low line.

24. INVITATIONS

Invitations are positions taken with the weapon, exposing a specific line, to induce the opponent to attack. There are four foil invitations: first, second, third, and fourth.

1) In the invitation in first (French high *septime*) the foil is shifted to the left of the line of offense, elbow flexed, and to the left, hand in third in fourth position, and shoulder high, point of the weapon below the hand, and describing a small, clockwise semicircle terminating a few centimeters to the left of the adversary's flank (Figs. 23-24). The invitation in first uncovers the flank or outside low line.

2) In the invitation in second the foil is carried to the right of the line of offense, elbow bent and in line with the flank, hand in fourth position (French *octave*), or elbow to the right, hand in second position (French *seconde*) and almost level with the flank, point of the weapon below the hand, and forming a tight, counterclockwise half-circle ending some centimeters to the right of the opponent's flank (Figs. 25-28). The invitation in second exposes the chest or high line.

Figure 24.

Invitation in First

Figure 23.

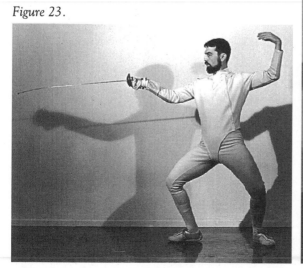

Invitation in Second (hand position in fourth)

Figure 25.

Figure 26.

Invitation in Second (hand position in second)

Figure 27.

Figure 28.

3) In the invitation in third the foil is moved to the right of the line of offense, elbow flexed, and in line with the flank, hand in fourth position (French *sixte*), or elbow to the right, hand in second in third position (French *tierce*), and chest high, point of the weapon above the hand, and a few centimeters to the right of the adversary's chest (Figs. 29-32). The invitation in third opens the chest or inside high line.

Figure 30.

Invitation in Third (hand position in fourth)

Figure 29.

Figure 32.

Invitation in Third (hand position in second in third)

Figure 31.

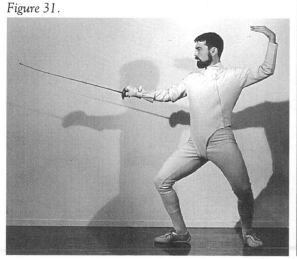

Invitation in Fourth

Figure 33.

Figure 34.

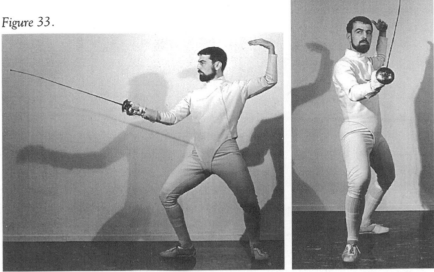

4) In the invitation in fourth (French *quarte*) the foil is brought to the left of the line of offense, elbow bent, and to the left, hand in third in fourth position, and chest high, point of the weapon above the hand, and some centimeters to the left of the opponent's right shoulder (Figs. 33-34). The invitation in fourth reveals the chest or outside high line.

Observation: It should be noted that in invitations in second and third, hand positions may be taken in either fourth or respectively, second and second in third. The present tendency among foil fencers is to employ only the hand position in fourth; this is true also of engagements and parries.

25. ENGAGEMENTS

Engagements are contact invitations in which the opposing steel is dominated and deviated from the line of offense. There are four engagements: first, second, third, and fourth. In these the hand and weapon assume exactly the same position they did in the invitations (Figs. 35-40).

The function of engagements is also the same as that of invitations: they open a particular line for attack.

Engagements are effected with the strong against the weak, if taken at correct or lunging distance; and with the medium against the weak, if made from out of distance.

Figure 35.
Engagement in
first.

Figure 36.
Engagement in
second.
(hand position
in fourth)

Figure 37.
Engagement in
second.
(hand position
in second)

Observation: The opposing steel is properly engaged when the adversary cannot force an entry in the line of engagement; the blade must be placed exactly as in the invitation, with the point and hand in the same line.

*Figure 38.
Engagement in
third.
(hand position
in fourth)*

*Figure 39.
Engagement in
third.
(hand position
in second in
third)*

*Figure 40.
Engagement in
fourth.*

26. Changes of Engagement

Changes of engagement are used to shift from one engagement to another. These movements are accomplished by passing the point over or under the opposing steel and carrying it to an opposite line of engagement. If the engagement is in the low line, the point passes over the hostile blade; if it is in the high line, it passes under.

Blade motion is effected with the fingers and wrist. The point is transferred in a small, semicircular movement, from one side of the opponent's steel to the other, and the blade carried, strong against weak, to the opposite line of engagement.

Single Changes of Engagement

In single changes of engagement the blade is shifted so that it engages the adversary's steel in a line opposite the original engagement. Single changes may be made from first to second and vice versa, or from third to fourth and vice versa. Single changes of engagement are identified by the line of engagement in which they finish: thus, the change from first to second is called the single change of engagement to second.

Observation: Changes of engagement from second to third and vice versa are also possible; however, those changes of engagement are less commonly used because they are more difficult to perform.

Double Changes of Engagement

In double changes of engagement the opponent's steel is carried to an opposite line, and then back again to the original line of engagement. Double changes may be effected from first to second to first, second to first to second, third to fourth to third, and fourth to third to fourth. Double changes of engagement are designated by the line of engagement in which they begin and end: thus, the changes from first to second to first are termed the double change of engagement to first.

Observation: Again, though not often employed, double changes of engagement from second to third to second, and third to second to third are possible.

27. TRANSPORTS

Transports carry the blade, strong against weak, without a break in contact, from one line of engagement to another. They may be executed from first to third and vice versa, or from second to fourth and vice versa. Transports are identified by the line of engagement in which they terminate: thus, the transport from first to third is called the transport to third.

28. ENVELOPMENTS

Envelopments are movements that encircle the opposing steel, so that the blade, in a continuous motion and without a loss of contact, returns to the original line of engagement. Envelopments may be accomplished in all lines. Envelopments are designated by the line of engagement in which they begin and end: thus, the envelopment from first to third to first is termed the envelopment in first.

Observation: Envelopments, in fact, consist of two transports: the first carries the opposing steel to a new line of engagement; the second brings it back to the original line of engagement. The two curved diagonal movements, when combined into a single motion, form an ellipse.

After the enveloping action has been mastered, it should be gradually tightened.

CHAPTER 4

OFFENSE

29. THE OFFENSE

The offense is the act of attacking the adversary.

30. SIMPLE ATTACKS

Offensive actions consisting of a single blade movement are called simple attacks.

In foil fencing there are four simple attacks: 1) the straight thrust, 2) the disengagement, 3) the glide, and 4) the cut-over.

Observation: Simple and compound attacks may terminate in either a lunge or a running attack. However, during the early phases of a fencer's development all offensive actions should be executed with a lunge.

31. THE STRAIGHT THRUST

The straight thrust is an action, without blade contact, in which the point of the weapon follows a straight line to the exposed target; it is a direct attack in one movement, and may be used when the adversary makes an invitation, or from one's own invitation or engagement. The straight thrust can be directed to each of the four lines: inside, outside, high, or low. It is effected from the guard at lunging distance, with the hand in fourth position (or second position if the thrust is aimed at the outside low line).

To execute the straight thrust, the sword arm is extended smoothly, with the hand rising gradually to shoulder level, thumb and index finger squeezing the blade as it advances, and attaining maximum pressure just before the lunge is completed, and the point reaches its destination. Throughout the action the right shoulder must be relaxed, so that the motion flows forward freely.

With the thrust the hand is shifted progressively to the right or left, depending upon the line of entry. These displacements of the hand are called oppositions, and their function is to provide protection by closing the line.

If the adversary invites in first, the thrust is directed to the outside low line, opposition to the right; if he invites in second, the thrust is aimed at the high line, opposition to the left; if he invites in third, the thrust is directed to the inside high line, opposition to the left; and if he invites in fourth, the thrust is aimed at the outside high line, opposition to the right.

From one's own engagement the blade is simply detached and the straight thrust directed to the exposed target. It should be noted, however, that the straight thrust from engagement in second is aimed at the high line, and the straight thrust from engagement in third is directed to the low line.

Since the straight thrust is easy to parry, its success depends upon speed; the faster the attack is, the more difficult it is to parry.

Observation: Coordination between arm extension and lunge is critical: the sword arm must be fully extended before the right foot moves. In other words, precedence should always be given to the point. If the arm and foot coordination is correct, the point of the weapon will arrive on target a fraction of a second before the right heel touches ground for the completion of the lunge.

When the thrust is executed, as it generally is, with the hand in fourth position, special care must be taken that the point of the weapon drops slightly below the level of the hand just before it reaches its destination, so that the blade will bend properly, with the point well fixed on the target.

32. THE DISENGAGEMENT

The disengagement is an action in which the blade, with a spiral motion of the point, is detached from the adversary's engagement, and directed to the exposed target; it is an indirect attack in one movement, and may be employed when the opponent engages blades. The disengagement can be aimed at each of the four lines: inside, outside, high, or low. It is accomplished from the guard at lunging distance, with the hand in fourth position (or second position if the thrust is directed to the outside low line).

To disengage or free the blade from the adversary's engagement, a tiny, semicircular motion of the point is effected with the fingers, foil arm extending easily, and hand rising gradually to shoulder height. Hand, wrist, arm, and right shoulder should not move; the fingers alone must guide the point in a closely controlled, spiral motion. As the point is liberated, and changing lines, it should penetrate steadily forward without wobbling. Correctly executed, the disengagement, arm extension, and lunge are accomplished in a single, unbroken movement.

With the disengagement the hand is moved progressively into opposition, closing to the right or left, depending upon the line of entry.

The disengagement from first travels downward, the disengagement from second, upward, and the disengagements from third and fourth, in a lateral direction, respectively from left to right, and vice versa.

If the opponent engages in first, the disengagement moves counterclockwise to the outside low line, opposition to the right; if he engages in second, the disengagement travels clockwise to the high line, opposition to the left; if he engages in third, the disengagement moves counterclockwise to the inside high line, opposition to the left; and if he engages in fourth, the disengagement travels clockwise to the outside high line, opposition to the right.

Observation: Particular care must be taken that the disengagement is kept as small as possible; the tighter it is, the more efficient it will be.

33. The Glide

The glide is an action in which the blade slides along the opposing steel to the exposed target; it is an attack in one movement that may be used when the adversary's blade is engaged. The glide assumes the name of the engagement from which it originates: first, second, third, and fourth. It is effected from the guard at lunging distance, with the hand in fourth position (or second position if the thrust is aimed at the outside low line).

To accomplish the action the sword arm is extended smoothly, blades touching, hand in opposition, and rising gradually to shoulder level. As the steel slips along the hostile blade it maintains constant contact, dominating and forcing it progressively to one side. Properly executed, the glide and lunge blend into a single, rapid motion.

If the opponent's blade is engaged in first, the hand is rotated from third in fourth to fourth position, and the glide is directed to the inside low line, opposition to the left; if it is engaged in second, the hand remains in fourth position, or is turned to second position, and the glide is aimed at the outside low line, opposition to the right; if it is engaged in third, the hand stays in fourth position, or is rotated to fourth position, and the glide is directed to the outside high line, opposition to the right; and if it is engaged in fourth, the hand is turned from third in fourth to fourth position, and the glide is aimed at the inside high line, opposition to the left.

Observation: Glides used in opposition to the adversary's imperfect or weak engagements are called forced glides. Their purpose is to regain opposition. In order to open the line, blade contact must be maintained and pressure exerted upon the opposing steel.

Forced glides resemble, in execution, the glides in first, second, third, and fourth described above. For example, if the opponent engages blades in fourth without closing the line sufficiently, the forced glide in fourth can be performed with strong opposition to the left.

THE FLANCONADE IN FOURTH

The flanconade in fourth, or external flanconade, is a glide to the adversary's flank, with the hand in fourth position, and opposition to the left.

From engagement in fourth, employing the point of blade contact as a fulcrum, the hand is simultaneously rotated in a helical motion to fourth position, and lowered slightly to dominate better the opposing steel; as the blade slips around the opponent's weapon, the point, in a small, counterclockwise movement, passes to the outside low line, where, without a break in continuity or blade contact, the thrust is effected with opposition to the left.

Observation: The cut-over is the fourth simple attack. Since it is a comparatively wide action in which the point is withdrawn from its threatening position, it presents certain risks, and therefore should be taught to the student only after he has mastered the simple and compound actions effected with the point in line.

Before concluding this section on simple attacks, mention must also be made of the thrust to low fourth. This action is used against the antagonist who exposes his low line by habitually keeping his hand high in the invitation, engagement, or parry of fourth. Instead of directing the thrust to the outside high line, it is aimed at the low line, with the hand in fourth position.

Plate I   Plate II

The Flanconade in Fourth

Plate III

CHAPTER 5

DEFENSE

34. THE DEFENSE

Blade motions that deviate the adversary's point before it reaches the target, or foot movements that remove the body from the range of attack, are called the defense. The first of these is designated the defense of steel, the second, the defense of measure. In the defense of steel the offensive response can be immediate; in the defense of measure it is always delayed, thus prolonging the encounter. From this it may be surmised that the defense of steel is the more efficient of the two.

35. PARRIES

Defensive movements of the blade that deflect the incoming steel are termed parries. These can be simple, circular, half circular, or ceding.

Simple, circular, and half circular parries may be executed either as opposition or beating motions; ceding parries can only be performed through opposition. In the one instance the adversary's steel is deviated merely by closing the line; in the other it is deflected by striking it to one side. From this it follows that opposition parries always terminate with blades in contact, and beating parries with blades separated.

36. SIMPLE PARRIES

Simple parries are protective displacements of the blade that cover exposed target areas by traveling the shortest route from one invitation or engagement to another.

In foil fencing there are four simple parries, each defending a certain portion or portions of the valid target: thus, the parry of first protects the inside high and low lines (Fig. 41), the parry of second, the outside low line (Figs. 42-43), the parry of third, the outside high line (Figs. 44-45), and the parry of fourth, the inside high line (Fig. 46).

Placement of the arm, hand, and weapon is the same as in invitations and engagements designated by the same number.

When the parrying action is correctly executed, the strong of the defending blade encounters the medium of the attacking steel.

Figure 42. Parry of second.
(hand position in fourth)

Figure 41. Parry of first.

Figure 43. Parry of second.
(hand position in second)

Figure 44. Parry of third.
(hand position in fourth)

Figure 45. Parry of third.
(hand position in second in third)

Figure 46. Parry of fourth.

Observation: Excessive dropping or raising of the point during the parry-ing action must be avoided; the point should always be close to the in-coming steel. The nearer the point is to the line of offense, the easier and faster it is to shift from defense to offense.

It is also important that the body remains in its low position while the parry is being executed; the tendency to rise with the parry must be kept in check.

37. PASSAGE FROM ONE SIMPLE PARRY TO ANOTHER

From the parry, invitation, or engagement in first, the movement to the parry of second is accomplished in one motion, rotating the hand to fourth or second position, and carrying the foil diagonally downward from left to right, hand almost level with the flank, point of the weapon lower than the hand, so that the opposing steel is met, strong against medium, and deflected to the right.

From the parry, invitation, or engagement in second, the passage to the parry of first is effected in one motion, turning the hand to third in fourth position, and shifting the foil diagonally upward from right to left, hand shoulder high, point of the weapon lower than the hand, so that the hostile blade is encountered, strong against medium, and deviated to the left.

From the parry, invitation, or engagement in third, the movement to the parry of fourth is achieved in one motion, rotating the hand to third in fourth position, and transporting the foil horizontally from right to left, hand chest high, point of the weapon higher than the hand, so that the opposing steel is met, strong against medium, and deflected to the left.

From the parry, invitation, or engagement in fourth, the passage to the parry of third is made in one motion, turning the hand to fourth or second in third position, and moving the foil horizontally from left to right, hand chest high, point of the weapon higher than the hand, so that the hostile blade is encountered, strong against medium, and deviated to the right.

It should be noted that the passage from the parry, invitation, or en-gagement in second to the parry of third and vice versa is also considered movement from one simple parry to another.

Observation: Placement of the sword arm and weapon is modified accord-ing to the deviation of the actual assault from the ideal line of attack. In other words, the hand may have to be raised or lowered slightly so that the parry can be effected with the strong of the blade in opposition to the medium of the incoming steel.

It should be further noted that the speed of the parry is in direct relation to the velocity of the attack.

38. CEDING PARRIES

Ceding parries are used in opposition to gliding actions in the low lines.
Instead of resisting the attack, it is yielded to, blades in constant contact,
hand lowered, wrist flexed, and point raised, so that the parry is assumed,
and the incoming steel deviated, just before the point reaches its destination.

There are two ceding parries in foil fencing: the ceding parry of third,
and the ceding parry of fourth. The ceding parry of third is employed against
the glide in first and the internal flanconade; the ceding parry of fourth, in
opposition to the glide in second, flanconade in second, and flanconade
in fourth.

39. THE RIPOSTE

The riposte is the thrust delivered immediately after the adversary's attack has been parried (Figs. 47-48). Ripostes may be simple or compound.

Opposition parries can be followed by ripostes in which the blade is
detached (straight thrust), or kept in contact (glide).

Observation: It should be noted that when the riposting action is effected
from the guard, as it generally is, the left hand and arm remain poised in
the guard position.

40. SIMPLE RIPOSTES

After the parry of first the riposte may be directed to the inside low line by
detaching the blade, or by maintaining contact.

After the parry of second the riposte may be aimed at the high line by
detaching the blade, or at the outside low line by maintaining contact.

After the parry of third the riposte may be directed to the low line by
detaching the blade, or to the outside high line by maintaining contact.

After the parry of fourth the riposte may be aimed at the inside high
line by detaching the blade, or by maintaining contact, or it can be directed to the outside low line with the flanconade in fourth.

Observation: The riposte must strike the attacker before he has time to
recover from the lunge.

Figure 47. Parry of fourth.

Figure 48. Simple riposte to the inside high line by detaching the blade.

COMPOUND ATTACKS

41. COMPOUND ATTACKS

Offensive actions consisting of two or more blade movements are called compound or composed attacks.

Observation: Compound or composed attacks may be divided into three groups: 1) feints, 2) actions on the blade, and 3) renewed attacks.

42. THE FEINT

The feint is a simulated thrust or menace that resembles so closely a genuine assault that the adversary is forced to parry. In contrast to a real attack, it does not end in a lunge or running attack.

Given proper accentuation, the feint will compel the opponent to move his blade in the direction of the presumed attack, thus uncovering a portion of the target for the actual thrust. The deeper, and more convincing the feint is, the greater the likelihood the adversary will react.

The feint is used when simple attacks no longer penetrate the opponent's defensive system, or when simple actions begin to be repetitious.

Observation: It is important to note that the number of blade motions in the attack must always exceed by one the number of parries. In other words, if there is one parry, the compound attack will consist of two movements, the feint and the thrust; if there are two parries, the compound attack will be composed of three motions, two feints and the thrust; and if there are three parries, the compound attack will be comprised of four movements, three feints and the thrust.

43. SINGLE FEINTS

Single or simple feints elude one parry; they are used in opposition to the invitation and engagement. Each feint is named after its first movement: we therefore speak of the feint direct, feint by disengagement, and feint by glide.

During execution of the feint the sword arm must be extended smoothly, so that the point penetrates in a steady forward motion without wobbling. Throughout the action the right shoulder should remain completely relaxed.

When single feints are employed with an advance, the feint coincides with the step forward or jump forward, and the thrust with the lunge. In every case, arm extension must precede foot movement.

44. ELUDING ONE SIMPLE PARRY

One simple parry is eluded by a single feint plus a disengagement. The disengagement enters a line opposite the line of the feint.

45. THE FEINT DIRECT

The feint direct is a simulated straight thrust that may be opposed to the adversary's invitations; it may be effected from one's own engagements, or it may follow a parry.

Whether the feint direct is accomplished from lunging distance, or with a step forward, it is an action in two movements, one for the feint, the other for the thrust.

During execution of the feint direct it is essential to give absolute precedence to the point; the feet must not move until the point is directed to the target and the arm well extended. From beginning to end, the attack should accelerate progressively, attaining maximum velocity as it reaches its final phase.

Observation: In this, and all compound actions consisting of one or more feints, point motion must be kept as tight as possible with the hand shifted progressively in opposition during the final movement of the attack.

46. THE FEINT DIRECT AND DISENGAGEMENT

1) In opposition to the invitation in first:

Master	*Pupil*
Invites in first.	First movement: simulates a straight thrust to the outside low line.
Parries second.	Second movement: eludes the parry of second with a disengagement clockwise to the high line.
Receives the touch.	

Observation: Movement of the weapon must originate in the fingers. The feint should be held long enough to provoke the parry; then, the instant before blade contact occurs, the point must be shifted upward and forward, in a tiny, semicircular motion. Timing is of primary importance: the first movement of the action should be long, the second, short.

2) In opposition to the invitation in second:

Master	Pupil
Invites in second.	First movement: simulates a straight thrust to the high line.
Parries first or third.	Second movement: eludes the parry of first with a disengagement counterclockwise to the outside low line; or eludes the parry of third with a disengagement counterclockwise to the low line or inside high line.
Receives the touch.	

3) In opposition to the invitation in third:

Master	Pupil
Invites in third.	First movement: simulates a straight thrust to the inside high line.
Parries fourth.	Second movement: eludes the parry of fourth with a disengagement clockwise to the outside high line.
Receives the touch.	

4) In opposition to the invitation in fourth:

Master	Pupil
Invites in fourth.	First movement: simulates a straight thrust to the outside high line.
Parries third.	Second movement: eludes the parry of third with a disengagement counterclockwise to the low line or inside high line.
Receives the touch.	

47. The Feint by Disengagement

The feint by disengagement is a simulated disengagement that may be opposed to the adversary's engagements. It is executed in the same manner as the feint direct.

48. The Feint by Disengagement and Disengagement

1) In opposition to the engagement in first:

Master	Pupil
Engages in first.	First movement: simulates a disengagement counterclockwise to the outside low line.
Parries second.	Second movement: eludes the parry of second with a disengagement clockwise to the high line.
Receives the touch.	

2) In opposition to the engagement in second:

Master	Pupil
Engages in second.	First movement: simulates a disengagement clockwise to the high line.
Parries first or third.	Second movement: eludes the parry of first with a disengagement counterclockwise to the outside low line; or eludes the parry of third with a disengagement counterclockwise to the low line or inside high line.
Receives the touch.	

3) In opposition to the engagement in third:

Master	Pupil
Engages in third.	First movement: simulates a disengagement counterclockwise to the inside high line.
Parries fourth.	Second movement: eludes the parry of fourth with a disengagement clockwise to the outside high line.
Receives the touch.	

4) In opposition to the engagement in fourth:

Master	Pupil
Engages in fourth.	First movement: simulates a disengagement clockwise to the outside high line.
Parries third.	Second movement: eludes the parry of third with a disengagement counterclockwise to the low line or inside high line.
Receives the touch.	

49. THE FEINT BY GLIDE

The feint by glide is a simulated glide that may be employed when the opponent's blade is engaged. It resembles in execution the feint direct and feint by disengagement.

50. THE FEINT BY GLIDE AND DISENGAGEMENT

1) From engagement in first:

Master	Pupil
	First movement: from his own engagement in first simulates a glide to the inside low line.
Parries first.	Second movement: eludes the parry of first with a disengagement counterclockwise to the outside low line.
Receives the touch.	

2) From engagement in second:

Master	Pupil
	First movement: from his own engagement in second simulates a glide to the outside low line.
Parries second.	Second movement: eludes the parry of second with a disengagement clockwise to the high line.
Receives the touch.	

3) From engagement in third:

Master	Pupil
	First movement: from his own engagement in third simulates a glide to the outside high line.
Parries third.	Second movement: eludes the parry of third with a disengagement counterclockwise to the low line or inside high line.
Receives the touch.	

4) From engagement in fourth:

Master	Pupil
	First movement: from his own engagement in fourth simulates a glide to the inside high line.
Parries fourth.	Second movement: eludes the parry of fourth with a disengagement clockwise to the outside high line.
Receives the touch.	

Observation: If the adversary effects weak engagements, his engagements are opposed with the feint by forced glide and disengagement.

THE FEINT BY FLANCONADE IN FOURTH AND DISENGAGEMENT

From engagement in fourth:

Master	Pupil
	First movement: from his own engagement in fourth simulates a glide to the outside low line (flanconade in fourth).
Parries second.	Second movement: eludes the parry of second with a disengagement clockwise to the high line.
Receives the touch.	

51. Compound Ripostes

Ripostes consisting of two or more blade motions are termed compound ripostes; their function is to elude one or more counterparries, that is, parries opposed to the riposte.

Observation: When the student has developed confidence in his attacks, and moves with speed and precision, the master may periodically parry the action and riposte, so that the pupil is forced, while still in the lunge position, to respond with the counterparry riposte.

52. Ripostes with Feints

After the parry of first, the feint direct or feint by glide may be directed to the inside low line, and the counterparry of first eluded with a disengagement traveling counterclockwise to the outside low line.

After the parry of second, the feint direct may be aimed at the high line, and the counterparry of third eluded with a disengagement moving counterclockwise to the low line, or to the inside high line; or the feint by glide may be directed to the outside low line, and the counterparry of second eluded with a disengagement traveling clockwise to the high line.

After the parry of third, the feint direct may be aimed at the low line, and the counterparry of second eluded with a disengagement moving clockwise to the high line; or the feint by glide may be directed to the outside high line, and the counterparry of third eluded with a disengagement traveling counterclockwise to the low line, or to the inside high line.

After the parry of fourth, the feint direct or feint by glide may be aimed at the inside high line, and the counterparry of fourth eluded with a disengagement moving clockwise to the outside high line; or with the feint by flanconade in fourth directed to the outside low line, and the counterparry of second eluded with a disengagement traveling clockwise to the high line.

53. Double Feints

Double feints elude two parries; they are employed in opposition to the invitation and engagement. Each feint is named after its initial movement: we therefore speak of the double feint direct, double feint by disengagement, and double feint by glide.

During execution of the double feint the sword arm must be extended gradually, so that the point moves progressively forward, penetrating with each feint deeper into the adversary's defensive system. From the point of view of efficiency, it is essential that the disengagements be kept as tight as possible.

When the double feint is coordinated with an advance, the two feints are completed with the step forward. The first feint should coincide with the motion of the right foot, the second with the movement of the left foot, and the final thrust with the lunge.

Observation: In coordinating the double feint with an advance it is important that the step forward be perfectly natural, and of normal length. The tendency to step too far forward with the right foot must be kept in check.

54. ELUDING TWO SIMPLE PARRIES

Two simple parries are eluded by a double feint plus a disengagement.

55. THE DOUBLE FEINT DIRECT AND DISENGAGEMENT

1) In opposition to the invitation in first:

Master	*Pupil*
Invites in first.	First movement: simulates a straight thrust to the outside low line.
Parries second.	Second movement: eludes the parry of second with a feint by disengagement clockwise to the high line.
Parries first or third.	Third movement: eludes the parry of first with a disengagement counterclockwise to the outside low line; or eludes the parry of third with a disengagement counterclockwise to the low line or inside high line.
Receives the touch.	

Observation: Again, particular care must be taken that point motion is effected with the fingers, and not with the wrist or shoulder. Once the action begins, the point should advance progressively through extension of the arm. Under no circumstances may the arm be withdrawn.

2) In opposition to the invitation in second:

Master	Pupil
Invites in second.	First movement: simulates a straight thrust to the high line.
Parries first or third.	Second movement: eludes the parry of first with a feint by disengagement counter-clockwise to the outside low line; or eludes the parry of third with a feint by disengagement counterclockwise to the low line or inside high line.
Parries second or fourth.	Third movement: eludes the parry of second with a disengagement clockwise to the high line; or eludes the parry of fourth with a disengagement clockwise to the outside high line.
Receives the touch.	

3) In opposition to the invitation in third:

Master	Pupil
Invites in third.	First movement: simulates a straight thrust to the inside high line.
Parries fourth.	Second movement: eludes the parry of fourth with a feint by disengagement clockwise to the outside high line.
Parries third.	Third movement: eludes the parry of third with a disengagement counterclockwise to the low line or inside high line.
Receives the touch.	

4) In opposition to the invitation in fourth:

Master	Pupil
Invites in fourth.	First movement: simulates a straight thrust to the outside high line.
Parries third.	Second movement: eludes the parry of third with a feint by disengagement counter-clockwise to the low line or inside high line.

| Parries second or fourth. | Third movement: eludes the parry of second with a disengagement clockwise to the high line; or eludes the parry of fourth with a disengagement clockwise to the outside high line. |
| Receives the touch. | |

56. THE DOUBLE FEINT BY DISENGAGEMENT AND DISENGAGEMENT

1) In opposition to the engagement in first:

Master	Pupil
Engages in first.	First movement: simulates a disengagement counterclockwise to the outside low line.
Parries second.	Second movement: eludes the parry of second with a feint by disengagement clockwise to the high line.
Parries first or third.	Third movement: eludes the parry of first with a disengagement counterclockwise to the outside low line; or eludes the parry of third with a disengagement counterclockwise to the low line or inside high line.
Receives the touch.	

2) In opposition to the engagement in second:

Master	Pupil
Engages in second.	First movement: simulates a disengagement clockwise to the high line.
Parries first or third.	Second movement: eludes the parry of first with a feint by disengagement counterclockwise to the outside low line; or eludes the parry of third with a feint by disengagement counterclockwise to the low line or inside high line.
Parries second or fourth.	Third movement: eludes the parry of second with a disengagement clockwise to the high line; or eludes the parry of fourth with a disengagement clockwise to the outside high line.
Receives the touch.	

3) In opposition to the engagement in third:

Master	Pupil
Engages in third.	First movement: simulates a disengagement counterclockwise to the inside high line.
Parries fourth.	Second movement: eludes the parry of fourth with a feint by disengagement clockwise to the outside high line.
Parries third.	Third movement: eludes the parry of third with a disengagement counterclockwise to the low line or inside high line.
Receives the touch.	

4) In opposition to the engagement in fourth:

Master	Pupil
Engages in fourth.	First movement: simulates a disengagement clockwise to the outside high line.
Parries third.	Second movement: eludes the parry of third with a feint by disengagement counterclockwise to the low line or inside high line.
Parries second or fourth.	Third movement: eludes the parry of second with a disengagement clockwise to the high line; or eludes the parry of fourth with a disengagement clockwise to the outside high line.
Receives the touch.	

57. THE DOUBLE FEINT BY GLIDE AND DISENGAGEMENT

1) From engagement in first:

Master	Pupil
	First movement: from his own engagement in first simulates a glide to the inside low line.
Parries first.	Second movement: eludes the parry of first with a feint by disengagement counterclockwise to the outside low line.

Parries second.

Receives the touch.

Third movement: eludes the parry of second with a disengagement clockwise to the high line.

2) From engagement in second:

Master	Pupil
	First movement: from his own engagement in second simulates a glide to the outside low line.
Parries second.	Second movement: eludes the parry of second with a feint by disengagement clockwise to the high line.
Parries first or third.	Third movement: eludes the parry of first with a disengagement counterclockwise to the outside low line; or eludes the parry of third with a disengagement counterclockwise to the low line or inside high line.
Receives the touch.	

3) From engagement in third:

Master	Pupil
	First movement: from his own engagement in third simulates a glide to the outside high line.
Parries third.	Second movement: eludes the parry of third with a feint by disengagement counterclockwise to the low line or inside high line.
Parries second or fourth.	Third movement: eludes the parry of second with a disengagement clockwise to the high line; or eludes the parry of fourth with a disengagement clockwise to the outside high line.
Receives the touch.	

4) From engagement in fourth:

Master	Pupil
	First movement: from his own engagement in fourth simulates a glide to the inside high line.
Parries fourth.	Second movement: eludes the parry of fourth with a feint by disengagement clockwise to the outside high line.
Parries third.	Third movement: eludes the parry of third with a disengagement counterclockwise to the low line or inside high line.
Receives the touch.	

Observation: If the opponent effects imperfect engagements, his engagements are opposed with the double feint by forced glide and disengagement.

THE DOUBLE FEINT BY FLANCONADE IN FOURTH AND DISENGAGEMENT

From engagement in fourth:

Master	Pupil
	First movement: from his own engagement in fourth simulates a glide to the outside low line (flanconade in fourth).
Parries second.	Second movement: eludes the parry of second with a feint by disengagement clockwise to the high line.
Parries first or third.	Third movement: eludes the parry of first with a disengagement counterclockwise to the outside low line; or eludes the parry of third with a disengagement counterclockwise to the low line or inside high line.
Receives the touch.	

58. CONVENTIONAL EXERCISES

Conventional exercises consist of pre-established actions executed by two fencers alternately assuming the role of attacker and defender. The purpose of the exercises is to perfect the various offensive and defensive movements studied in the lesson, and to develop, through practice, a sense of fencing measure and time.

Observation: During the exercises, care must be taken that the guard position and lunge are correct in every detail.

EXERCISES WITH SIMPLE PARRIES

FIRST EXERCISE

The straight thrust in opposition to the four invitations:

A	B
Invites.	Directs a straight thrust to the exposed target.
Executes a simple parry and ripostes by detaching the blade, or by maintaining contact.	Receives the touch.

SECOND EXERCISE

The disengagement in opposition to the four engagements:

A	B
Engages.	Directs a disengagement to the exposed target.
Executes a simple parry and ripostes by detaching the blade, or by maintaining contact.	Receives the touch.

Third Exercise

The straight thrust or feint direct and disengagement in opposition to the four invitations:

A	B
Invites.	Directs a straight thrust or feint direct and disengagement to the exposed target.
Executes one simple parry if the attack is a straight thrust, or two simple parries if it is a feint direct and disengagement, and ripostes by detaching the blade, or by maintaining contact.	Receives the touch or opposes the riposte with the counterparry riposte.

Fourth Exercise

The disengagement or feint by disengagement and disengagement in opposition to the four engagements:

A	B
Engages.	Directs a disengagement or feint by disengagement and disengagement to the exposed target.
Executes one simple parry if the attack is a disengagement, or two simple parries if it is a feint by disengagement and disengagement, and ripostes by detaching the blade, or by maintaining contact.	Receives the touch or opposes the riposte with the counterparry riposte.

Fifth Exercise

The single or double feint direct and disengagement is opposed to the four invitations, first from correct, or lunging distance, then from out of distance, with a step forward and lunge; the single feint is countered with two simple parries, the double feint with three simple parries.

Sixth Exercise

The single or double feint by disengagement and disengagement is opposed to the four engagements, first from correct, or lunging distance, then from out of distance, with a step forward and lunge; the single feint is countered with two simple parries, the double feint with three simple parries.

Observation: In the above exercises care should be taken that the feints are properly stressed, and the parries kept tight. Each of the actions must be performed with the utmost precision.

CHAPTER 7

CIRCULAR ATTACKS

59. CIRCULAR PARRIES

Circular parries are defensive blade movements in which the point describes a tight, complete circle around the incoming steel, intercepting and transferring it to the opposite line. At the completion of the action the point is in exactly the same position it was before the parry was executed.

The circular parry in foil is effected by keeping the hand fixed in its position of invitation or engagement, while the point is set in motion by the fingers and wrist.

In foil fencing there are four circular parries, each protecting a certain area or areas of the valid target: thus, the parry of counter of first defends the outside low line, the parry of counter of second, the high and inside low lines, the parry of counter of third, the inside high line, and the parry of counter of fourth, the outside high line.

As in the preceding parries, the strong of the defending blade must encounter the medium of the attacking steel.

From the invitation or engagement in first the parry of counter of first is accomplished in one motion, with the point moving clockwise over the adversary's blade.

From the invitation or engagement in second the parry of counter of second is effected in one movement, with the point traveling counterclockwise over the opponent's steel.

From the invitation or engagement in third the parry of counter of third is achieved in one motion, with the point moving clockwise under the adversary's blade.

From the invitation or engagement in fourth the parry of counter of fourth is made in one movement, with the point traveling counterclockwise under the opponent's steel.

60. HALF CIRCULAR PARRIES

Half circular parries are defensive displacements of the blade along a diagonal semicircular route from a high to a low line and vice versa. They represent one half of a circular parry.

In foil fencing half circular parries are formed by moving from second to fourth, and from third to first.

Observation: The movement from fourth to second in opposition to the cut-over to the flank may also be considered a half circular parry.

61. CIRCULAR ATTACKS

Circular attacks are used in opposition to circular parries. In these compound offensive actions the feint provokes a circular parry, which is then deceived by a circular thrust moving in the same direction as the parry.

The circular thrust or deceive may be preceded by a feint direct, feint by disengagement, or feint by glide, depending upon placement of the adversary's weapon.

Observation: The deceive, like the disengagement, must be kept as tight as possible; correctly executed, it is a tiny, spiral action that moves progressively forward. At the completion of the action the point will have returned to the exact line in which the movement began. Viewed on a two-dimensional surface, the deceive is a perfect circle.

62. ELUDING ONE CIRCULAR PARRY

One circular parry is eluded by a single feint plus a deceive. The deceive is completed in the same line as the feint.

63. THE FEINT DIRECT AND DECEIVE

1) In opposition to the invitation in first:

Master	Pupil
Invites in first.	First movement: simulates a straight thrust to the outside low line.
Parries counter of first.	Second movement: eludes the parry of counter of first with a deceive counterclockwise to the outside low line.
Receives the touch.	

2) In opposition to the invitation in second:

Master	Pupil
Invites in second.	First movement: simulates a straight thrust to the high line.
Parries counter of second.	Second movement: eludes the parry of counter of second with a deceive clockwise to the high line.
Receives the touch.	

Observation: In opposition to the feint to the high line the master could also have executed the half circular parry of fourth; the parry would, in this case, be eluded with a disengagement clockwise to the outside high line.

3) In opposition to the invitation in third:

Master	Pupil
Invites in third.	First movement: simulates a straight thrust to the inside high line.
Parries counter of third.	Second movement: eludes the parry of counter of third with a deceive counter-clockwise to the inside high line.
Receives the touch.	

Observation: In opposition to the feint to the inside high line the master could also have executed the half circular parry of first; the parry would, in this instance, be eluded with a disengagement counterclockwise to the outside low line.

4) In opposition to the invitation in fourth:

Master	Pupil
Invites in fourth.	First movement: simulates a straight thrust to the outside high line.
Parries counter of fourth.	Second movement: eludes the parry of counter of fourth with a deceive clockwise to the outside high line.
Receives the touch.	

64. THE FEINT BY DISENGAGEMENT AND DECEIVE

1) In opposition to the engagement in first:

Master	Pupil
Engages in first.	First movement: simulates a disengagement counterclockwise to the outside low line.
Parries counter of first.	Second movement: eludes the parry of counter of first with a deceive counterclockwise to the outside low line.
Receives the touch.	

2) In opposition to the engagement in second:

Master	Pupil
Engages in second.	First movement: simulates a disengagement clockwise to the high line.
Parries counter of second.	Second movement: eludes the parry of counter of second with a deceive clockwise to the high line.
Receives the touch.	

3) In opposition to the engagement in third:

Master	Pupil
Engages in third.	First movement: simulates a disengagement counterclockwise to the inside high line.
Parries counter of third.	Second movement: eludes the parry of counter of third with a deceive counterclockwise to the inside high line.
Receives the touch.	

4) In opposition to the engagement in fourth:

Master	Pupil
Engages in fourth.	First movement: simulates a disengagement clockwise to the outside high line.
Parries counter of fourth.	Second movement: eludes the parry of counter of fourth with a deceive clockwise to the outside high line.
Receives the touch.	

65. The Feint by Glide and Deceive

1) From engagement in first:

Master	Pupil
	First movement: from his own engagement in first simulates a glide to the inside low line.
Parries counter of second.	Second movement: eludes the parry of counter of second with a deceive clockwise to the inside low line.
Receives the touch.	

2) From engagement in second:

Master	Pupil
	First movement: from his own engagement in second simulates a glide to the outside low line.
Parries counter of first.	Second movement: eludes the parry of counter of first with a deceive counterclockwise to the outside low line.
Receives the touch.	

3) From engagement in third:

Master	Pupil
	First movement: from his own engagement in third simulates a glide to the outside high line.
Parries counter of fourth.	Second movement: eludes the parry of counter of fourth with a deceive clockwise to the outside high line.
Receives the touch.	

4) From engagement in fourth:

Master	Pupil
	First movement: from his own engagement in fourth simulates a glide to the inside high line.

Parries counter of third.

Receives the touch.

Second movement: eludes the parry of counter of third with a deceive counterclockwise to the inside high line.

Observation: If the adversary effects weak engagements, his engagements are opposed with the feint by forced glide and deceive.

THE FEINT BY FLANCONADE IN FOURTH AND DECEIVE

From engagement in fourth:

Master	Pupil
	First movement: from his own engagement in fourth simulates a glide to the outside low line (flanconade in fourth).
Parries counter of first.	Second movement: eludes the parry of counter of first with a deceive counterclockwise to the outside low line.
Receives the touch.	

66. ELUDING ONE CIRCULAR AND ONE SIMPLE PARRY

One circular and one simple parry are eluded by a feint direct, feint by disengagement, or feint by glide, depending upon placement of the adversary's weapon, followed by a feint by deceive, and disengagement.

67. THE FEINT DIRECT, DECEIVE, AND DISENGAGEMENT

1) In opposition to the invitation in first:

Master	Pupil
Invites in first.	First movement: simulates a straight thrust to the outside low line.
Parries counter of first.	Second movement: eludes the parry of counter of first with a feint by deceive counterclockwise to the outside low line.
Parries second.	Third movement: eludes the parry of second with a disengagement clockwise to the high line.
Receives the touch.	

2) In opposition to the invitation in second:

Master	Pupil
Invites in second.	First movement: simulates a straight thrust to the high line.
Parries counter of second.	Second movement: eludes the parry of counter of second with a feint by deceive clockwise to the high line
Parries first or third.	Third movement: eludes the parry of first with a disengagement counterclockwise to the outside low line; or eludes the parry of third with a disengagement counterclockwise to the low line or inside high line.
Receives the touch.	

3) In opposition to the invitation in third:

Master	Pupil
Invites in third.	First movement: simulates a straight thrust to the inside high line.
Parries counter of third.	Second movement: eludes the parry of counter of third with a feint by deceive counterclockwise to the inside high line.
Parries fourth.	Third movement: eludes the parry of fourth with a disengagement clockwise to the outside high line.
Receives the touch.	

4) In opposition to the invitation in fourth:

Master	Pupil
Invites in fourth.	First movement: simulates a straight thrust to the outside high line.
Parries counter of fourth.	Second movement: eludes the parry of counter of fourth with a feint by deceive clockwise to the outside high line.
Parries third.	Third movement: eludes the parry of third with a disengagement counterclockwise to the low line or inside high line.
Receives the touch.	

68. THE FEINT BY DISENGAGEMENT, DECEIVE, AND DISENGAGEMENT

1) In opposition to the engagement in first:

Master	Pupil
Engages in first.	First movement: simulates a disengagement counterclockwise to the outside low line.
Parries counter of first.	Second movement: eludes the parry of counter of first with a feint by deceive counterclockwise to the outside low line.
Parries second.	Third movement: eludes the parry of second with a disengagement clockwise to the high line.
Receives the touch.	

2) In opposition to the engagement in second:

Master	Pupil
Engages in second.	First movement: simulates a disengagement clockwise to the high line.
Parries counter of second.	Second movement: eludes the parry of counter of second with a feint by deceive clockwise to the high line.
Parries first or third.	Third movement: eludes the parry of first with a disengagement counterclockwise to the outside low line; or eludes the parry of third with a disengagement counterclockwise to the low line or inside high line.
Receives the touch.	

3) In opposition to the engagement in third:

Master	Pupil
Engages in third.	First movement: simulates a disengagement counterclockwise to the inside high line.
Parries counter of third.	Second movement: eludes the parry of counter of third with a feint by deceive counterclockwise to the inside high line.

| Parries fourth. | Third movement: eludes the parry of fourth with a disengagement clockwise to the outside high line. |
| Receives the touch. | |

4) In opposition to the engagement in fourth:

Master	Pupil
Engages in fourth.	First movement: simulates a disengagement clockwise to the outside high line.
Parries counter of fourth.	Second movement: eludes the parry of counter of fourth with a feint by deceive clockwise to the outside high line.
Parries third.	Third movement: eludes the parry of third with a disengagement counterclockwise to the low line or inside high line.
Receives the touch.	

69. THE FEINT BY GLIDE, DECEIVE, AND DISENGAGEMENT

1) From engagement in first:

Master	Pupil
	First movement: from his own engagement in first simulates a glide to the inside low line.
Parries counter of second.	Second movement: eludes the parry of counter of second with a feint by deceive clockwise to the inside low line.
Parries first.	Third movement: eludes the parry of first with a disengagement counterclockwise to the outside low line.
Receives the touch.	

2) From engagement in second:

Master	Pupil
	First movement: from his own engagement in second simulates a glide to the outside low line.

Parries counter of first.	Second movement: eludes the parry of counter of first with a feint by deceive counterclockwise to the outside low line.
Parries second.	Third movement: eludes the parry of second with a disengagement clockwise to the high line.
Receives the touch.	

3) From engagement in third:

Master	Pupil
	First movement: from his own engagement in third simulates a glide to the outside high line.
Parries counter of fourth.	Second movement: eludes the parry of counter of fourth with a feint by deceive clockwise to the outside high line.
Parries third.	Third movement: eludes the parry of third with a disengagement counterclockwise to the low line or inside high line.
Receives the touch.	

4) From engagement in fourth:

Master	Pupil
	First movement: from his own engagement in fourth simulates a glide to the inside high line.
Parries counter of third.	Second movement: eludes the parry of counter of third with a feint by deceive counterclockwise to the inside high line.
Parries fourth.	Third movement: eludes the parry of fourth with a disengagement clockwise to the outside high line.
Receives the touch.	

Observation: If the opponent effects imperfect engagements, his engagements are opposed with the feint by forced glide, deceive, and disengagement.

THE FEINT BY FLANCONADE IN FOURTH, DECEIVE, AND DISENGAGEMENT

From engagement in fourth:

Master	Pupil
	First movement: from his own engagement in fourth simulates a glide to the outside low line (flanconade in fourth).
Parries counter of first.	Second movement: eludes the parry of counter of first with a feint by deceive counterclockwise to the outside low line.
Parries second.	Third movement: eludes the parry of second with a disengagement clockwise to the high line.
Receives the touch.	

70. ELUDING ONE SIMPLE AND ONE CIRCULAR PARRY

One simple and one circular parry are eluded by a double feint plus a deceive.

71. THE DOUBLE FEINT DIRECT AND DECEIVE

1) In opposition to the invitation in first:

Master	Pupil
Invites in first.	First movement: simulates a straight thrust to the outside low line.
Parries second.	Second movement: eludes the parry of second with a feint by disengagement clockwise to the high line.
Parries counter of second.	Third movement: eludes the parry of counter of second with a deceive clockwise to the high line.
Receives the touch.	

2) In opposition to the invitation in second:

Master	Pupil
Invites in second.	First movement: simulates a straight thrust to the high line.
Parries first or third.	Second movement: eludes the parry of first with a feint by disengagement counterclockwise to the outside low line; or eludes the parry of third with a feint by disengagement counterclockwise to the inside high line.
Parries counter of first or counter of third.	Third movement: eludes the parry of counter of first with a deceive counterclockwise to the outside low line; or eludes the parry of counter of third with a deceive counterclockwise to the inside high line.
Receives the touch.	

3) In opposition to the invitation in third:

Master	Pupil
Invites in third.	First movement: simulates a straight thrust to the inside high line.
Parries fourth.	Second movement: eludes the parry of fourth with a feint by disengagement clockwise to the outside high line.
Parries counter of fourth.	Third movement: eludes the parry of counter of fourth with a deceive clockwise to the outside high line.
Receives the touch.	

4) In opposition to the invitation in fourth:

Master	Pupil
Invites in fourth.	First movement: simulates a straight thrust to the outside high line.
Parries third.	Second movement: eludes the parry of third with a feint by disengagement counterclockwise to the inside high line.

| Parries counter of third. | Third movement: eludes the parry of counter of third with a deceive counterclockwise to the inside high line. |
| Receives the touch. | |

72. THE DOUBLE FEINT BY DISENGAGEMENT AND DECEIVE

1) In opposition to the engagement in first:

Master	Pupil
Engages in first.	First movement: simulates a disengagement counterclockwise to the outside low line.
Parries second.	Second movement: eludes the parry of second with a feint by disengagement clockwise to the high line.
Parries counter of second.	Third movement: eludes the parry of counter of second with a deceive clockwise to the high line.
Receives the touch.	

2) In opposition to the engagement in second:

Master	Pupil
Engages in second.	First movement: simulates a disengagement clockwise to the high line.
Parries first or third.	Second movement: eludes the parry of first with a feint by disengagement counterclockwise to the outside low line; or eludes the parry of third with a feint by disengagement counterclockwise to the inside high line.
Parries counter of first or counter of third.	Third movement: eludes the parry of counter of first with a deceive counterclockwise to the outside low line; or eludes the parry of counter of third with a deceive counterclockwise to the inside high line.
Receives the touch.	

3) In opposition to the engagement in third:

Master	Pupil
Engages in third.	First movement: simulates a disengagement counterclockwise to the inside high line.
Parries fourth.	Second movement: eludes the parry of fourth with a feint by disengagement clockwise to the outside high line.
Parries counter of fourth.	Third movement: eludes the parry of counter of fourth with a deceive clockwise to the outside high line.
Receives the touch.	

4) In opposition to the engagement in fourth:

Master	Pupil
Engages in fourth.	First movement: simulates a disengagement clockwise to the outside high line.
Parries third.	Second movement: eludes the parry of third with a feint by disengagement counterclockwise to the inside high line.
Parries counter of third.	Third movement: eludes the parry of counter of third with a deceive counterclockwise to the inside high line.
Receives the touch.	

73. THE DOUBLE FEINT BY GLIDE AND DECEIVE

1) From engagement in first:

Master	Pupil
	First movement: from his own engagement in first simulates a glide to the inside low line.
Parries first.	Second movement: eludes the parry of first with a feint by disengagement counterclockwise to the outside low line.

Parries counter of first.	Third movement: eludes the parry of counter of first with a deceive counterclockwise to the outside low line.
Receives the touch.	

2) From engagement in second:

Master	Pupil
	First movement: from his own engagement in second simulates a glide to the outside low line.
Parries second.	Second movement: eludes the parry of second with a feint by disengagement clockwise to the high line.
Parries counter of second.	Third movement: eludes the parry of counter of second with a deceive clockwise to the high line.
Receives the touch.	

3) From engagement in third:

Master	Pupil
	First movement: from his own engagement in third simulates a glide to the outside high line.
Parries third.	Second movement: eludes the parry of third with a feint by disengagement counterclockwise to the inside high line.
Parries counter of third.	Third movement: eludes the parry of counter of third with a deceive counterclockwise to the inside high line.
Receives the touch.	

4) From engagement in fourth:

Master	Pupil
	First movement: from his own engagement in fourth simulates a glide to the inside high line.

Parries fourth.	Second movement: eludes the parry of fourth with a feint by disengagement clockwise to the outside high line.
Parries counter of fourth.	Third movement: eludes the parry of counter of fourth with a deceive clockwise to the outside high line.
Receives the touch.	

Observation: If the adversary effects weak engagements, his engagements are opposed with the double feint by forced glide and deceive.

THE DOUBLE FEINT BY FLANCONADE IN FOURTH AND DECEIVE

From engagement in fourth:

Master	Pupil
	First movement: from his own engagement in fourth simulates a glide to the outside low line (flanconade in fourth).
Parries second.	Second movement: eludes the parry of second with a feint by disengagement clockwise to the high line.
Parries counter of second.	Third movement: eludes the parry of counter of second with a deceive clockwise to the high line.
Receives the touch.	

74. ELUDING TWO CIRCULAR PARRIES

Two circular parries are eluded by a feint direct, feint by disengagement, or feint by glide, depending upon placement of the opponent's weapon, followed by a feint by deceive and deceive. The final deceive terminates in the same line as the initial feint.

75. THE FEINT DIRECT AND DOUBLE DECEIVE

1) In opposition to the invitation in first:

Master	Pupil
Invites in first.	First movement: simulates a straight thrust to the outside low line.

Parries counter of first.	Second movement: eludes the parry of counter of first with a feint by deceive counterclockwise to the outside low line.
Parries counter of first.	Third movement: eludes the parry of counter of first with a deceive counterclockwise to the outside low line.
Receives the touch.	

2) In opposition to the invitation in second:

Master	Pupil
Invites in second.	First movement: simulates a straight thrust to the high line.
Parries counter of second.	Second movement: eludes the parry of counter of second with a feint by deceive clockwise to the high line.
Parries counter of second.	Third movement: eludes the parry of counter of second with a deceive clockwise to the high line.
Receives the touch.	

3) In opposition to the invitation in third:

Master	Pupil
Invites in third.	First movement: simulates a straight thrust to the inside high line.
Parries counter of third.	Second movement: eludes the parry of counter of third with a feint by deceive counterclockwise to the inside high line.
Parries counter of third.	Third movement: eludes the parry of counter of third with a deceive counterclockwise to the inside high line.
Receives the touch.	

4) In opposition to the invitation in fourth:

Master	Pupil
Invites in fourth.	First movement: simulates a straight thrust to the outside high line.

Parries counter of fourth.	Second movement: eludes the parry of counter of fourth with a feint by deceive clockwise to the outside high line.
Parries counter of fourth.	Third movement: eludes the parry of counter of fourth with a deceive clockwise to the outside high line.
Receives the touch.	

76. THE FEINT BY DISENGAGEMENT AND DOUBLE DECEIVE

1) In opposition to the engagement in first:

Master	Pupil
Engages in first.	First movement: simulates a disengagement counterclockwise to the outside low line.
Parries counter of first.	Second movement: eludes the parry of counter of first with a feint by deceive counterclockwise to the outside low line.
Parries counter of first.	Third movement: eludes the parry of counter of first with a deceive counterclockwise to the outside low line.
Receives the touch.	

2) In opposition to the engagement in second:

Master	Pupil
Engages in second.	First movement: simulates a disengagement clockwise to the high line.
Parries counter of second.	Second movement: eludes the parry of counter of second with a feint by deceive clockwise to the high line.
Parries counter of second.	Third movement: eludes the parry of counter of second with a deceive clockwise to the high line.
Receives the touch.	

3) In opposition to the engagement in third:

Master	Pupil
Engages in third.	First movement: simulates a disengagement counterclockwise to the inside high line.

Parries counter of third.	Second movement: eludes the parry of counter of third with a feint by deceive counterclockwise to the inside high line.
Parries counter of third.	Third movement: eludes the parry of counter of third with a deceive counter-clockwise to the inside high line.
Receives the touch.	

4) In opposition to the engagement in fourth:

Master	Pupil
Engages in fourth.	First movement: simulates a disengagement clockwise to the outside high line.
Parries counter of fourth.	Second movement: eludes the parry of counter of fourth with a feint by deceive clockwise to the outside high line.
Parries counter of fourth.	Third movement: eludes the parry of counter of fourth with a deceive clockwise to the outside high line.
Receives the touch.	

77. THE FEINT BY GLIDE AND DOUBLE DECEIVE

1) From engagement in first:

Master	Pupil
	First movement: from his own engagement in first, simulates a glide to the inside low line.
Parries counter of second.	Second movement: eludes the parry of counter of second with a feint by deceive clockwise to the inside low line.
Parries counter of second.	Third movement: eludes the parry of counter of second with a deceive clockwise to the inside low line.
Receives the touch.	

2) From engagement in second:

Master	Pupil
	First movement: from his own engagement in second simulates a glide to the outside low line.
Parries counter of first.	Second movement: eludes the parry of counter of first with a feint by deceive counterclockwise to the outside low line.
Parries counter of first.	Third movement: eludes the parry of counter of first with a deceive counterclockwise to the outside low line.
Receives the touch.	

3) From engagement in third:

Master	Pupil
	First movement: from his own engagement in third simulates a glide to the outside high line.
Parries counter of fourth.	Second movement: eludes the parry of counter of fourth with a feint by deceive clockwise to the outside high line.
Parries counter of fourth.	Third movement: eludes the parry of counter of fourth with a deceive clockwise to the outside high line.
Receives the touch.	

4) From engagement in fourth:

Master	Pupil
	First movement: from his own engagement in fourth simulates a glide to the inside high line.
Parries counter of third.	Second movement: eludes the parry of counter of third with a feint by deceive counterclockwise to the inside high line.

Parries counter of third.	Third movement: eludes the parry of counter of third with a deceive counter-clockwise to the inside high line.
Receives the touch.	

Observation: If the opponent effects imperfect engagements, his engagements are opposed with the feint by forced glide and double deceive.

THE FEINT BY FLANCONADE IN FOURTH AND DOUBLE DECEIVE

From engagement in fourth:

Master	*Pupil*
	First movement: from his own engagement in fourth simulates a glide to the outside low line (flanconade in fourth).
Parries counter of first.	Second movement: eludes the parry of counter of first with a feint by deceive counterclockwise to the outside low line.
Parries counter of first.	Third movement: eludes the parry of counter of first with a deceive counterclockwise to the outside low line.
Receives the touch.	

78. TRIPLE FEINTS

Triple feints elude three parries; they are used in opposition to the invitation and engagement.

The feints are executed with a gradual extension of the sword arm, and may be coordinated with an advance. The first feint is made with the motion of the right foot, the second with the movement of the left foot, the third from immobility, and the final thrust with the lunge.

Observation: As a rule, it is advisable to avoid triple feints in combat since they expose the attacker to counterattacks; but they are useful in the lesson as an exercise in point control.

79. ELUDING ONE SIMPLE, ONE CIRCULAR, AND ONE SIMPLE PARRY

One simple, one circular, and one simple parry can be eluded by a double feint followed by a feint by deceive and disengagement.

80. The Double Feint Direct, Deceive, and Disengagement

1) In opposition to the invitation in first:

Master	Pupil
Invites in first.	First movement: simulates a straight thrust to the outside low line.
Parries second.	Second movement: eludes the parry of second with a feint by disengagement clockwise to the high line.
Parries counter of second.	Third movement: eludes the parry of counter of second with a feint by deceive clockwise to the high line.
Parries first or third.	Fourth movement: eludes the parry of first with a disengagement counterclockwise to the outside low line; or eludes the parry of third with a disengagement counterclockwise to the low line or inside high line.
Receives the touch.	

Observation: Correctly executed, multiple feints are very tight, and are kept in close proximity to the opposing steel. Each feint must be directed with precision to the appropriate target area, so that it draws the exact parry desired. Careful timing is of the utmost importance: if the feints are not held long enough, they will not provoke parries; if they are held too long, they will be caught by the parries. An attack consisting of multiple feints can only succeed if every movement of the action is properly coordinated with the adversary's parries.

2) In opposition to the invitation in second:

Master	Pupil
Invites in second.	First movement: simulates a straight thrust to the high line.
Parries first or third.	Second movement: eludes the parry of first with a feint by disengagement counterclockwise to the outside low line; or eludes the parry of third with a feint by disengagement counterclockwise to the inside high line.

Parries counter of first or counter of third.	Third movement: eludes the parry of counter of first with a feint by deceive counterclockwise to the outside low line; or eludes the parry of counter of third with the feint by deceive counterclockwise to the inside high line.
Parries second or fourth.	Fourth movement: eludes the parry of second with a disengagement clockwise to the high line; or eludes the parry of fourth with a disengagement clockwise to the outside high line.
Receives the touch.	

3) In opposition to the invitation in third:

Master	*Pupil*
Invites in third.	First movement: simulates a straight thrust to the inside high line.
Parries fourth.	Second movement: eludes the parry of fourth with a feint by disengagement clockwise to the outside high line.
Parries counter of fourth.	Third movement: eludes the parry of counter of fourth with a feint by deceive clockwise to the outside high line.
Parries third.	Fourth movement: eludes the parry of third with a disengagement counterclockwise to the low line or inside high line.
Receives the touch.	

4) In opposition to the invitation in fourth:

Master	*Pupil*
Invites in fourth.	First movement: simulates a straight thrust to the outside high line.
Parries third.	Second movement: eludes the parry of third with a feint by disengagement counterclockwise to the inside high line.
Parries counter of third.	Third movement: eludes the parry of counter of third with a feint by deceive counterclockwise to the inside high line.

Parries fourth.	Fourth movement: eludes the parry of fourth with a disengagement clockwise to the outside high line.
Receives the touch.	

81. THE DOUBLE FEINT BY DISENGAGEMENT, DECEIVE, AND DISENGAGEMENT

1) In opposition to the engagement in first:

Master	Pupil
Engages in first.	First movement: simulates a disengagement counterclockwise to the outside low line.
Parries second.	Second movement: eludes the parry of second with a feint by disengagement clockwise to the high line.
Parries counter of second.	Third movement: eludes the parry of counter of second with a feint by deceive clockwise to the high line.
Parries first or third.	Fourth movement: eludes the parry of first with a disengagement counterclockwise to the outside low line; or eludes the parry of third with a disengagement counterclockwise to the low line or inside high line.
Receives the touch.	

2) In opposition to the engagement in second:

Master	Pupil
Engages in second.	First movement: simulates a disengagement clockwise to the high line.
Parries first or third.	Second movement: eludes the parry of first with a feint by disengagement counterclockwise to the outside low line; or eludes the parry of third with a feint by disengagement counterclockwise to the inside high line.
Parries counter of first or counter of third.	Third movement: eludes the parry of counter of first with a feint by deceive coun-

	terclockwise to the outside low line; or eludes the parry of counter of third with the feint by deceive counterclockwise to the inside high line.
Parries second or fourth.	Fourth movement: eludes the parry of second with a disengagement clockwise to the high line; or eludes the parry of fourth with a disengagement clockwise to the outside high line.
Receives the touch.	

3) In opposition to the engagement in third:

Master	*Pupil*
Engages in third.	First movement: simulates a disengagement counterclockwise to the inside high line.
Parries fourth.	Second movement: eludes the parry of fourth with a feint by disengagement clockwise to the outside high line.
Parries counter of fourth.	Third movement: eludes the parry of counter of fourth with a feint by deceive clockwise to the outside high line.
Parries third.	Fourth movement: eludes the parry of third with a disengagement counterclockwise to the low line or inside high line.
Receives the touch.	

4) In opposition to the engagement in fourth:

Master	*Pupil*
Engages in fourth.	First movement: simulates a disengagement clockwise to the outside high line.
Parries third.	Second movement: eludes the parry of third with a feint by disengagement counterclockwise to the inside high line.
Parries counter of third.	Third movement: eludes the parry of counter of third with a feint by deceive counterclockwise to the inside high line.

Parries fourth.	Fourth movement: eludes the parry of fourth with a disengagement clockwise to the outside high line.
Receives the touch.	

82. THE DOUBLE FEINT BY GLIDE, DECEIVE, AND DISENGAGEMENT

1) From engagement in first:

Master	Pupil
	First movement: from his own engagement in first simulates a glide to the inside low line.
Parries first.	Second movement: eludes the parry of first with a feint by disengagement counterclockwise to the outside low line.
Parries counter of first.	Third movement: eludes the parry of counter of first with a feint by deceive counterclockwise to the outside low line.
Parries second.	Fourth movement: eludes the parry of second with a disengagement clockwise to the high line.
Receives the touch.	

2) From engagement in second:

Master	Pupil
	First movement: from his own engagement in second simulates a glide to the outside low line.
Parries second.	Second movement: eludes the parry of second with a feint by disengagement clockwise to the high line.
Parries counter of second.	Third movement: eludes the parry of counter of second with a feint by deceive clockwise to the high line.
Parries first or third.	Fourth movement: eludes the parry of first with a disengagement counterclockwise to

| | the outside low line; or eludes the parry of third with a disengagement counterclockwise to the low line or inside high line. |
| Receives the touch. | |

3) From engagement in third:

Master	Pupil
	First movement: from his own engagement in third simulates a glide to the outside high line.
Parries third.	Second movement: eludes the parry of third with a feint by disengagement counterclockwise to the inside high line.
Parries counter of third.	Third movement: eludes the parry of counter of third with a feint by deceive counterclockwise to the inside high line.
Parries fourth.	Fourth movement: eludes the parry of fourth with a disengagement clockwise to the outside high line.
Receives the touch.	

4) From engagement in fourth:

Master	Pupil
	First movement: from his own engagement in fourth simulates a glide to the inside high line.
Parries fourth.	Second movement: eludes the parry of fourth with a feint by disengagement clockwise to the outside high line.
Parries counter of fourth.	Third movement: eludes the parry of counter of fourth with a feint by deceive clockwise to the outside high line.
Parries third.	Fourth movement: eludes the parry of third with a disengagement counterclockwise to the low line or inside high line.
Receives the touch.	

Observation: If the adversary effects weak engagements, his engagements are opposed with the double feint by forced glide, deceive, and disengagement.

THE DOUBLE FEINT BY FLANCONADE IN FOURTH, DECEIVE, AND DISENGAGEMENT

From engagement in fourth:

Master	Pupil
	First movement: from his own engagement in fourth simulates a glide to the outside low line (flanconade in fourth).
Parries second.	Second movement: eludes the parry of second with a feint by disengagement clockwise to the high line.
Parries counter of second.	Third movement: eludes the parry of counter of second with a feint by deceive clockwise to the high line.
Parries first or third.	Fourth movement: eludes the parry of first with a disengagement counterclockwise to the outside low line; or eludes the parry of third with a disengagement counterclockwise to the low line or inside high line.
Receives the touch.	

83. ELUDING ONE CIRCULAR, ONE SIMPLE, AND ONE CIRCULAR PARRY

One circular, one simple, and one circular parry can be eluded by a feint direct, feint by disengagement, or feint by glide, depending upon placement of the opponent's weapon, succeeded by a feint by deceive, feint by disengagement, and deceive.

84. THE FEINT DIRECT, DECEIVE, DISENGAGEMENT, AND DECEIVE

1) In opposition to the invitation in first:

Master	Pupil
Invites in first.	First movement: simulates a straight thrust to the outside low line.

Parries counter of first.	Second movement: eludes the parry of counter of first with a feint by deceive counterclockwise to the outside low line.
Parries second.	Third movement: eludes the parry of second with a feint by disengagement clockwise to the high line.
Parries counter of second.	Fourth movement: eludes the parry of counter of second with a deceive clockwise to the high line.
Receives the touch.	

2) In opposition to the invitation in second:

Master	Pupil
Invites in second.	First movement: simulates a straight thrust to the high line.
Parries counter of second.	Second movement: eludes the parry of counter of second with a feint by deceive clockwise to the high line.
Parries first or third.	Third movement: eludes the parry of first with a feint by disengagement counterclockwise to the outside low line; or eludes the parry of third with a feint by disengagement counterclockwise to the inside high line.
Parries counter of first or counter of third.	Fourth movement: eludes the parry of counter of first with a deceive counterclockwise to the outside low line; or eludes the parry of counter of third with a deceive counterclockwise to the inside high line.
Receives the touch.	

3) In opposition to the invitation in third:

Master	Pupil
Invites in third.	First movement: simulates a straight thrust to the inside high line.
Parries counter of third.	Second movement: eludes the parry of counter of third with a feint by deceive counterclockwise to the inside high line.

Parries fourth.	Third movement: eludes the parry of fourth with a feint by disengagement clockwise to the outside high line.
Parries counter of fourth.	Fourth movement: eludes the parry of counter of fourth with a deceive clockwise to the outside high line.
Receives the touch.	

4) In opposition to the invitation in fourth:

Master	Pupil
Invites in fourth.	First movement: simulates a straight thrust to the outside high line.
Parries counter of fourth.	Second movement: eludes the parry of counter of fourth with a feint by deceive clockwise to the outside high line.
Parries third.	Third movement: eludes the parry of third with a feint by disengagement counterclockwise to the inside high line.
Parries counter of third.	Fourth movement: eludes the parry of counter of third with a deceive counterclockwise to the inside high line.
Receives the touch.	

85. The Feint by Disengagement, Deceive, Disengagement, and Deceive

1) In opposition to the engagement in first:

Master	Pupil
Engages in first.	First movement: simulates a disengagement counterclockwise to the outside low line.
Parries counter of first.	Second movement: eludes the parry of counter of first with a feint by deceive counterclockwise to the outside low line.
Parries second.	Third movement: eludes the parry of second with a feint by disengagement clockwise to the high line.

| Parries counter of second. | Fourth movement: eludes the parry of counter of second with a deceive clockwise to the high line. |
| Receives the touch. | |

2) In opposition to the engagement in second:

Master	Pupil
Engages in second.	First movement: simulates a disengagement clockwise to the high line.
Parries counter of second.	Second movement: eludes the parry of counter of second with a feint by deceive clockwise to the high line.
Parries first or third.	Third movement: eludes the parry of first with a feint by disengagement counterclockwise to the outside low line; or eludes the parry of third with a feint by disengagement counterclockwise to the inside high line.
Parries counter of first or counter of third.	Fourth movement: eludes the parry of counter of first with a deceive counterclockwise to the outside low line; or eludes the parry of counter of third with a deceive counterclockwise to the inside high line.
Receives the touch.	

3) In opposition to the engagement in third:

Master	Pupil
Engages in third.	First movement: simulates a disengagement counterclockwise to the inside high line.
Parries counter of third.	Second movement: eludes the parry of counter of third with a feint by deceive counterclockwise to the inside high line.
Parries fourth.	Third movement: eludes the parry of fourth with a feint by disengagement clockwise to the outside high line.

Parries counter of fourth.	Fourth movement: eludes the parry of counter of fourth with a deceive clockwise to the outside high line.
Receives the touch.	

4) In opposition to the engagement in fourth:

Master	Pupil
Engages in fourth.	First movement: simulates a disengagement clockwise to the outside high line.
Parries counter of fourth.	Second movement: eludes the parry of counter of fourth with a feint by deceive clockwise to the outside high line.
Parries third.	Third movement: eludes the parry of third with a feint by disengagement counter-clockwise to the inside high line.
Parries counter of third.	Fourth movement: eludes the parry of counter of third with a deceive counter-clockwise to the inside high line.
Receives the touch.	

86. THE FEINT BY GLIDE, DECEIVE, DISENGAGEMENT, AND DECEIVE

1) From engagement in first:

Master	Pupil
	First movement: from his own engagement in first simulates a glide to the inside low line.
Parries counter of second.	Second movement: eludes the parry of counter of second with a feint by deceive clockwise to the inside low line.
Parries first.	Third movement: eludes the parry of first with a feint by disengagement counter-clockwise to the outside low line.
Parries counter of first.	Fourth movement: eludes the parry of counter of first with a deceive counterclock-wise to the outside low line.
Receives the touch.	

2) From engagement in second:

Master	Pupil
	First movement: from his own engagement in second simulates a glide to the outside low line.
Parries counter of first.	Second movement: eludes the parry of counter of first with a feint by deceive counterclockwise to the outside low line.
Parries second.	Third movement: eludes the parry of second with a feint by disengagement clockwise to the high line.
Parries counter of second.	Fourth movement: eludes the parry of counter of second with a deceive clockwise to the high line.
Receives the touch.	

3) From engagement in third:

Master	Pupil
	First movement: from his own engagement in third simulates a glide to the outside high line.
Parries counter of fourth.	Second movement: eludes the parry of counter of fourth with a feint by deceive clockwise to the outside high line.
Parries third.	Third movement: eludes the parry of third with a feint by disengagement counterclockwise to the inside high line.
Parries counter of third.	Fourth movement: eludes the parry of counter of third with a deceive counterclockwise to the inside high line.
Receives the touch.	

4) From engagement in fourth:

Master	Pupil
	First movement: from his own engagement in fourth simulates a glide to the inside high line.

Parries counter of third.	Second movement: eludes the parry of counter of third with a feint by deceive counterclockwise to the inside high line.
Parries fourth.	Third movement: eludes the parry of fourth with a feint by disengagement clockwise to the outside high line.
Parries counter of fourth.	Fourth movement: eludes the parry of counter of fourth with a deceive clockwise to the outside high line.
Receives the touch.	

Observation: If the opponent effects imperfect engagements, his engagements are opposed with the feint by forced glide, deceive, disengagement, and deceive.

THE FEINT BY FLANCONADE IN FOURTH, DECEIVE, DISENGAGEMENT, AND DECEIVE

From engagement in fourth:

Master	*Pupil*
	First movement: from his own engagement in fourth simulates a glide to the outside low line (flanconade in fourth).
Parries counter of first.	Second movement: eludes the parry of counter of first with a feint by deceive counterclockwise to the outside low line.
Parries second.	Third movement: eludes the parry of second with a feint by disengagement clockwise to the high line.
Parries counter of second.	Fourth movement: eludes the parry of counter of second with a deceive clockwise to the high line.
Receives the touch.	

Observation: In addition to the two defensive systems just mentioned, combining three parries, a simple parry followed by a circular parry, and a simple parry, or a circular parry succeeded by a simple parry, and a circular parry, there is yet another system, less commonly encountered, which consists of a circular parry followed by two simple parries. This defense is opposed with a feint direct, feint by disengagement, or feint by glide, depending upon placement of the adversary's weapon, succeeded by a feint by deceive, feint by disengagement, and disengagement. For example, in opposition to the master's invitation in third, the pupil simulates a straight thrust to the inside high line, the parry of counter of third is eluded with a feint by deceive counterclockwise to the inside high line, the parry of fourth is eluded with a feint by disengagement clockwise to the outside high line, and the parry of third is eluded with a disengagement counterclockwise to the inside high line.

87. Exercises with Circular Parries

First Exercise

The straight thrust in opposition to the four invitations:

A	B
Invites.	Directs a straight thrust to the exposed target.
Executes a circular parry and ripostes by detaching the blade, or by maintaining contact.	Receives the touch.

Second Exercise

The disengagement in opposition to the four engagements:

A	B
Engages.	Directs a disengagement to the exposed target.
Executes a circular parry and ripostes by detaching the blade, or by maintaining contact.	Receives the touch.

THIRD EXERCISE

The straight thrust or feint direct and deceive in opposition to the four invitations:

A	B
Invites.	Directs a straight thrust or feint direct and deceive to the exposed target.
Executes one circular parry if the attack is a straight thrust, or two circular parries if it is a feint direct and deceive, and ripostes by detaching the blade, or by maintaining contact.	Receives the touch or opposes the riposte with the counter-parry riposte.

FOURTH EXERCISE

The disengagement or feint by disengagement and deceive in opposition to the four engagements:

A	B
Engages.	Directs a disengagement or feint by disengagement and deceive to the exposed target.
Executes one circular parry if the attack is a disengagement, or two circular parries if it is a feint by disengagement and deceive, and ripostes by detaching the blade, or by maintaining contact.	Receives the touch or opposes the riposte with the counter-parry riposte.

Observation: It should be noted that the feint direct and deceive, and the feint by disengagement and deceive, may be parried either with two circular parries, or with one circular and one simple parry.

88. CIRCULAR RIPOSTES

Circular ripostes, like circular attacks, are used in opposition to circular parries. If, for example, an attacker, whose assault has been parried, defends himself with a circular counterparry, his counterparry can be eluded with a compound riposte consisting of a feint and deceive. This is executed in exactly the same way as a compound circular attack.

CHAPTER 8

THE CUT-OVER

89. THE CUT-OVER

After examining simple and compound attacks with the point in line, it is appropriate to turn to the cut-over, an action in which the point is momentarily withdrawn from the line of offense. The cut-over is a disengagement over the blade; it is an indirect attack executed in one movement, and may be used when the adversary engages in either third or fourth. The cut-over can be directed to the inside and outside high lines, and to the outside low line. It is effected from the guard at lunging distance, with the hand in fourth position (or third position if the thrust is aimed at the outside low line).

To liberate the blade from the opponent's engagement, the point is lifted over the opposing steel (Fig. 49), and dropped in the line opposite the original engagement; as the point nears the line of assault the sword arm is extended, hand rising gradually to shoulder height, and the thrust delivered. Blade motion is accomplished primarily through finger and wrist action, with some assistance from the elbow. Timing of the lunge is critical: to ensure correct placement of the point the lunge must be delayed until the arm is completely straight. When the cut-over is properly executed, there is little point vibration, and the thrust terminates with the point of the weapon firmly fixed on the target.

From the adversary's engagement in third the cut-over is directed to the inside high line, opposition to the left; and from his engagement in fourth it is aimed at either the outside high line, opposition to the right, or low line, hand in line with the right shoulder. When the thrust is directed to the low line the point travels counterclockwise in a semicircular movement, with the hand rotating at the wrist from fourth to third position.

Observation: It should be noted that during execution of the cut-over the point is momentarily lifted from its threatening position, and the arm withdrawn, thus exposing the attacker to a possible counterattack. For this reason it is prudent to avoid repeated use of the cut-over. To minimize the danger of exposure to a counterattack during execution of the cut-over, the point must be lifted just enough to pass over the opposing steel; the tighter the movement is, the faster and more secure the action will be.

Figure 49. The cut-over.

90. Compound Attacks with the Cut-over

The cut-over may also be employed in a compound attack. It can be preceded by a single feint, or it may serve as a feint before a disengagement.

Double feints with the cut-over should be avoided because of the exposure to counterattacks.

In a compound attack the cut-over is useful against the opponent who alternates simple, circular, and half circular parries.

91. The Feint Direct and Cut-over

1) In opposition to the invitation in third:

Master	Pupil
Invites in third.	First movement: simulates a straight thrust to the inside high line.
Parries fourth.	Second movement: eludes the parry of fourth with a cut-over to the outside high line or to the low line.
Receives the touch.	

Observation: Care must be taken that the feint to the high line is placed with precision; if it is too low, the cut-over may be caught by the parry.

2) In opposition to the invitation in fourth:

Master	Pupil
Invites in fourth.	First movement: simulates a straight thrust to the outside high line.
Parries third.	Second movement: eludes the parry of third with a cut-over to the inside high line.
Receives the touch.	

92. THE FEINT BY DISENGAGEMENT AND CUT-OVER

1) In opposition to the engagement in third:

Master	Pupil
Engages in third.	First movement: simulates a disengagement counterclockwise to the inside high line.
Parries fourth.	Second movement: eludes the parry of fourth with a cut-over to the outside high line or to the low line.
Receives the touch.	

2) In opposition to the engagement in fourth:

Master	Pupil
Engages in fourth.	First movement: simulates a disengagement clockwise to the outside high line.
Parries third.	Second movement: eludes the parry of third with a cut-over to the inside high line.
Receives the touch.	

93. THE FEINT BY GLIDE AND CUT-OVER

1) From engagement in third:

Master	Pupil
	First movement: from his own engagement in third simulates a glide to the outside high line.
Parries third.	Second movement: eludes the parry of third with a cut-over to the inside high line.
Receives the touch.	

2) From engagement in fourth:

Master	Pupil
	First movement: from his own engagement in fourth simulates a glide to the inside high line.
Parries fourth.	Second movement: eludes the parry of fourth with a cut-over to the outside high line or to the low line.
Receives the touch.	

Observation: If the adversary effects weak engagements, his engagements are opposed with the feint by forced glide and cut-over.

94. THE FEINT BY CUT-OVER AND DISENGAGEMENT

1) In opposition to the engagement in third:

Master	Pupil
Engages in third.	First movement: simulates a cut-over to the inside high line.
Parries fourth.	Second movement: eludes the parry of fourth with a disengagement clockwise to the outside high line.
Receives the touch.	

2) In opposition to the engagement in fourth:

Master	Pupil
Engages in fourth.	First movement: simulates a cut-over to the outside high or low line.
Parries third or second.	Second movement: eludes the parry of third with a disengagement counterclockwise to the low line or inside high line; or eludes the parry of second with a disengagement clockwise to the high line.
Receives the touch.	

Observation: When the feint by cut-over is directed to the low line, the hand may be kept in fourth position.

If the action is combined with an advance, the step forward must be delayed until the sword arm is fully extended.

To develop further the student's point control the teacher can add to the above compound attacks with two blade movements, compound attacks with three blade motions, such as the double feint direct and cut-over; double feint by disengagement and cut-over; double feint by glide and cut-over; the feint by cut-over, feint by disengagement, and disengagement; and the feint by cut-over, feint by disengagement, and deceive.

95. RIPOSTES WITH THE CUT-OVER

The cut-over may be used as a riposte after the parries of third, fourth, counter of third, and counter of fourth.

Observation: Ripostes with the cut-over are particularly effective at close range because it is easier to pass the point over the opposing steel than to disengage under it.

CHAPTER 9

ACTIONS ON THE BLADE

96. ACTIONS ON THE BLADE

Actions on the blade are movements that deviate or deflect the opposing steel during the attack. For example, the glide is an action on the blade that is accomplished in one movement. In the development of the attack the opposing steel is forced aside through opposition.

Blade seizure, changes of engagement, transports, envelopments, beats, expulsions, pressures, blade cover, and disarmaments are actions on the blade used in attacks of two or more blade motions to deviate or deflect the opposing steel so that a thrust or feint may be executed.

With the exception of glides and disarmaments, the movements listed above can be combined with an advance. In each case the action on the blade is coordinated with the step forward.

Observation: The glide is a simple attack when it commences from engagement and is effected in one movement; it is a compound attack when it is preceded by the act of engagement, and is accomplished in two or more motions.

97. BLADE SEIZURE

Blade seizure is an action on the blade opposed to the adversary's weapon in line; it consists of an engagement usually combined with an advance, and followed by a straight thrust, glide, or feint. The complete action is comprised of two or more motions. Blade seizure can be effected in each of the four engagements. We therefore speak of blade seizure in first, second, third, and fourth.

In the first movement the opposing steel is contacted, as the step forward is made, and deviated from its placement in line through gradual and accentuated pressure of the strong against the weak; in the second motion a straight thrust, glide, or feint is directed to the exposed target.

Observation: It should be noted that blade seizure is most effective when it is succeeded by a glide. In executing this action care must be taken that the engagement is smooth, and that the glide is accomplished with strong opposition.

In the case of an advanced student already familiar with the counterattacks and countertime, the master may periodically execute a disengagement in time in opposition to blade seizure so that the pupil will learn to make the shift from the attack to countertime. For instance, after having permitted the student to effect blade seizure in fourth with a glide, the teacher can disengage in time to the outside high line; the instant the pupil fails to contact the opposing blade, he must be directed to pause at the completion of his step forward and parry counter of fourth with an immediate riposte to the inside high line.

98. CHANGES OF ENGAGEMENT FOLLOWED BY GLIDES

Single or double changes of engagement followed by glides may be employed when the opponent's steel is engaged or in line. In every case the hostile blade must be engaged strong against weak, and carried with decision to the new line of engagement before the glide is effected.

Changes of engagement succeeded by glides are accomplished in two or more movements.

When a single change of engagement is followed by a glide, the attack terminates in the line opposite the initial engagement. From engagement in first the opposing steel is transferred from left to right, with the glide in second, and opposition to the right; from engagement in second the hostile blade is shifted from right to left, with the glide in first, and opposition to the left; from engagement in third the opposing steel is moved from right to left, with the glide in fourth or flanconade in fourth, and opposition to the left; and from engagement in fourth the hostile blade is carried from left to right, with the glide in third and opposition to the right.

When a double change of engagement is succeeded by a glide, the assault ends in the original line of engagement. From engagement in first the opposing steel is transferred to second, and then back to first, with the glide in first, and opposition to the left; from engagement in second the hostile blade is shifted to first, and then back to second, with the glide in second, and opposition to the right; from engagement in third the opposing steel is moved to fourth, and then back to third, with the glide in third, and opposition to the right; and from engagement in fourth the hostile blade is carried to third, and then back to fourth, with the glide in fourth or flanconade in fourth, and opposition to the left.

99. Transports Followed by Glides

Transports followed by glides may be used when the adversary's steel is engaged.

These actions are accomplished from engagement in two movements, without a break in blade contact. Correctly executed, the transport and glide fuse in a rapid and continuous motion. The hand is shifted so that the blade pivots, strong against weak, in a tight, spiral movement around the opponent's steel, transporting it to the new line of engagement, arm moving gradually to full extension; then, without interrupting the flow of motion, the thrust is effected along the adversary's blade.

From engagement in first the opposing steel is transferred from left to right, with the glide in third, and opposition to the right; from engagement in second the hostile blade is carried from right to left, with the glide in fourth, and opposition to the left; from engagement in third the opposing steel is moved from right to left, with the glide in first, and opposition to the left; and from engagement in fourth the hostile blade is shifted from left to right, with the glide in second, and opposition to the right.

The transport to first and glide to the inside low line is called the internal flanconade; the transport to second and glide to the outside low line is known as the flanconade in second. In the internal flanconade the hand stays in fourth position, and the blade glides along the inside of the opposing steel; in the flanconade in second it may remain in fourth position, or it can be rotated to second position, and the blade glides along the outside of the opposing steel.

Observation: Transports from first to third and second to fourth followed by glides may also be used effectively as ripostes; the internal flanconade and flanconade in second, however, must not be employed as ripostes since, during the transporting action, they can easily carry the opponent's point to one's own leg.

The internal flanconade and flanconade in second are generally combined with an advance. In adding the step forward particular care should be taken that blade motion precedes foot movement.

100. Envelopments Followed by Glides

Envelopments in first, second, third, and fourth followed by glides may be employed when the adversary's steel is engaged.

These actions are made from engagement in two movements, without a break in blade contact. Properly executed, the envelopment and glide blend in a swift and continuous motion. The hand is shifted so that the blade pivots, strong against weak, in a close spiral movement around the opponent's steel, transporting it to the high or low line, and then back again to its initial position, arm advancing gradually to complete extension; immediately on regaining the original line, and without interrupting the flow of motion, the thrust is effected along the adversary's blade.

From engagement in first the point travels clockwise around the opposing steel, carrying the blade in an elliptical movement from first to third to first, and ending with the glide in first, and opposition to the left; from engagement in second the point moves counterclockwise around the hostile blade, transporting the steel in an elliptical motion from second to fourth to second, and terminating with the glide in second, and opposition to the right; from engagement in third the point travels clockwise around the opposing steel, carrying the blade in an elliptical movement from third to first to third, and ending with the glide in third, and opposition to the right; from engagement in fourth the point moves counterclockwise around the hostile blade, transporting the steel in an elliptical motion from fourth to second to fourth, and terminating with the glide in fourth, and opposition to the left.

Observation: Throughout the enveloping action movement of the point must be kept as tight as possible; the smaller the point motion is, the more efficient the action will be.

101. BEATS

Beats are blows of measured violence delivered with the strong of the blade against the medium of the adversary's steel to dislodge it from engagement or its position in line. The line in which the attacking blade encounters the opposing steel identifies the beat: we therefore speak of beats in first, second, third, and fourth. There are four classifications of beats: simple beats, change beats, circular beats, and grazing beats. With the exception of grazing beats, beats are accomplished by striking the opponent's blade at one point only. The blow must be sharp and produce a clicking sound.

Attacks with beats are performed in two or more movements, with the beat representing the first motion, and the straight thrust, disengagement, or feint, the second.

Beats are executed with the sword arm flexed. Blade movement is effected primarily through finger pressure and wrist action, with some assistance from the forearm. The beat should be kept as tight as possible, with the steel stopping dead on contact, and then moving forward instantly for the second motion of the assault. The shorter the delay between the beat and the succeeding blade movement, the more efficient the attack will be.

102. SIMPLE BEATS

Simple beats are effected by moving the blade the shortest distance necessary to encounter the opposing steel. They may be executed from an invitation or engagement; the engagement can be one's own, or the adversary's. In the latter case the beat is called a false beat.

When simple beats are made from engagement the blade must be lifted slightly from the opposing steel to gain momentum for the blow; this should be accomplished without alerting the opponent of the impending attack.

103. THE SIMPLE BEAT AND STRAIGHT THRUST

1) The simple beat in first:

   First movement: from the invitation in second the hand is rotated to third in fourth position, and the opposing steel is deflected with a blow diagonally upward to the left.

   Second movement: the sword arm is extended immediately, and a straight thrust delivered to the inside low line, hand in fourth position.

2) The simple beat in second:

   First movement: from the invitation in first the hand is turned to fourth or second position, and the hostile blade deviated with a blow diagonally downward to the right.

   Second movement: the sword arm is straightened promptly, and a straight thrust directed to the high line, hand in fourth position, or to the outside low line, hand in fourth or second position.

3) The simple beat in third:

   First movement: from the invitation in fourth the hand is rotated to fourth position, and the opposing steel deflected with a blow to the right.

Second movement: the sword arm is extended immediately, and a straight thrust delivered to the outside high line, hand in fourth position, or to the low line, hand in fourth or second position.

4) The simple beat in fourth:

First movement: from the invitation in third the hand is turned to third in fourth position, and the hostile blade deviated with a blow to the left.

Second movement: the sword arm is straightened promptly, and a straight thrust directed to the inside high line, hand in fourth position.

Observation: The simple beat in fourth and straight thrust is often combined with a jump lunge. In performing this action strict attention must be paid to hand and foot coordination: correctly timed, blade contact and completion of the jump occur simultaneously.

It should also be noted that simple, change, and circular beats in third can be executed with the hand rotated to second in third position; but this is not commonly encountered in today's foil fencing.

104. THE SIMPLE BEAT AND DISENGAGEMENT

In the event the adversary, on sensing the beat, tends to shift his blade in the direction of the concussion to parry the thrust, his defensive reaction should be provoked with a light beat, and the parry eluded with a disengagement.

The simple beat in third is followed by disengagement to the inside high line, or to the low line; the simple beat in fourth is succeeded by disengagement to the outside high line.

105. CHANGE BEATS

Change beats are made from one's own or the adversary's engagement by carrying the point over or under the opposing steel, and striking it on the opposite side.

106. THE CHANGE BEAT AND STRAIGHT THRUST

1) The change beat in first:

First movement: from engagement in second the point is brought clockwise over the hostile blade, hand rotated to third in fourth position, and the opposing steel deflected with a blow diagonally upward to the left.

Second movement: the sword arm is extended immediately, and a straight thrust delivered to the inside low line, hand in fourth position.

2) The change beat in second:

First movement: from engagement in first the point is shifted counterclockwise over the hostile blade, hand turned to fourth or second position, and the opposing steel deviated with a blow diagonally downward to the right.

Second movement: the sword arm is straightened promptly, and a straight thrust directed to the high line, hand in fourth position, or to the outside low line, hand in fourth or second position.

3) The change beat in third:

First movement: from engagement in fourth the point is transferred clockwise under the hostile blade, hand rotated to fourth position, and the opposing steel deflected with a blow to the right.

Second movement: the sword arm is extended immediately, and a straight thrust delivered to the outside high line, hand in fourth position, or to the low line, hand in fourth or second position.

4) The change beat in fourth:

First movement: from engagement in third the point is carried counterclockwise under the hostile blade, hand turned to third in fourth position, and the opposing steel deviated with a blow to the left.

Second movement: the sword arm is straightened promptly, and a straight thrust directed to the inside high line, hand in fourth position.

107. CIRCULAR BEATS

Circular beats are executed in precisely the same manner as circular parries: the hand remains fixed in its position of invitation or engagement, while the point, set in motion by the fingers and wrist, describes a tight, complete circle around the adversary's extended blade, beating it in the direction of the invitation or engagement.

108. THE CIRCULAR BEAT AND STRAIGHT THRUST

1) The circular beat in first:

First movement: from the invitation or engagement in first the point is brought clockwise over the hostile blade, and the opposing steel deflected with a blow to the left.

Second movement: the sword arm is extended immediately, and a straight thrust delivered to the inside low line, hand in fourth position.

2) The circular beat in second:

First movement: from the invitation or engagement in second the point is shifted counterclockwise over the hostile blade, and the opposing steel deviated with a blow to the right.

Second movement: the sword arm is straightened promptly, and a straight thrust directed to the high line, hand in fourth position, or to the outside low line, hand in fourth or second position.

3) The circular beat in third:

First movement: from the invitation or engagement in third, the point is transferred clockwise under the hostile blade, and the opposing steel deflected with a blow to the right.

Second movement: the sword arm is extended immediately, and a straight thrust delivered to the outside high line, hand in fourth position, or to the low line, hand in fourth or second position.

4) The circular beat in fourth:

> First movement: from the invitation or engagement in fourth the point is carried counterclockwise under the hostile blade, and the opposing steel deviated with a blow to the left.

> Second movement: the sword arm is straightened promptly, and a straight thrust directed to the inside high line, hand in fourth position.

109. GRAZING BEATS

Grazing beats are sliding beats in which the point is withdrawn, and the line changed by passing over the opposing steel. The beat, transfer of line, and thrust must appear to be a single, continuous movement. The end result is the same as that of a simple beat and disengagement, except that the grazing action is faster.

The grazing beat in third is followed by a thrust to the inside high line; the grazing beat in fourth is succeeded by a thrust to the low line.

Observation: The grazing beat is, in fact, a beat and cut-over.

110. EXPULSIONS

Expulsions are powerful sliding beats in which the strong of the attacking weapon is forced along the opposing steel, expelling it from its position in engagement or line. Expulsions can be effected in any of the four lines, but they are most commonly used in third and fourth.

Attacks with expulsions are performed in two or more movements, with the sliding beat representing the first motion, and the straight thrust or feint, the second.

Expulsions are executed by flexing the elbow, raising the point slightly in engagements in third and fourth, or lowering the point a little in engagements in first and second, and then, with sudden violence, pressing the strong of the blade forward against the weak and medium of the opposing steel, driving it diagonally to one side. Care must be taken that the point of the attacking blade does not pass beyond the limits of the target area, otherwise time will be lost in returning to line for the thrust or feint.

The principal advantage of expulsions over beats in which blade contact is broken is that expulsions cannot be countered with the disengagement in time.

Observation: The expulsion in third is especially effective if the hand is rotated from fourth to third position as the arm extends. This action is so powerful that it will either loosen the opponent's grip on his weapon or disarm him.

111. PRESSURES

Pressures are gradual applications of force with the strong or medium of the blade against the adversary's weak to deviate it from its position in line. Like beats, they are identified by the line in which they encounter the opposing steel: first, second, third, and fourth. From correct distance, pressures are effected strong against weak, and from out of distance, medium against weak.

Attacks with pressures are made in two or more movements, with the pressure representing the first motion, and the straight thrust, disengagement, glide, or feint, the second.

Blade movement in pressures is accomplished through finger and wrist action, with some assistance from the forearm. The sword arm should begin to extend with the pressure, so that the point of the weapon moves progressively forward. As opposition is gained, and the opposing steel forced aside, the target is exposed. Throughout the action, the point must remain close to the hostile blade.

Observation: The distinction between blade seizure and pressures is subtle: in the first instance the opposing steel is forced aside by engagement, while advancing, so that an immediate attack can be launched; in the second, it is deviated by pressure, from immobility or with a step forward, in order to test the adversary's reaction. If he submits to the pressure, he may be hit with a straight thrust or glide; if he applies a counter-pressure, he can be touched with a disengagement.

112. BLADE COVER

Blade cover is an action in which the blade slides over the opposing steel, gaining in opposition, and deviating it from its position in line.

The attack with blade cover is accomplished in two or more movements, with the covering action representing the first motion, and the straight thrust or feint, the second.

In the first movement the hand is rotated to second position, sword arm extending so that the weapon slides on the opposing steel, strong against weak and medium, pressing it lightly to the left and downward, with the point of the attacking blade a little higher than the hand, and aimed at the adversary's right shoulder; in the second motion the hand is turned quickly to fourth position, and the thrust or feint directed to the inside high line.

Observation: Blade cover is usually combined with an advance. Here, again, blade motion must precede foot movement.

113. DISARMAMENTS

Disarmaments are violent attacks on the opposing steel to disarm the adversary, or make him lose control of his weapon, so that he is no longer able to defend himself. The blade motion during the disarmament is either vertical or spiral.

Attacks with disarmament are effected in two movements, with the assault on the blade representing the first motion, and the straight thrust, the second.

The first movement of the vertical disarmament is executed from the opponent's engagement in first, or from one's own engagement in third, by rotating the hand to third position, simultaneously raising the point of the weapon with a slight flexing of the arm and wrist, and then striking forcefully downward with the strong of the blade against the medium of the opposing steel, driving it to the floor; in the second motion, the straight thrust is directed to the high line, hand in fourth position.

The first movement of the spiral disarmament to the left is performed from one's own engagement in third, or against the adversary's blade in line, by pressing with increasing force in a clockwise spiral direction, hand turning to third in fourth position, so that the strong of the blade slides along the weak and medium of the opposing steel, whipping it to the left; in the second motion, the straight thrust is aimed at the inside high line, hand in fourth position.

The first movement of the spiral disarmament to the right is made from one's own engagement in fourth, or in opposition to the opponent's blade in line, by pressing with increasing force in a counterclockwise spiral direction, hand rotating to second position, so that the strong of the blade slides along the weak and medium of the opposing steel, whipping it to the right; in the second motion, the straight thrust is directed to the low line, hand in second position, or to the high line, hand in fourth position.

114. Changes of Engagement Followed by Feints

Single or double changes of engagement may be followed by one or more feints. For example, single or double changes of engagement in first, second, third, or fourth can be succeeded by the feint direct and disengagement, feint by glide and disengagement, feint direct and deceive, or feint by glide and deceive.

The adversary's weapon is first engaged, and then the single or double change of engagement is effected. From the final position of engagement the blade is either detached for a feint direct, or left in contact for a feint by glide. If the opponent reacts with a simple parry, the defense is eluded with a disengagement; if he responds with a circular parry, the defense is eluded with a deceive.

Observation: As an exercise in point control, double changes of engagement may be followed by double feints. For example, the student can be directed to execute a double change of engagement in fourth succeeded by a double feint direct and disengagement, or a double feint direct and deceive. In the first instance he eludes parries of fourth and third; in the second, parries of fourth and counter of fourth.

Care must be taken that the opposing steel is carried smoothly from one engagement to another, and that the sword arm is well extended during the feinting actions. The point, with tight motion, should advance progressively.

Cadence is an important factor in the success of these actions. Double changes of engagement must be accomplished in leisurely fashion, so that the adversary will be caught off guard when he is suddenly confronted with the initial feint of the attack.

115. Transports Followed by Feints

Transports may be followed by one or more feints. For instance, transports in first, second, third, or fourth can be succeeded by the feint by glide and disengagement, or feint by glide and deceive.

The adversary's foil is first engaged, and then the transport is executed. From the new position of engagement the blade is either detached for a feint direct, or left in contact for a feint by glide. Again, the opponent's defensive reaction will determine whether the final movement of the attack will be a disengagement or a deceive.

116. Beats Followed by Feints

Beats may be followed by one or more feints. For example, simple beats in
first and second can be succeeded by the feint direct and disengagement,
or feint direct and deceive; simple beats in third and fourth may be followed by the feint direct and disengagement, feint direct and deceive, or
feint direct and cut-over. The beat must be light, so that the feint can be
placed with precision.

117. Simple Beat, Feint Direct, and Disengagement

1) In opposition to the threat in first:

Master	Pupil
Places the weapon in line.	First movement: executes a beat in first.
Submits to the effect of the beat.	Second movement: simulates a straight thrust to the inside low line.
Parries first.	Third movement: eludes the parry of first with a disengagement counterclockwise to the outside low line.
Receives the touch.	

2) In opposition to the threat in second:

Master	Pupil
Places the weapon in line.	First movement: executes a beat in second.
Submits to the effect of the beat.	Second movement: simulates a straight thrust to the outside low line.
Parries second.	Third movement: eludes the parry of sec- ond with a disengagement clockwise to the high line.
Receives the touch.	

3) In opposition to the threat in third:

Master	Pupil
Places the weapon in line.	First movement: executes a beat in third.
Submits to the effect of the beat.	Second movement: simulates a straight thrust to the outside high line.

Parries third.	Third movement: eludes the parry of third with a disengagement counterclockwise to the low line or inside high line.
Receives the touch.	

4) In opposition to the threat in fourth:

Master	Pupil
Places the weapon in line.	First movement: executes a beat in fourth.
Submits to the effect of the beat.	Second movement: simulates a straight thrust to the inside high line.
Parries fourth.	Third movement: eludes the parry of fourth with a disengagement clockwise to the outside high line.
Receives the touch.	

118. SIMPLE BEAT, FEINT DIRECT, AND DECEIVE

1) In opposition to the threat in first:

Master	Pupil
Places the weapon in line.	First movement: executes a beat in first.
Submits to the effect of the beat.	Second movement: simulates a straight thrust to the inside low line.
Parries counter of second.	Third movement: eludes the parry of counter of second with a deceive clockwise to the inside low line.
Receives the touch.	

2) In opposition to the threat in second:

Master	Pupil
Places the weapon in line.	First movement: executes a beat in second.
Submits to the effect of the beat.	Second movement: simulates a straight thrust to the outside low line.
Parries counter of first.	Third movement: eludes the parry of counter of first with a deceive counterclockwise to the outside low line.
Receives the touch.	

3) In opposition to the threat in third:

Master	Pupil
Places the weapon in line.	First movement: executes a beat in third.
Submits to the effect of the beat.	Second movement: simulates a straight thrust to the outside high line.
Parries counter of fourth.	Third movement: eludes the parry of counter of fourth with a deceive clockwise to the outside high line.
Receives the touch.	

4) In opposition to the threat in fourth:

Master	Pupil
Places the weapon in line.	First movement: executes a beat in fourth.
Submits to the effect of the beat.	Second movement: simulates a straight thrust to the inside high line.
Parries counter of third.	Third movement: eludes the parry of counter of third with a deceive counter-clockwise to the inside high line.
Receives the touch.	

119. SIMPLE BEAT, FEINT DIRECT, AND CUT-OVER

1) In opposition to the threat in third:

Master	Pupil
Places the weapon in line.	First movement: executes a beat in third.
Submits to the effect of the beat.	Second movement: simulates a straight thrust to the outside high line.
Parries third.	Third movement: eludes the parry of third with a cut-over to the inside high line.
Receives the touch.	

2) In opposition to the threat in fourth:

Master	Pupil
Places the weapon in line.	First movement: executes a beat in fourth.
Submits to the effect of the beat.	Second movement: simulates a straight thrust to the inside high line.
Parries fourth.	Third movement: eludes the parry of fourth with a cut-over to the outside high line or to the low line.
Receives the touch.	

Observation: It is, of course, also possible to follow change beats and circular beats with the feint direct and disengagement, feint direct and deceive, or feint direct and cut-over; or with the feint by disengagement and disengagement, feint by disengagement and deceive, or feint by disengagement and cut-over.

120. PRESSURES FOLLOWED BY FEINTS

Pressures may be followed by one or more feints. For example, pressures in first, second, third, or fourth can be succeeded by the feint direct and disengagement, feint by glide and disengagement, feint direct and deceive, or feint by glide and deceive. In every case the pressure forces the adversary's blade out of line, thus opening the target for a feint direct or feint by glide. The opponent's defensive response will, again, determine whether the last movement of the attack will be a disengagement or a deceive.

Observation: As an exercise in point control, pressures may be followed by double feints. For example, the student can be instructed to execute a pressure in fourth succeeded by a double feint direct and disengagement, or a double feint direct and deceive. In the first instance, he eludes parries of fourth and third; in the second, parries of fourth and counter of fourth.

121. BLADE COVER FOLLOWED BY FEINTS

Blade cover may be followed by one or more feints. For instance, blade cover can be succeeded by the feint direct and disengagement, or feint direct and deceive.

122. BLADE COVER, FEINT DIRECT, AND DISENGAGEMENT

In opposition to the threat in fourth:

Master	Pupil
Places the weapon in line.	First movement: executes blade cover.
Submits to the effect of blade cover.	Second movement: simulates a straight thrust to the inside high line.
Parries fourth.	Third movement: eludes the parry of fourth with a disengagement clockwise to the outside high line.
Receives the touch.	

123. BLADE COVER, FEINT DIRECT, AND DECEIVE

In opposition to the threat in fourth:

Master	Pupil
Places the weapon in line.	First movement: executes blade cover.
Submits to the effect of blade cover.	Second movement: simulates a straight thrust to the inside high line.
Parries counter of third.	Third movement: eludes the parry of counter of third with a deceive counterclockwise to the inside high line.
Receives the touch.	

124. RENEWED ATTACKS

Renewed attacks are second offensive actions launched against an opponent who, having parried the initial assault, either hesitates or fails to respond. The second thrust is executed in opposition to the placement of the adversary's weapon at the completion of the parry.

Depending upon fencing measure, renewed attacks may be effected from the lunge, with a second lunge, or with a step forward and lunge.

1) If the opponent parries from a stationary position, the renewed assault is accomplished from the lunge with an appel of the right foot, and second thrust to the target area opposite the line in which the original attack was parried.

2) If the adversary retreats with his parry, the renewed assault is performed by recovering forward to the guard position, and then attacking with a second lunge. The renewed assault may also consist of a single or double feint, or an action on the blade if the opposing steel is in line.

3) If the opponent, after parrying, uses the defense of measure, and steps out of distance, the renewed attack is made by recovering forward to the guard position, and then attacking with a step forward and lunge.

Renewed attacks can also be effected by gaining on the lunge, or with a running attack, directly from the lunge, or after resuming the guard position with the left foot.

Observation: When the second thrust is executed from the lunge it is called a replacement.

For the advanced student the most useful drills involving renewed attacks are those in which there is a recovery forward and second lunge or running attack. For example, in opposition to the master's invitation in third the pupil may be directed to execute a straight thrust to the inside high line; on the teacher's parry of fourth in retreat and hesitation, the student recovers forward quickly with a tight feint by disengagement to the outside high line. The instructor's parry of third is then eluded with a disengagement to the inside high line and second lunge. When the action has been mastered by the pupil, the second lunge may be substituted with a running attack passing on the master's inside, that is to say, the side opposite the hostile blade.

In a variation of the action the student, after his initial assault with the straight thrust has been parried, recovers forward with a feint by disengagement to the outside high line, and the teacher, instead of parrying third, parries counter of fourth so that the pupil must elude the circular parry with a deceive to the outside high line. Again, the action terminates in a second lunge or running attack passing on the instructor's outside.

In each case, with the recovery forward, the student's rear arm returns to its elevated position and the feet assume their correct placement on guard in preparation for the second lunge or running attack.

When the pupil is secure in these actions the master may alternate his second parry, sometimes employing a simple, sometimes a circular parry, thus forcing the student to follow his feint by disengagement with either a disengagement or deceive, depending upon the defensive response.

CHAPTER 10

COUNTEROFFENSE

125. TIME, VELOCITY, AND MEASURE

The three fundamental elements of fencing are time, velocity, and measure.

Time in fencing signifies the favorable moment at which an offensive action will catch the adversary off guard.

Velocity refers to the minimum time necessary to complete an offensive, defensive, or counteroffensive movement.

Measure is the distance that must be covered to reach the target with a thrust. See pages 16 and 17.

126. FENCING TIME

Each fencing movement represents one unit of fencing time; consequently, the straight thrust requires, in execution, one unit; the feint direct and disengagement, two units; and the double feint direct and disengagement, three units. The number of units of fencing time establishes the priority of hits.

Observation: Although simple attacks executed from lunging distance are made in one movement, or one unit of fencing time, the same actions, accomplished from out of distance with an advance, require two movements, or two units of fencing time, the first, for the step forward, the second, for the thrust.

In contrast, compound attacks with an advance do not require more movements, or units of fencing time, since the step forward is coordinated with one or more blade motions. For example, the feint direct and disengagement with an advance consists of two blade motions and a step forward, yet it is effected in only two movements because the feint and step forward are combined in the first movement of the action.

Because compound attacks require two or more units of fencing time, they are susceptible to interruption by counterthrusts. But the counterthrust or counterattack is correct only if it arrives on target one unit of fencing time before the attack. For instance, in a compound attack consisting of two motions, the counterthrust must arrive before initiation of the second movement.

Simple attacks, on the other hand, are not, as a rule, anticipated by a counterattack. According to the conventions of foil fencing, the attack has the right of way because it is executed in a single unit of fencing time. However, if the simple attack is defective, that is, slow, then the loss of fencing time can result in the counterthrust arriving first. This may occur, for example, when the arm is withdrawn during execution of a disengagement, or when there is a break in time as the point is raised and lowered in a cut-over. Still, correct simple attacks may be opposed with counterattacks that either remove the target (inquartata and passata sotto), or block the line of entry and divert the incoming steel (imbroccata and time thrust).

127. COUNTERATTACKS

Counterattacks are offensive actions opposed to attacks. The attack, instead of being parried, is met with a counterthrust. Such an action may be employed against compound attacks, or faulty simple attacks in which the movement is slowed down or interrupted. To be valid the counterattack must arrive at the target before the attack is completed.

In general, counterattacks are used against the adversary who tends to be repetitive in his actions, or gives away his intentions.

Counterattacks are said to be performed in the first, second, or third unit of time, depending upon whether the counterthrust catches the opponent on his first, second, or third movement.

There are seven counterattacks in foil fencing: 1) the arrest, 2) the disengagement in time, 3) the appuntata, 4) the imbroccata, 5) the inquartata, 6) the passata sotto, and 7) the time thrust.

128. THE ARREST

The arrest is a counterattack that interrupts completion of a compound attack with feints. Attacks with a single feint are arrested on the first movement; attacks with a double feint, on either the first or second movement.

When the arrest is made on the first movement of an attack with an advance, it is generally executed with a half lunge; when it is made on the second motion, it is accomplished from the guard.

In opposition to the feint direct and disengagement, or feint by disengagement and disengagement, the arrest is made on the first movement of the attack. From one's own invitation or engagement in first, the arrest is directed to the high line, hand in fourth position, opposition to the right; from one's own invitation or engagement in second, the arrest is aimed at the low line, hand in fourth or second position, opposition to the right;

from one's own invitation or engagement in third, the arrest is directed to the outside high line, hand in fourth position, opposition to the right; and from one's own invitation or engagement in fourth, the arrest is aimed at the low line, hand in fourth or second position, opposition to the right.

Against the double feint direct and disengagement, or double feint by disengagement and disengagement, the arrest may be executed on the second movement of the attack. From one's own invitation or engagement in first, the parry of second, after failing to encounter the opposing steel, is followed by the arrest in the low line, hand in fourth or second position, opposition to the right; from one's own invitation or engagement in second, the parry of third, after failing to meet the hostile blade is succeeded by the arrest in the high line, hand in fourth position, opposition to the right; from one's own invitation or engagement in third, the parry of fourth, after failing to catch the opposing steel, is followed by the arrest in the low line, hand in fourth or second position, opposition to the right; and from one's own invitation or engagement in fourth, the parry of third, after failing to contact the hostile blade, is succeeded by the arrest in the outside high line, hand in fourth position, opposition to the right.

Observation: The arrest may also be used in opposition to the delayed cut-over.

129. THE DISENGAGEMENT IN TIME

The disengagement in time is a counterattack against actions on the blade. Generally, it is executed with the weapon in line, but it may also be effected from one's own invitation or engagement.

Disengagement is accomplished as the adversary attempts to deviate or deflect the blade. For example, if the opponent initiates his attack with a simple beat or pressure in fourth, his action on the blade can be avoided by a disengagement in time to the outside high line, opposition to the right.

Success depends upon timing and point control: the disengagement should be timed to elude the opposing steel the instant before blade contact occurs; the hand must be fixed, and the sword arm fully extended. Correctly executed, the semicircular movement of the point is so small that it is barely perceptible. As the point changes lines, the hand is shifted in opposition and the action completed with a rapid lunge.

130. THE APPUNTATA

The appuntata is a counterattack in opposition to the compound riposte. It is employed against the adversary who habitually follows his parry with one or more feints.

Since the appuntata is executed from the lunge with an appel to accent the second thrust, it resembles the renewed attack from the lunge. The difference, however, is that the second thrust in the appuntata is directed to the same line as the original attack, and is intended to anticipate the second movement of the compound riposte. For instance, if the opponent parries fourth, deflecting an assault to the inside high line, and then ripostes with the feint direct, the second thrust is aimed at the same line as the initial attack, that is, the inside high line, with the hand in fourth position, and opposition to the right.

131. THE IMBROCCATA

The imbroccata is a counterattack against gliding attacks and ripostes that end in the outside low line, that is, the external flanconade, and the flanconade in second.

Plate IV. The imbroccata.

Figure 50. The inquartata.

The action is effected from the guard position with the hand either in fourth or second position. As the adversary is in the act of completing his attack or riposte, a counterthrust, with opposition to the right, is directed along the incoming steel to the outside low line.

132. THE INQUARTATA

The inquartata is a counterattack in opposition to both simple and compound attacks terminating in the inside high line (Fig. 50).

Against a simple attack, the counterattack is delivered as soon as the opponent initiates his movement. From an invitation or engagement in third, the attack with a straight thrust or disengagement to the inside high line is opposed with the counterthrust to the same line, hand in fourth position, opposition to the left, left leg extended backward, as in a lunge, and left foot shifted approximately forty-five degrees to the right of the line of direction.

In opposition to a compound attack, the counterattack follows a parry. From an invitation or engagement in fourth, the attack with a feint to the outside high line is opposed with the parry of third, and counterthrust to the inside high line as described above.

133. THE PASSATA SOTTO

The passata sotto is a counterattack against both simple and compound attacks ending in the outside high line.

In opposition to a simple attack, the counterattack is delivered as the adversary begins his action. From an invitation or engagement in second or fourth, the attack with a straight thrust or disengagement to the high line, or the outside high line, is opposed with the counterthrust to the low line, hand in second position, opposition to the right, left leg extended backward along the line of direction, and body lowered, with the chest close to the right thigh, and left hand resting on the floor near the right foot.

Against a compound attack, the counterattack follows a parry. From an invitation or engagement in first or third, the attack with a feint to the outside low line, or to the inside high line, is opposed with the parry of second or fourth, and the counterthrust to the low line as described above.

Plate V. The passata sotto.

Observation: Because of the awkwardness of the posture and difficulty in returning quickly to the guard, the passata sotto tends to be little used in contemporary fencing.

134. THE TIME THRUST

The time thrust is a counterattack that precedes the final movement of the attack. It is accomplished from the guard position, and may be executed in all lines against both simple and compound attacks.

In opposition to a simple attack, the counterthrust is directed along the same line as the assault, with exactly enough opposition to deviate the incoming steel.

Against a compound attack, after one or more parries fail to catch the opposing blade, the counterthrust is effected as described above.

Observation: In general, it is difficult to perform the time thrust against a simple attack, unless the offensive action is unusually slow.

135. COUNTERTIME

Actions in countertime are movements used in opposition to counterattacks. They are simulated attacks designed to provoke the opponent's counterthrusts, thus exposing him to the parry and riposte, or to the counterattack into the counterattack.

The initial motion of the action in countertime must be sufficiently clear to induce the adversary to counterattack, without being so obvious that he suspects a trap. This can be accomplished by combining an accented feint or attack on the blade with an advance. The feint direct, feint by disengagement, or simple beat, executed with a step forward, provide excellent bait for the counterattacker.

In opposition to the opponent's invitation or engagement in first, a feint may be directed to his outside low line to draw an arrest to the high line; as he counterattacks, his action can be countered with the parry of third and riposte to the low line.

Against the adversary's invitation or engagement in second, a feint may be aimed at his high line to prompt an arrest to the low line; as he counterattacks, his action can be opposed with the parry of second and riposte to the high line.

In opposition to the opponent's invitation or engagement in third, a feint may be directed to his low line to draw an arrest to the high line; as he counterattacks, his action can be countered with the parry of third and riposte to the low line.

Against the adversary's invitation or engagement in fourth, a feint may be aimed at his outside high line to prompt an arrest to the low line; as he counterattacks, his action can be opposed with the parry of second and riposte to the high line.

In opposition to the opponent's weapon in line, a beat in fourth may be effected to draw his disengagement in time to the outside high line; as he counterattacks, his action can be countered with the parry of counter of fourth and riposte to the inside high line, or with the time thrust in third, hand in fourth position, opposition to the right.

Observation: For every action in fencing there is a counteraction. These opposing movements are termed contraries. The contrary of the counter-attack is the action in countertime; the contrary of the action in countertime is the feint in time.

136. THE FEINT IN TIME

The feint in time is a movement opposed to actions in countertime. It is a feigned arrest or disengagement in time intended to provoke the adversary's action in countertime, so that this may be opposed with a disengagement or deceive in time.

If the feint in time is derived from an arrest, it is a feint direct; if it stems from a disengagement in time, it is a feint by disengagement.

Execution of the feint in time is the same as in a feint direct or feint by disengagement as already described in offensive actions: the feint, or simulated counterattack, is directed to the opponent's exposed target; as he parries in countertime, his parry is eluded with a disengagement or deceive, depending upon whether he uses a simple or a circular parry.

Since the adversary's parry in countertime is performed from the guard position, the final motion of the feint in time must be effected with a lunge.

137. THE ARREST IN COUNTERTIME

The arrest in countertime is an action opposed to the single or double feint in time. It is executed in the same manner as an arrest against a compound attack.

If the opponent avoids a beat in first or third with a feint by disengagement in time, his movement is countered with an arrest in countertime to the high line; if he eludes a beat in second or fourth with a feint by disengagement in time, his action is opposed with an arrest in countertime to the low line.

CHAPTER 11

ACTIONS IN TIME

138. PROBING ACTIONS

Probing actions are feigned attacks that test the adversary's defensive and counteroffensive responses. His reactions to simulated assaults with feints and beats will indicate whether he defends himself with simple or circular parries or, instead, has a tendency to counterattack.

139. ACTIONS OF CONCEALMENT

Actions of concealment are movements used to confuse the opponent and hide one's own intentions. These consist of changes in placement of the weapon, transports, envelopments, pressures, and tight disengagements that move rapidly around the opposing steel, combined with small forward and backward steps.

140. INITIATIVE FOR THE ATTACK

Attacks may be executed on one's own initiative, or on the adversary's. In the first instance it is one's own selection of time that determines the moment of the assault; in the second, it is the opponent's movement of his weapon that prompts the attack.

141. ATTACKS IN TIME

Attacks in time are offensive actions effected while the adversary is in the act of changing the placement of his weapon. In other words, the attack is executed just as the opposing steel is moved from an invitation to an engagement or vice versa, or put in line.

The straight thrust or feint direct becomes an action in time if it is accomplished the instant the hostile blade is shifted from an engagement to an invitation; the disengagement or feint by disengagement becomes an action in time if it is performed the moment the opposing steel is moved from an invitation to an engagement; and the beat preceding a straight thrust, disengagement, or feint becomes an action in time if it is made the instant the hostile blade is placed in line.

Observation: Attacks in time must be delayed until the final stage of the lesson when the student is thoroughly warmed up, and his reflex actions are sharpest.

142. THE COUNTER-DISENGAGEMENT

The counter-disengagement is an action in time opposed to the disengagement. It is employed against the adversary who repeatedly frees his blade from engagement, or disengages in time to avoid contact.

The action is accomplished in one movement with a lunge. As the opponent disengages, a complete circle is made, following the direction of the disengagement, and returning the blades to their original positions. Correctly executed, the counter-disengagement penetrates forward in a tight, spiral movement, arm extending smoothly, and hand shifting in opposition.

If the adversary disengages to the inside high line, the counter-disengagement travels clockwise to the outside high line, opposition to the right; and if he disengages to the outside high line, the counter-disengagement moves counterclockwise to the inside high line, opposition to the left.

Observation: It should be noted that the most common use of the counter-disengagement is to deceive a circular parry. In compound attacks it is, in fact, called a deceive.

143. FIRST AND SECOND INTENTION

Every simple and compound offensive action may be accomplished in first or second intention. In first intention the movement is executed with the intent of reaching the target directly through the action itself. In second intention the movement is performed with the express purpose of provoking defensive responses against which counteractions can be applied. Second intention is especially useful in opposition to the adversary who, following a particular parry, always ripostes in the same line. For example, after the opponent parries fourth and ripostes direct, one remains in the lunge and counterparries fourth, ripostes direct, counterparries fourth, and ripostes by disengagement. The first counterparry riposte serves to provoke a counterparry riposte in the same line, so that the opposing final counterparry of fourth can be eluded with the riposte by disengagement.

Observation: The distinction between second intention and countertime is that second intention prompts a parry and riposte which is opposed with the counterparry and riposte, while countertime provokes a counterattack which is countered with the parry and riposte, or with another counterattack.

CHAPTER 12

PEDAGOGY

144. THE TEACHING POSITION

Because of the physical strain involved in holding the traditional guard position for prolonged periods of time, the master should adopt an erect posture, torso inclined a little forward, right arm well extended, hand chest high, left arm bent, hand in front of the left breast, ready to deliver signals, weight distributed equally between the legs, knees slightly flexed, and feet comfortably spaced, right foot following the line of direction, left foot pointing away from the line of direction at about a forty-five degree angle.

Since the lunge is too tiring to perform throughout a teaching session, it is replaced with a carefully measured advance.

145. METHOD OF INSTRUCTION

The master must have complete control of the lesson; at no time should the student be permitted to act on his own. Commands must be given in a clear and authoritative manner. Voice and hand signals should be used to urge the pupil forward, or to hold him back. On the command, "Via!" the attack must be launched and the lunge position held until the order, "On guard!" is given. If the student begins to move before the command, "Via!" he should be restrained with the order, "Steady!"

Initially, each action must be broken into its component parts. This is possible even with simple attacks. For instance, the straight thrust can be demonstrated in two motions: first, the sword arm is extended, and then the lunge is effected. Once the action is executed smoothly, and with precedence of point, the two movements may be fused into one.

Observation: The teacher's voice will help establish the proper cadence for each phase of the lesson. To quicken the pace, he need only shorten the time between the command, "Via!" and the word, "Hup!" which is uttered as the hit arrives.

A typical lesson begins with the orders: "First position!" (Fig. 51) "Salute!" "Mask on!" (Fig. 52) "On!" (Fig. 53) "Guard!" (Fig. 54) "Straight thrust, via!"; "Hup!" (Fig. 55); "On guard!"; "Disengagement, via!"; "Hup!";

"On guard!"; "Glide, via!" (if the attack is parried and a riposte delivered); "Remain in the lunge position!"; "Counterparry second and riposte to the high line, via!"; "Hup!"; "On guard!"; "First position, rest!" etc.

During the course of the lesson the student should be directed periodically to advance and retreat so that he develops mobility on the fencing strip.

Fencing movements must be repeated until the pupil executes them correctly. This usually necessitates practicing an action five or six times, or for approximately one length of the fencing strip. If, after these initial attempts, the student still has not grasped the mechanics of the movement, it should be set aside and repeated in the following lesson. The same action must be performed in at least three consecutive training sessions to guarantee that it is fixed in the pupil's mind.

Every error in the lesson should be drawn to the student's attention and corrected in a constructive and friendly manner; the lesson must be an exercise in precision. Rest pauses should be carefully spaced and brief so that the continuity of the lesson is unbroken.

In working with experienced fencers, point control can be developed by moving progressively from single to triple feints. For example, in the initial lesson of a group of related lessons, the pupil may be directed, in opposition to the invitation in first, to execute the feint direct and disengagement; the double feint direct and disengagement; the feint direct and deceive; the feint direct, deceive, and disengagement; the double feint direct and deceive; the feint direct and double deceive; the double feint direct, deceive, and disengagement; and the feint direct, deceive, disengagement, and deceive. In succeeding lessons the same actions can be effected in opposition to invitations in second, third, and fourth. At first the attacks should be performed from immobility, then with an advance, and finally, when the student is secure in his hand and foot coordination, in time, and with mobility on the fencing strip.

Precision and a fine tactile sense can be developed by having the pupil retreat one step back parrying double counter of second, followed by a transport to fourth and riposte along the blade to the inside high line. When this has been mastered, the riposte can be accomplished with the flanconade in fourth, or by disengagement, feint by disengagement and disengagement, and feint by disengagement and deceive. Periodically, the master can step back on the riposte so that the student must lunge.

An effective way to teach the pupil to execute the disengagement in time is to instruct him to advance the length of the fencing strip with his sword arm completely extended and point in line. The teacher retreats, stopping from time to time to engage or beat the threatening steel in fourth.

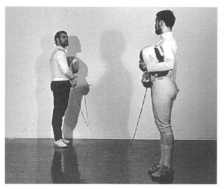

Figure 51. "First position!"

Figure 52. "Mask on!"

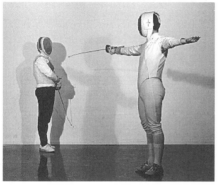

Figure 53. "On!"

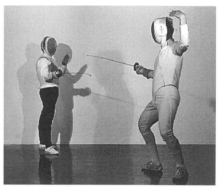

Figure 54. "Guard!"

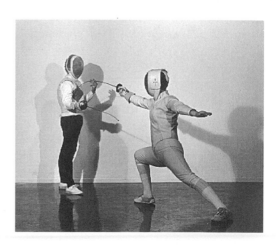

Figure 55.
"Straight thrust, via!" "Hup!"

The instant before contact occurs, the student must disengage clockwise with a tiny motion of the point, closing the line progressively to the outside, and lunge. Throughout the action the point should move steadily forward.

Second intention can be taught by instructing the pupil, in opposition to the teacher's blade in line, or placement of the blade in line, to execute a simple beat in fourth with advance, and deep feint direct, drawing the instructor's parry of fourth and direct riposte, so that this, in turn, may be countered by the student with the counterparry of fourth and riposte by disengagement to the outside high line with a lunge. When the action has been mastered, the teacher, on the pupil's final motion, can counterparry third and riposte with the feint by disengagement and deceive to the inside high line, prompting the student, as he recovers, to counterparry double counter of third and riposte by glide in third with a lunge. As an alternative, the pupil may be directed to follow his circular parries with a change of engagement to fourth and riposte by glide in fourth, or flanconade in fourth. Although complex, these actions are invaluable in preparing fencers for competition.

146. Organization of the Lesson

Every lesson must move progressively from simple to compound actions. The student should be led slowly, in stages, from immobility to intense activity, and then back again to immobility. During this process the arm and leg muscles must warm up gradually.

The logical connection between movement and countermovement should be stressed so that the pupil understands why an action is employed, and how it may be countered. For example, it is appropriate to follow the attack by feint direct and disengagement with an exercise consisting of two simple parries, or one simple and one circular parry.

Offensive and defensive movements must be alternated in the lesson to give the student an opportunity to catch his breath after each series of lunges. In this way attacks and parries combined respectively with an advance and retreat will carry the pupil forward and backward across the entire length of the fencing strip.

Observation: The following sequence of actions should be followed in the complete advanced lesson: 1) simple attacks, 2) parries, 3) ripostes, 4) compound attacks, 5) counterattacks, 6) countertime, and 7) second intention. Obviously, with beginners, only the first few segments of the lesson can be accomplished.

147. Preparation for Combat

When the student has been taught all of the offensive, defensive, and counteroffensive actions listed above, he is ready to begin exercises in preparation for combat.

First Group of Exercises

The pupil executes pre-established offensive actions, on his own initiative, from immobility, and with an advance. For instance, the student may be directed to attack with a feint by glide. His assault must be launched with maximum decision, so that he eludes the master's simple parry.

Second Group of Exercises

The pupil performs whatever offensive actions he wishes, on his own initiative, without knowing what the defense will be. For example, the teacher may invite, engage, or place his blade in line; the student must then adopt an appropriate probing action and attack in opposition to the master's reaction.

Observation: Meaningless movements of either the body or weapon should be avoided; every motion must serve a particular end.

Third Group of Exercises

The actions in the first and second groups of exercises are effected in time.

When the pupil has learned to attack with confidence, the teacher can parry the assault and add the counterparry riposte to each of the exercises.

148. Free Fencing

Free fencing should begin with the master. The student must be encouraged to keep his actions simple and to attack with decision. At first the teacher should use only simple parries. Later, when the pupil is more secure in his offensive actions, circular parries may be added. Counterattacks, on the other hand, must be avoided because they intimidate the beginner.

The length of time this introduction to free fencing takes depends upon the individual student; for some it is a matter of weeks, for others, months. In general, there is less harm in prolonging the training period than in abandoning the pupil too early and running the risk of having him develop defects in combat.

149. THE ASSAULT

Combat between two fencers is called an assault or bout. This is the practical application of what has been learned in the lesson.

In combat the following rules should be kept in mind:

1) A correct guard position must be maintained throughout the assault.

2) The bout should receive total concentration.

3) Maximum attention must be given to fencing measure.

4) The adversary should be faced with absolute calm.

5) The opponent's offensive, defensive, and counter-offensive tendencies must be determined with probing actions so that they may be opposed with appropriate contraries.

6) An unknown adversary should first be assaulted with simple attacks.

7) Ripostes must be rapid in order to minimize the possibility of replacements.

8) Both offensive and defensive actions should be varied so that the opponent cannot predict what will occur next.

9) The adversary who is prone to attacking must be countered with actions in time or counterattacks.

10) Countertime and second intention should be used respectively against opponents who tend to counterattack or riposte in the same line.

Observation: During the assault, only those actions that have been perfected in the lesson should be employed. Every fencing movement must be executed in a natural and spontaneous manner. Emphasis should be placed on decision and speed.

150. Double Hits

The basic principle of fencing is to hit the adversary without being touched by him. Yet, during the course of an assault, double hits occur. In such cases it is necessary to determine, according to the conventions of foil fencing, which of the fencers should be considered touched.

If both foilsmen launch attacks at exactly the same moment (*tempo comune*), or execute simultaneous replacements, neither fencer's action may be given precedence, and each hit is annulled. But in all other instances one of the foilsmen is held responsible for the double hit.

1)   The attacker is at fault if, in the development of a compound action, his blade is met by the defender and the immediate riposte and final motion of the attack result in a double hit.

2)   The attacker is in error if his attack on the opposing blade (whether it is in line or not) fails to make contact, and he continues the action, disregarding the counterattack, and provokes a double hit.

3)   The defender is at fault if, in opposition to a compound attack, he attempts to parry, and without encountering the incoming steel, ripostes, causing a double hit.

4)   The counterattacker is in error if the attack and counterattack terminate in a double hit.

151. The Left-handed Opponent

The right-handed fencer, in his first encounter with a left-handed adversary, generally finds the reversed target confusing. This difficulty can be overcome if the target is viewed in exactly the same way that it is on a right-handed opponent.

Beginning with simple attacks, if the adversary invites in first, the straight thrust is directed to the outside low line, opposition to the left; if he invites in second, the straight thrust is aimed at the high line, opposition to the right; if he invites in third, the straight thrust is directed to the inside high line, opposition to the right; and if he invites in fourth, the straight thrust is aimed at the outside high line, opposition to the left.

If the opponent engages in first, the disengagement moves clockwise to the outside low line, opposition to the left; if he engages in second, the disengagement travels counterclockwise to the high line, opposition to the right; if he engages in third, the disengagement moves clockwise to the inside high line, opposition to the right; and if he engages in fourth, the disengagement travels counterclockwise to the outside high line, opposition to the left.

If the adversary's blade is engaged in first, the glide is directed to the outside low line, opposition to the left; if it is engaged in second, the glide is aimed at the inside low line, opposition to the right; if it is engaged in third, the glide is directed to the inside high line, opposition to the right; and if it is engaged in fourth, the glide is aimed at the outside high line, opposition to the left. The flanconade in fourth is directed to the inside low line, opposition to the left.

Like simple attacks, ripostes may also terminate in a different line.

After the parry of first the riposte may be directed to the outside low line by detaching the blade, or by maintaining contact.

After the parry of second the riposte may be aimed at the high line by detaching the blade, or at the inside low line by maintaining contact.

After the parry of third the riposte may be directed to the low line by detaching the blade, or to the inside high line by maintaining contact.

After the parry of fourth the riposte may be aimed at the low line by detaching the blade, or at the outside high line by detaching the blade, or by maintaining contact.

Compound attacks with single and double feints follow the same pattern as simple attacks.

If the opponent invites in first, the single feint is directed to the outside low line, and the parry of second eluded with a disengagement moving counterclockwise to the high line; with the double feint the action terminates in the low line.

If the adversary invites in second, the single feint is aimed at the high line, and the parry of third is eluded with a disengagement traveling clockwise to the low line; with the double feint the movement ends in the high line.

If the opponent invites in third, the single feint is directed to the inside high line, and the parry of fourth eluded with a disengagement moving counterclockwise to the outside high line; with the double feint the action terminates in the inside high line.

If the adversary invites in fourth, the single feint is aimed at the outside high line, and the parry of third is eluded with a disengagement traveling clockwise to the inside high line; with the double feint the movement ends in the outside high line.

Circular attacks are treated in similar fashion.

If the opponent invites in first, the feint is directed to the outside low line, and the parry of counter of first eluded with a deceive moving clock-wise to the outside low line.

If the adversary invites in second, the feint is aimed at the high line, and the parry of counter of second eluded with a deceive traveling counterclockwise to the high line.

If the opponent invites in third, the feint is directed to the inside high line, and the parry of counter of third eluded with a deceive moving clock-wise to the inside high line.

If the adversary invites in fourth, the feint is aimed at the outside high line, and the parry of counter of fourth eluded with a deceive traveling counterclockwise to the outside high line.

Actions on the blade are also affected by the reversed target.

In the case of transports followed by glides, if the opponent's blade is engaged in first, the opposing steel is transported from left to right, with the glide in the inside high line, opposition to the right; if it is engaged in second, the hostile blade is shifted from right to left, with the glide to the outside high line, opposition to the left; if it is engaged in third, the opposing steel is transferred from right to left, with the glide to the outside low line, opposition to the left; and if it is engaged in fourth, the hostile blade is carried from left to right, with the glide to the inside low line, opposition to the right.

With beats, the beat in first is followed by a thrust to the outside low line; the beat in second, by a thrust to the high line; the beat in third, by a thrust to the inside high line; and the beat in fourth, by a thrust to the low line, or to the outside high line.

The attack with blade cover, instead of ending in the inside high line, terminates in the low line.

Similarly, adjustments must be made with counterattacks such as the arrest and the inquartata.

From an invitation or engagement in first, the arrest is in the high line; from an invitation or engagement in second, the arrest is in the low line; from an invitation or engagement in third, the arrest is in the low line; and from an invitation or engagement in fourth, the arrest is in the inside high line.

The inquartata, rather than being directed to the inside high line, is aimed at the low line.

As concerns two left-handed fencers, they oppose one another in the usual way; any awkwardness they may sense at first generally stems from the fact that their early fencing experience is gained largely from encounters with right-handed adversaries.

152. Fencing Tactics

Every opponent is likely to have a weakness. To discover this, his method of swordplay must be analyzed. The procedure of analysis is the same for each adversary: a number of questions should be asked. Does he repeat certain attacks? Which parry combinations does he favor? Does he always riposte to the same line? Is he apt to counterattack?

From the beginning of the encounter to the end, the opponent must be placed on the defensive with continuous threats. He should be frustrated at every turn, so that his will to resist is broken. Under steady pressure it is probable that he will become reckless and expose himself.

The moment conditions are propitious, the assault must be launched at top speed, with precedence of point, and sword arm fully extended. The ideal time to strike is when the adversary steps forward.

Paradoxical as it may seem, the best defense is a powerful offense. As long as the opponent is preoccupied with protecting himself, he is at a disadvantage. If, however, he manages to seize the initiative, and parries are required, they must be varied in such a way that he cannot guess which combination will be used. In this regard, it should be noted that combined simple and circular parries provide a particularly effective defense.

SYNOPTIC TABLES

The tables that follow provide an overview of the principal offensive actions, and the defensive and counteroffensive actions with which they may be opposed. From left to right the tables contain the number assigned to an action in the text, the name of the action, the number of movements comprising the action, the invitation or engagement from which the action is executed, the parry or parries it eludes, the final line of attack, the final parry that may be used in opposition to the action, the riposte that may follow the final parry, and the counterattacks that may be opposed to the action in the first movement, in the second movement, and in the third movement.

TABLE I: PRINCIPAL SIMPLE ATTACKS						
NO.		OFFENSIVE ACTION	NUMBER OF MOVEMENTS COMPRISING ACTION	INVITATION OR ENGAGEMENT FROM WHICH THE ACTION IS EXECUTED	PARRY OR PARRIES ELUDED	FINAL LINE OF ATTACK
31.	1)	Straight thrust to the outside low line	One	From the adversary's invitation in first		Outside low line
	2)	Straight thrust to the high line	One	From the opponent's invitation in second		High line
	3)	Straight thrust to the inside high line	One	From the adversary's invitation in third		Inside high line
	4)	Straight thrust to the outside high line	One	From the opponent's invitation in fourth		Outside high line
32.	1)	Disengagement to the outside low line	One	From the adversary's engagement in first		Outside low line
	2)	Disengagement to the high line	One	From the opponent's engagement in second		High line
	3)	Disengagement to the inside high line	One	From the adversary's engagement in third		Inside high line
	4)	Disengagement to the outside high line	One	From the opponent's engagement in fourth		Outside high line

FINAL PARRY THAT MAY BE USED IN OPPOSITION TO THE ACTION	RIPOSTE THAT MAY FOLLOW THE FINAL PARRY	COUNTERATTACKS THAT MAY BE OPPOSED TO THE ACTION IN FIRST MOVEMENT	COUNTERATTACKS THAT MAY BE OPPOSED TO THE ACTION IN SECOND MOVEMENT	COUNTERATTACKS THAT MAY BE OPPOSED TO THE ACTION IN THIRD MOVEMENT
Second or Counter of first	To the high line (detached) or outside low line (contact) To the inside low line (detached or contact)			
First or Third or Fourth	To the inside low line (detached or contact) To the low line (detached) or outside high line (contact) To the inside high line (detached or contact) or outside low line (flanconade in fourth)			
Fourth or Counter of third	To the inside high line (detached or contact) or outside low line (flanconade in fourth) To the low line (detached) or outside high line (contact)			
Third or Counter of fourth	To the low line (detached) or outside high line (contact) To the inside high line (detached or contact) or outside low line (flanconade in fourth)			
Second or Counter of first	To the high line (detached) or outside low line (contact) To the inside low line (detached or contact)			
First or Third or Fourth	To the inside low line (detached or contact) To the low line (detached) or outside high line (contact) To the inside high line (detached or contact) or outside low line (flanconade in fourth)			
Fourth or Counter of third	To the inside high line (detached or contact) or outside low line (flanconade in fourth) To the low line (detached) or outside high line (contact)			
Third or Counter of fourth	To the low line (detached) or outside high line (contact) To the inside high line (detached or contact) or outside low line (flanconade in fourth)			

		NUMBER OF MOVEMENTS COMPRISING	INVITATION OR ENGAGEMENT FROM WHICH THE ACTION IS	PARRY OR PARRIES	
NO.	OFFENSIVE ACTION	ACTION	EXECUTED	ELUDED	FINAL LINE OF ATTACK
33.	1) Glide to the inside low line	One	From one's own engagement in first		Inside low line
	2) Glide to the outside low line	One	From one's own engagement in second		Outside low line
	3) Glide to the outside high line	One	From one's own engagement in third		Outside high line
	4) Glide to the inside high line	One	From one's own engagement in fourth		Inside high line
	Flanconade in fourth	One	From one's own engagement in fourth		Outside low line

TABLE I: PRINCIPAL SIMPLE ATTACKS (CONTINUED)

FINAL PARRY THAT MAY BE USED IN OPPOSITION TO THE ACTION	RIPOSTE THAT MAY FOLLOW THE FINAL PARRY	COUNTERATTACKS THAT MAY BE OPPOSED TO THE ACTION IN FIRST MOVEMENT	COUNTERATTACKS THAT MAY BE OPPOSED TO THE ACTION IN SECOND MOVEMENT	COUNTERATTACKS THAT MAY BE OPPOSED TO THE ACTION IN THIRD MOVEMENT
First or Ceding third or Counter of second	To the inside low line (detached or concact) To the low line (detached) or outside high line (contact) To the high line (detached) or outside low line (contact)	Inquartata		
Second or Ceding fourth	To the high line (detached) or outside low line (contact) To the inside high line (detached or contact) or outside low line (flanconade in fourth)	Time thrust		
Third or Counter of fourth	To the low line (detached) or outside high line (contact) To the inside high line (detached or contact) or outside low line (flanconade in fourth)	Time thrust or Passata sotto		
Fourth or Counter of third	To the inside high line (detached or contact) or outside low line (flanconade in fourth) To the low line (detached) or outside high line (contact)	Inquartata		
Second or Ceding fourth	To the high line (detached) or outside low line (contact) To the inside high line (detached or contact) or outside low line (flanconade in fourth)	Imbroccata		

TABLE II: PRINCIPAL COMPOUND ATTACKS WITH FEINTS OPPOSED TO SIMPLE PARRIES					
NO.		OFFENSIVE ACTION	NUMBER OF MOVEMENTS COMPRISING ACTION	INVITATION OR ENGAGEMENT FROM WHICH THE ACTION IS EXECUTED	PARRY OR PARRIES ELUDED	FINAL LINE OF ATTACK
46.	1)	Feint direct to the outside low line	Two	From the adversary's invitation in first	Second	High line
	2)	Feint direct to the high line	Two	From the opponent's invitation in second	First or third	a) Low line (eludes first or third) b) Inside high line (eludes third)
	3)	Feint direct to the inside high line	Two	From the adversary's invitation in third	Fourth	Outside high line
	4)	Feint direct to the outside high line	Two	From the opponent's invitation in fourth	Third	Inside high line
48.	1)	Feint by disengagement to the outside low line	Two	From the adversary's engagement in first	Second	High line
	2)	Feint by disengagement to the high line	Two	From the opponent's engagement in second	First or third	a) Low line (eludes first or third) b) Inside high line (eludes third)
	3)	Feint by disengagement to the inside high line	Two	From the adversary's engagement in third	Fourth	Outside high line

FINAL PARRY THAT MAY BE USED IN OPPOSITION TO THE ACTION	RIPOSTE THAT MAY FOLLOW THE FINAL PARRY	COUNTERATTACKS THAT MAY BE OPPOSED TO THE ACTION IN FIRST MOVEMENT	COUNTERATTACKS THAT MAY BE OPPOSED TO THE ACTION IN SECOND MOVEMENT	COUNTERATTACKS THAT MAY BE OPPOSED TO THE ACTION IN THIRD MOVEMENT
First or Third or Fourth	To the inside low line (detached or contact) To the low line (detached) or outside high line (contact) To the inside high line (detached or contact) or outside low line (flanconade in fourth)	Arrest to the high line	Time thrust or Passata sotto	
Second Fourth or Counter of third	To the high line (detached) or outside low line (contact) To the inside high line (detached or contact) or outside low line (flanonade in fourth) To the low line (detached) or outside high line (contact)	Arrest to the low line	Time thrust Inquartata	
Third or Counter of fourth	To the low line (detached) or outside high line (contact) To the inside high line (detached or contact) or outside low line (flanconade in fourth)	Arrest to the high line	Time thrust or Passata sotto	
Fourth or Counter of third	To the inside high line (detached or contact) or outside low line (flanconade in fourth) To the low line (detached) or outside high line (contact)	Arrest to the low line	Time thrust or Inquartata	
First or Third or Fourth	To the inside low line (detached or contact) To the low line (detached) or outside high line (contact) To the inside high line (detached or contact) or outside low line (flanconade in fourth)	Arrest to the high line	Time thrust or Passata sotto	
Second Fourth or Counter of third	To the high line (detached) or outside low line (contact) To the inside high line (detached or contact) or outside low line (flanconade in fourth) To the low line (detached) or outside high line (contact)	Arrest to the low line	Time thrust Inquartata	
Third or Counter of fourth	To the low line (detached) or outside high line (contact) To the inside high line (detached or contact) or outside low line (flanconade in fourth)	Arrest to the high line	Time thrust or Passata sotto	

TABLE II: PRINCIPAL COMPOUND ATTACKS WITH FEINTS OPPOSED TO SIMPLE PARRIES (CONTINUED)

NO.		OFFENSIVE ACTION	NUMBER OF MOVEMENTS COMPRISING ACTION	INVITATION OR ENGAGEMENT FROM WHICH THE ACTION IS EXECUTED	PARRY OR PARRIES ELUDED	FINAL LINE OF ATTACK
48.	4)	Feint by disengagement to the outside high line	Two	From the opponent's engagement in fourth	Third	Inside high line
50.	1)	Feint by glide to the inside low line	Two	From one's own engagement in first	First	Outside low line
	2)	Feint by glide to the outside low line	Two	From one's own engagement in second	Second	High line
	3)	Feint by glide to the outside high line	Two	From one's own engagement in third	Third	a) Low line b) Inside high line
	4)	Feint by glide to the inside high line	Two	From one's own engagement in fourth	Fourth	Outside high line
		Feint by flanconade in fourth	Two	From one's own engagement in fourth	Second	High line
55.	1)	Double feint direct to the outside low line	Three	From the adversary's invitation in first	Second and first or third	a) Low line (eludes second and first or third) b) Inside high line (eludes second and third)

FINAL PARRY THAT MAY BE USED IN OPPOSITION TO THE ACTION	RIPOSTE THAT MAY FOLLOW THE FINAL PARRY	COUNTERATTACKS THAT MAY BE OPPOSED TO THE ACTION IN FIRST MOVEMENT	COUNTERATTACKS THAT MAY BE OPPOSED TO THE ACTION IN SECOND MOVEMENT	COUNTERATTACKS THAT MAY BE OPPOSED TO THE ACTION IN THIRD MOVEMENT
Fourth or Counter of third	To the inside high line (detached or contact) or outside low line (flanconade in fourth) To the low line (detached) or outside high line (contact)	Arrest to the low line	Time thrust or Inquartata	
Second or Counter of first	To the high line (detached) or outside low line (contact) To the inside low line (detached or contact)	Arrest to the inside	Time thrust	
First or Third or Fourth	To the inside low line (detached or contact) To the low line (detached) or outside high line (contact) To the inside high line (detached or contact) or outside low line (flanconade in fourth)	Arrest to the high line	Time thrust or Passata sotto	
Second Fourth or Counter of third	To the high line (detached) or outside low line (contact) To the inside high line (detached or contact) or outside low line (flanconade in fourth) To the low line (detached) or outside high line (contact)	Arrest to the low line	Time thrust Inquartata	
Third or Counter of fourth	To the low line (detached) or outside high line (contact) To the inside high line (detached or contact) or outside low line (flanconade in fourth)	Arrest to the high line	Time thrust or Passata sotto	
First or Third or Fourth	To the inside low line detached or contact) To the low line (detached) or outside high line (contact) To the inside high line (detached or contact) or outside low line (flanconade in fourth)	Arrest by disengagement to the high line	Time thrust or Passata sotto	
Second Fourth or Counter of third	To the high line (detached) or outside low line (contact) To the inside high line (detached or contact) or outside low line (flanconade in fourth) To the low line (detached) or outside high line (contact)	Arrest to the high line	Arrest to the low line	Time thrust Inquartata

		NUMBER OF MOVEMENTS COMPRISING	INVITATION OR ENGAGEMENT FROM WHICH THE ACTION IS	PARRY OR PARRIES	
NO.	OFFENSIVE ACTION	ACTION	EXECUTED	ELUDED	FINAL LINE OF ATTACK
55.	2) Double feint direct to the high line	Three	From the opponent's invitation in second	First or third and second or third and fourth	a) High line (eludes first or third and second) b) Outside high line (eludes third and fourth)
	3) Double feint direct to the inside high line	Three	From the adversary's invitation in third	Fourth and third	Inside high line
	4) Double feint direct to the outside high line	Three	From the opponent's invitation in fourth	Third and fourth	Outside high line
56.	1) Double feint by disengagement to the outside low line	Three	From the adversary's engagement in first	Second and first or third	a) Low line (eludes second and first or third b) Inside high line (eludes second and third)
	2) Double feint by disengagement to the high line	Three	From the opponent's engagement in second	First or third and second or third and fourth	a) High line (eludes first or third and second) b) Outside high line (eludes third and fourth)
	3) Double feint by disengagement to the inside high line	Three	From the adversary's engagement in third	Fourth and third	Inside high line

TABLE II: PRINCIPAL COMPOUND ATTACKS WITH FEINTS OPPOSED TO SIMPLE PARRIES (CONTINUED)

FINAL PARRY THAT MAY BE USED IN OPPOSITION TO THE ACTION	RIPOSTE THAT MAY FOLLOW THE FINAL PARRY	COUNTERATTACKS THAT MAY BE OPPOSED TO THE ACTION IN FIRST MOVEMENT	COUNTERATTACKS THAT MAY BE OPPOSED TO THE ACTION IN SECOND MOVEMENT	COUNTERATTACKS THAT MAY BE OPPOSED TO THE ACTION IN THIRD MOVEMENT
First or Third or Fourth	To the inside low line (detached or contact) To the low line (detached) or outside high line (contact) To the inside high line (detached or contact) or outside low line (flanconade in fourth)	Arrest to the low line	Arrest to the high line	Time thrust or Passata sotto
Third or Counter of fourth	To the low line (detached) or outside high line (contact) To the inside high line (detached or contact) or outside low line (flanconade in fourth)			
Fourth or Counter of third	To the inside high line (detached or contact) or outside low line (flanconade in fourth) To the low line (detached) or outside high line (contact)	Arrest to the high line	Arrest to the low line	Time thrust or Inquartata
Third or Counter of fourth	To the low line (detached) or outside high line (contact) To the inside high line (detached or contact) or outside low line (flanconade in fourth)	Arrest to the low line	Arrest to the high line	Time thrust or Passata sotto
Second	To the high line (detached) or outside low line (contact)	Arrest to the high line	Arrest to the low line	Time thrust
Fourth or Counter of third	To the inside high line (detached or contact) or outside low line (flanconade in fourth) To the low line (detached) or outside high line (contact)			Inquartata
First or Third or Fourth	To the inside low line (detached or contact) To the low line (detached) or outside high line (contact) To the inside high line (detached or contact) or outside low line (flanconade in fourth)	Arrest to the low line	Arrest to the high line	Time thrust or Passata sotto
Third or Counter of fourth	To the low line (detached) or outside high line (contact) To the inside high line (detached or contact) or outside low line (flanconade in fourth)			
Fourth or Counter of third	To the inside high line (detached or contact) or outside low line (flanconade in fourth) To the low line (detached) or outside high line (contact)	Arrest to the high line	Arrest to the low line	Time thrust or Inquartata

NO.		OFFENSIVE ACTION	NUMBER OF MOVEMENTS COMPRISING ACTION	INVITATION OR ENGAGEMENT FROM WHICH THE ACTION IS EXECUTED	PARRY OR PARRIES ELUDED	FINAL LINE OF ATTACK
TABLE II: PRINCIPAL COMPOUND ATTACKS WITH FEINTS OPPOSED TO SIMPLE PARRIES (CONTINUED)						
56.	4)	Double feint by disengagement to the outside high line	Three	From the opponent's engagement in fourth	Third and fourth	Outside high line
57.	1)	Double feint by glide to the inside low line	Three	From one's own engagement in first	First and second	High line
	2)	Double feint by glide to the outside low line	Three	From one's own engagement in second	Second and first or third	a) Low line (eludes second and first or third) b) Inside high line (eludes second and third)
	3)	Double feint by glide to the outside high line	Three	From one's own engagement in third	Third and second or fourth	a) High line (eludes third and second) b) Outside high line (eludes third and fourth)
	4)	Double feint by glide to the inside high line	Three	From one's own engagement in fourth	Fourth and third	a) Low line b) Inside high line
		Double feint by flanconade in fourth	Three	From one's own engagement in fourth	Second and first or third	a) Low line (eludes second and first or third) b) Inside high line (eludes second and third)

FINAL PARRY THAT MAY BE USED IN OPPOSITION TO THE ACTION	RIPOSTE THAT MAY FOLLOW THE FINAL PARRY	COUNTERATTACKS THAT MAY BE OPPOSED TO THE ACTION IN FIRST MOVEMENT	COUNTERATTACKS THAT MAY BE OPPOSED TO THE ACTION IN SECOND MOVEMENT	COUNTERATTACKS THAT MAY BE OPPOSED TO THE ACTION IN THIRD MOVEMENT
Third or Counter of fourth	To the low line (detached) or outside high line (contact) To the inside high line (detached or contact) or outside low line (flanconade in fourth)	Arrest to the low line	Arrest to the high line	Time thrust or Passata sotto
First or Third or Fourth	To the inside low line (detached or contact) To the low line (detached) or outside high line (contact) To the inside high line (detached or contact) or outside low line (flanconade in fourth)	Arrest to the inside	Arrest to the high line	Time thrust or Passata sotto
Second	To the high line (detached) or outside low line (contact)	Arrest to the high line	Arrest to the low line	Time thrust
Fourth or Counter of third	To the inside high line (detached or contact) or outside low line (flanconade in fourth) To the low line (detached) or outside high line (contact)			Inquartata
First or Third or Fourth	To the inside low line (detached or contact) To the low line (detached) or outside high line (contact) To the inside high line (detached or contact) or outside low line (flanconade in fourth)	Arrest by disengagement to the low line	Arrest to the high line	Time thrust or Passata sotto
Third or Counter of fourth	To the low line (detached) or outside high line (contact) To the inside high line (detached or contact) or outside low line (flanconade in fourth)			
Second	To the high line (detached) or outside low line (contact)	Arrest to the high line	Arrest to the low line	Time thrust
Fourth or Counter of third	To the inside high line (detached or contact) or outside low line (flanconade in fourth) To the low line (detached) or outside high line (contact)			Inquartata
Second	To the high line (detached) or outside low line (contact)	Arrest by disengagement to the high line	Arrest to the low line	Time thrust
Fourth or Counter of third	To the inside high line (detached or contact) or outside low line (flanconade in fourth) To the low line (detached) or outside high line (contact)			Inquartata

NO.	OFFENSIVE ACTION	NUMBER OF MOVEMENTS COMPRISING ACTION	INVITATION OR ENGAGEMENT FROM WHICH THE ACTION IS EXECUTED	PARRY OR PARRIES ELUDED	FINAL LINE OF ATTACK
	TABLE III: PRINCIPAL COMPOUND ATTACKS WITH FEINTS OPPOSED TO CIRCULAR PARRIES				
63.	1) Feint direct to the outside low line and deceive	Two	From the adversary's invitation in first	Counter of first	Outside low line
	2) Feint direct to the high line and deceive	Two	From the opponent's invitation in second	Counter of second	High line
	3) Feint direct to the inside high line and deceive	Two	From the adversary's invitation in third	Counter of third	Inside high line
	4) Feint direct to the outside high line and deceive	Two	From the opponent's invitation in fourth	Counter of fourth	Outside high line
64.	1) Feint by disengagement to the outside low line and deceive	Two	From the adversary's engagement in first	Counter of first	Outside low line
	2) Feint by disengagement to the high line and deceive	Two	From the opponent's engagement in second	Counter of second	High line
	3) Feint by disengagement to the inside high line and deceive	Two	From the adversary's engagement in third	Counter of third	Inside high line
	4) Feint by disengagement to the outside high line and deceive	Two	From the opponent's engagement in fourth	Counter of fourth	Outside high line

FINAL PARRY THAT MAY BE USED IN OPPOSITION TO THE ACTION	RIPOSTE THAT MAY FOLLOW THE FINAL PARRY	COUNTERATTACKS THAT MAY BE OPPOSED TO THE ACTION IN FIRST MOVEMENT	COUNTERATTACKS THAT MAY BE OPPOSED TO THE ACTION IN SECOND MOVEMENT	COUNTERATTACKS THAT MAY BE OPPOSED TO THE ACTION IN THIRD MOVEMENT
Second or Counter of first	To the high line (detached) or outside low line (contact) To the inside low line (detached or contact)	Arrest to the high line	Time thrust	
First or Third or Fourth	To the inside low line (detached or contact) To the low line (detached) or outside high line (contact) To the inside high line (detached or contact) or outside low line (flanconade in fourth)	Arrest to the low line	Time thrust or Passata sotto	
Fourth or Counter of third	To the inside high line (detached or contact) or outside low line (flanconade in fourth) To the low line (detached) or outside high line (contact)	Arrest to the high line	Time thrust or Inquartata	
Third or Counter of fourth	To the low line (detached) or outside high line (contact) To the inside high line (detached or contact) or outside low line (flanconade in fourth)	Arrest to the low line	Time thrust or Passata sotto	
Second or Counter of first	To the high line (detached) or outside low line (contact) To the inside low line (detached or contact)	Arrest to the high line	Time thrust	
First or Third or Fourth	To the inside low line (detached or contact) To the low line (detached) or outside high line (contact) To the inside high line (detached or contact) or outside low line (flanconade in fourth)	Arrest to the low line	Time thrust or Passata sotto	
Fourth or Counter of third	To the inside high line (detached or contact) or outside low line (flanconade in fourth) To the low line (detached) or outside high line (contact)	Arrest to the high line	Time thrust or Inquartata	
Third or Counter of fourth	To the low line (detached) or outside high line (contact) To the inside high line (detached or contact) or outside low line (flanconade in fourth)	Arrest to the low line	Time thrust or Passata sotto	

		NUMBER OF MOVEMENTS COMPRISING	INVITATION OR ENGAGEMENT FROM WHICH THE ACTION IS	PARRY OR PARRIES	
NO.	OFFENSIVE ACTION	ACTION	EXECUTED	ELUDED	FINAL LINE OF ATTACK
65.	1) Feint by glide to the inside low line and deceive	Two	From one's own engagement in first	Counter of second	Inside low line
	2) Feint by glide to the outside low line and deceive	Two	From one's own engagement in second	Counter of first	Outside low line
	3) Feint by glide to the outside high line and deceive	Two	From one's own engagement in third	Counter of fourth	Outside high line
	4) Feint by glide to the inside high line and deceive	Two	From one's own engagement in fourth	Counter of third	Inside high line
	Feint by flanconade in fourth and deceive	Two	From one's own engagement in fourth	Counter of first	Outside low line
67.	1) Feint direct to the outside low line, deceive and disengagement	Three	From the adversary's invitation in first	Counter of first and second	High line
	2) Feint direct to the high line, deceive and disengagement	Three	From the opponent's invitation in second	Counter of second and first	Outside low line
	3) Feint direct to the inside high line, deceive and disengagement	Three	From the adversary's invitation in third	Counter of third and fourth	Outside high line
	4) Feint direct to the outside high line, deceive and disengagement	Three	From the opponent's invitation in fourth	Counter of fourth and third	Inside high line

TABLE III: PRINCIPAL COMPOUND ATTACKS WITH FEINTS OPPOSED TO CIRCULAR PARRIES (CONTINUED)

FINAL PARRY THAT MAY BE USED IN OPPOSITION TO THE ACTION	RIPOSTE THAT MAY FOLLOW THE FINAL PARRY	COUNTERATTACKS THAT MAY BE OPPOSED TO THE ACTION IN FIRST MOVEMENT	COUNTERATTACKS THAT MAY BE OPPOSED TO THE ACTION IN SECOND MOVEMENT	COUNTERATTACKS THAT MAY BE OPPOSED TO THE ACTION IN THIRD MOVEMENT
First or Counter of second	To the inside low line (detached or contact) To the high line (detached) or outside low line (contact)	Arrest to the inside	Time thrust	
Second or Counter of first	To the high line (detached) or outside low line (contact) To the inside low line (detached or contact)	Arrest to the high line	Time thrust	
Third or Counter of fourth	To the low line (detached) or outside high line (contact) To the inside high line (detached or contact) or outside low line (flanconade in fourth)	Arrest to the low line	Time thrust or Passata sotto	
Fourth or Counter of third	To the inside high line (detached or contact) or outside low line (flanconade in fourth) To the low line (detached) or outside high line (contact)	Arrest to the high line	Time thrust or Inquartata	
Second or Counter of first	To the high line (detached) or outside low line (contact) To the inside low line (detached or contact)	Arrest by disengagement to the high line	Time thrust	
First or Third or Fourth	To the inside low line (detached or contact) To the low line (detached) or outside high line (contact) To the inside high line (detached or contact) or outside low line (flanconade in fourth)	Arrest to the high line	Arrest to the high line	Time thrust or Passata sotto
Second or Counter of first	To the high line (detached) or outside low line (contact) To the inside low line (detached or contact)	Arrest to the low line	Arrest to the low line	Time thrust
Third or Counter of fourth	To the low line (detached) or outside high line (contact) To the inside high line (detached or contact) or outside low line (flanconade in fourth)	Arrest to the high line	Arrest to the high line	Time thrust or Passata sotto
Fourth or Counter of third	To the inside high line (detached or contact) or outside low line (flanconade in fourth) To the low line (detached) or outside high line (contact)	Arrest to the low line	Arrest to the low line	Time thrust or Inquartata

TABLE III: PRINCIPAL COMPOUND ATTACKS WITH FEINTS OPPOSED TO CIRCULAR PARRIES (CONTINUED)					
NO.		OFFENSIVE ACTION	NUMBER OF MOVEMENTS COMPRISING ACTION	INVITATION OR ENGAGEMENT FROM WHICH THE ACTION IS EXECUTED	PARRY OR PARRIES ELUDED	FINAL LINE OF ATTACK
68.	1)	Feint by disengagement to the outside low line, deceive and disengagement	Three	From the adversary's engagement in first	Counter of first and second	High line
	2)	Feint by disengagement to the high line, deceive and disengagement	Three	From the opponent's engagement in second	Counter of second and first	Outside low line
	3)	Feint by disengagement to the inside high line, deceive and disengagement	Three	From the adversary's engagement in third	Counter of third and fourth	Outside high line
	4)	Feint by disengagement to the outside high line, deceive and disengagement	Three	From the opponent's engagement in fourth	Counter of fourth and third	Inside high line
69.	1)	Feint by glide to the inside low line, deceive and disengagement	Three	From one's own engagement in first	Counter of second and first	Outside low line
	2)	Feint by glide to the outside low line, deceive and disengagement	Three	From one's own engagement in second	Counter of first and second	High line
	3)	Feint by glide to the outside high line, deceive and disengagement	Three	From one's own engagement in third	Counter of fourth and third	Inside high line
	4)	Feint by glide to the inside high line, deceive and disengagement	Three	From one's own engagement in fourth	Counter of third and fourth	Outside high line
		Feint by flanconade in fourth, deceive and disengagement	Three	From one's own engagement in fourth	Counter of first and second	High line

FINAL PARRY THAT MAY BE USED IN OPPOSITION TO THE ACTION	RIPOSTE THAT MAY FOLLOW THE FINAL PARRY	COUNTERATTACKS THAT MAY BE OPPOSED TO THE ACTION IN FIRST MOVEMENT	COUNTERATTACKS THAT MAY BE OPPOSED TO THE ACTION IN SECOND MOVEMENT	COUNTERATTACKS THAT MAY BE OPPOSED TO THE ACTION IN THIRD MOVEMENT
First or Third or Fourth	To the inside low line (detached or contact) To the low line (detached) or outside high line (contact) To the inside high line (detached or contact) or outside low line (flanconade in fourth)	Arrest to the high line	Arrest to the high line	Time thrust or Passata sotto
Second or Counter of first	To the high line (detached) or outside low line (contact) To the inside low line (detached or contact)	Arrest to the low line	Arrest to the low line	Time thrust
Third or Counter of fourth	To the low line (detached) or outside high line (contact) To the inside high line (detached or contact) or outside low line (flanconade in fourth)	Arrest to the high line	Arrest to the high line	Time thrust or Passata sotto
Fourth or Counter of third	To the inside high line (detached or contact) or outside low line (flanconade in fourth) To the low line (detached) or outside high line (contact)	Arrest to the low line	Arrest to the low line	Time thrust or Inquartata
Second or Counter of first	To the high line (detached) or outside low line (contact) To the inside low line (detached or contact)	Arrest to the inside	Arrest to the high line	Time thrust
First or Third or Fourth	To the inside low line (detached or contact) To the low line (detached) or outside high line (contact) To the inside high line (detached or contact) or outside low line (flanconade in fourth)	Arrest to the high line	Arrest to the high line	Time thrust or Passata sotto
Fourth or Counter of third	To the inside high line (detached or contact) or outside low line (flanconade in fourth) To the low line (detached) or outside high line (contact)	Arrest to the low line	Arrest to the low line	Time thrust or Inquartata
Third or Counter of fourth	To the low line (detached) or outside high line (contact) To the inside high line (detached or contact) or outside low line (flanconade in fourth)	Arrest to the high line	Arrest to the high line	Time thrust or Passata sotto
First or Third or Fourth	To the inside low line (detached or contact) To the low line (detached) or outside high line (contact) To the inside high line (detached or contact) or outside low line (flanconade in fourth)	Arrest by disengagement to the high line	Arrest to the high line	Time thrust or Passata sotto

NO.	OFFENSIVE ACTION	NUMBER OF MOVEMENTS COMPRISING ACTION	INVITATION OR ENGAGEMENT FROM WHICH THE ACTION IS EXECUTED	PARRY OR PARRIES ELUDED	FINAL LINE OF ATTACK
TABLE III: PRINCIPAL COMPOUND ATTACKS WITH FEINTS OPPOSED TO CIRCULAR PARRIES (CONTINUED)					
71.	1) Double feint direct to the outside low line and deceive	Three	From the adversary's invitation in first	Second and counter of second	High line
	2) Double feint direct to the high line and deceive	Three	From the opponent's invitation in second	First and counter of first or third and counter of third	a) Outside low line b) Inside high line
	3) Double feint direct to the inside high line and deceive	Three	From the adversary's invitation in third	Fourth and counter of fourth	Outside high line
	4) Double feint direct to the outside high line and deceive	Three	From the opponent's invitation in fourth	Third and counter of third	Inside high line
72.	1) Double feint by disengagement to the outside low line and deceive	Three	From the adversary's engagement in first	Second and counter of second	High line
	2) Double feint by disengagement to the high line and deceive	Three	From the opponent's engagement in second	First and counter of first or third and counter of third	a) Outside low line b) Inside high line

FINAL PARRY THAT MAY BE USED IN OPPOSITION TO THE ACTION	RIPOSTE THAT MAY FOLLOW THE FINAL PARRY	COUNTERATTACKS THAT MAY BE OPPOSED TO THE ACTION IN FIRST MOVEMENT	COUNTERATTACKS THAT MAY BE OPPOSED TO THE ACTION IN SECOND MOVEMENT	COUNTERATTACKS THAT MAY BE OPPOSED TO THE ACTION IN THIRD MOVEMENT
First or Third or Fourth	To the inside low line (detached or contact) To the low line (detached) or outside high line (contact) To the inside high line (detached or contact) or outside low line (flanconade in fourth)	Arrest to the high line	Arrest to the low line	Time thrust or Passata sotto
Second or Counter of first Fourth or Counter of third	To the high line (detached) or outside low line (contact) To the inside low line (detached or contact) To the inside high line (detached or contact) or outside low line (flanconade in fourth) To the low line (detached) or outside high line (contact)	Arrest to the low line	Arrest to the high line	Time thrust Inquartata
Third or Counter of fourth	To the low line (detached) or outside high line (contact) To the inside high line (detached or contact) or outside low line (flanconade in fourth)	Arrest to the high line	Arrest to the low line	Time thrust or Passata sotto
Fourth or Counter of third	To the inside high line (detached or contact) or outside low line (flanconade in fourth) To the low line (detached) or outside high line (contact)	Arrest to the low line	Arrest to the high line	Time thrust or Inquartata
First or Third or Fourth	To the inside low line (detached or contact) To the low line (detached) or outside high line (contact) To the inside high line (detached or contact) or outside low line (flanconade in fourth)	Arrest to the high line	Arrest to the low line	Time thrust or Passata sotto
Second or Counter of first Fourth or Counter of third	To the high line (detached) or outside low line (contact) To the inside low line (detached or contact) To the inside high line (detached or contact) or outside low line (flanconade in fourth) To the low line (detached) or outside high line (contact)	Arrest to the low line	Arrest to the high line	Time thrust Inquartata

NO.	OFFENSIVE ACTION	NUMBER OF MOVEMENTS COMPRISING ACTION	INVITATION OR ENGAGEMENT FROM WHICH THE ACTION IS EXECUTED	PARRY OR PARRIES ELUDED	FINAL LINE OF ATTACK
			TABLE III: PRINCIPAL COMPOUND ATTACKS WITH FEINTS OPPOSED TO CIRCULAR PARRIES (CONTINUED)		
72.	3) Double feint by disengagement to the inside high line and deceive	Three	From the adversary's engagement in third	Fourth and counter of fourth	Outside high line
	4) Double feint by disengagement to the outside high line and deceive	Three	From the opponent's engagement in fourth	Third and counter of third	Inside high line
73.	1) Double feint by glide to the inside low line and deceive	Three	From one's own engagement in first	First and counter of first	Outside low line
	2) Double feint by glide to the outside low line and deceive	Three	From one's own engagement in second	Second and counter of second	High line
	3) Double feint by glide to the outside high line and deceive	Three	From one's own engagement in third	Third and counter of third	Inside high line
	4) Double feint by glide to the inside high line and deceive	Three	From one's own engagement in fourth	Fourth and counter of fourth	Outside high line
	Double feint by flanconade in fourth and deceive	Three	From one's own engagement in fourth	Second and counter of second	High line

FINAL PARRY THAT MAY BE USED IN OPPOSITION TO THE ACTION	RIPOSTE THAT MAY FOLLOW THE FINAL PARRY	COUNTERATTACKS THAT MAY BE OPPOSED TO THE ACTION IN FIRST MOVEMENT	COUNTERATTACKS THAT MAY BE OPPOSED TO THE ACTION IN SECOND MOVEMENT	COUNTERATTACKS THAT MAY BE OPPOSED TO THE ACTION IN THIRD MOVEMENT
Third or Counter of fourth	To the low line (detached) or outside high line (contact) To the inside high line (detached or contact) or outside low line (flanconade in fourth)	Arrest to the high line	Arrest to the low line	Time thrust or Passata sotto
Fourth or Counter of third	To the inside high line (detached or contact) or outside low line (flanconade in fourth) To the low line (detached) or outside high line (contact)	Arrest to the low line	Arrest to the high line	Time thrust or Inquartata
Second or Counter of first	To the high line (detached) or outside low line (contact) To the inside low line (detached or contact)	Arrest to the inside	Arrest to the high line	Time thrust
First or Third or Fourth	To the inside low line (detached or contact) To the low line (detached) or outside high line (contact) To the inside high line (detached or contact) or outside low line (flanconade in fourth)	Arrest to the high line	Arrest to the low line	Time thrust or Passata sotto
Fourth or Counter of third	To the inside high line (detached or contact) or outside low line (flanconade in fourth) To the low line (detached) or outside high line (contact)	Arrest to the low line	Arrest to the high line	Time thrust or Inquartata
Third or Counter of fourth	To the low line (detached) or outside high line (contact) To the inside high line (detached or contact) or outside low line (flanconade in fourth)	Arrest to the high line	Arrest to the low line	Time thrust or Passata sotto
First or Third or Fourth	To the inside low line (detached or contact) To the low line (detached) or outside high line (contact) To the inside high line (detached or contact) or outside low line (flanconade in fourth)	Arrest by disengagement to the high line	Arrest to the low line	Time thrust or Passata sotto

TABLE III: PRINCIPAL COMPOUND ATTACKS WITH FEINTS OPPOSED TO CIRCULAR PARRIES (CONTINUED)					
NO.	OFFENSIVE ACTION	NUMBER OF MOVEMENTS COMPRISING ACTION	INVITATION OR ENGAGEMENT FROM WHICH THE ACTION IS EXECUTED	PARRY OR PARRIES ELUDED	FINAL LINE OF ATTACK
75.	1) Feint direct to the outside low line and double deceive	Three	From the adversary's invitation in first	Double counter of first	Outside low line
	2) Feint direct to the high line and double deceive	Three	From the opponent's invitation in second	Double counter of second	High line
	3) Feint direct to the inside high line and double deceive	Three	From the adversary's invitation in third	Double counter of third	Inside high line
	4) Feint direct to the outside high line and double deceive	Three	From the opponent's invitation in fourth	Double counter of fourth	Outside high line
76.	1) Feint by disengagement to the outside low line and double deceive	Three	From the adversary's engagement in first	Double counter of first	Outside low line
	2) Feint by disengagement to the high line and double deceive	Three	From the opponent's engagement in second	Double counter of second	High line
	3) Feint by disengagement to the inside high line and double deceive	Three	From the adversary's engagement in third	Double counter of third	Inside high line
	4) Feint by disengagement to the outside high line and double deceive	Three	From the opponent's engagement in fourth	Double counter of fourth	Outside high line

FINAL PARRY THAT MAY BE USED IN OPPOSITION TO THE ACTION	RIPOSTE THAT MAY FOLLOW THE FINAL PARRY	COUNTERATTACKS THAT MAY BE OPPOSED TO THE ACTION IN FIRST MOVEMENT	COUNTERATTACKS THAT MAY BE OPPOSED TO THE ACTION IN SECOND MOVEMENT	COUNTERATTACKS THAT MAY BE OPPOSED TO THE ACTION IN THIRD MOVEMENT
Second or Counter of first	To the high line (detached) or outside low line (contact) To the inside low line (detached or contact)	Arrest to the high line	Arrest to the high line	Time thrust
First or Third or Fourth	To the inside low line (detached or contact) To the low line (detached) or outside high line (contact) To the inside high line (detached or contact) or outside low line (flanconade in fourth)	Arrest to the low line	Arrest to the low line	Time thrust or Passata sotto
Fourth or Counter of third	To the inside high line (detached or contact) or outside low line (flanconade in fourth) To the low line (detached) or outside high line (contact)	Arrest to the high line	Arrest to the high line	Time thrust or Inquartata
Third or Counter of fourth	To the low line (detached) or outside high line (contact) To the inside high line (detached or contact) or outside low line (flanconade in fourth)	Arrest to the low line	Arrest to the low line	Time thrust or Passata sotto
Second or Counter of first	To the high line (detached) or outside low line (contact) To the inside low line (detached or contact) .	Arrest to the high line	Arrest to the high line	Time thrust
First or Third or Fourth	To the inside low line (detached or contact) To the low line (detached) or outside high line (contact) To the inside high line (detached or contact) or outside low line (flanconade in fourth)	Arrest to the low line	Arrest to the low line	Time thrust or Passata sotto
Fourth or Counter of third	To the inside high line (detached or contact) or outside low line (flanconade in fourth) To the low line (detached) or outside high line (contact)	Arrest to the high line	Arrest to the high line	Time thrust or Inquartata
Third or Counter of fourth	To the low line (detached) or outside high line (contact) To the inside high line (detached or contact) or outside low line (flanconade in fourth)	Arrest to the low line	Arrest to the low line	Time thrust or Passata sotto

TABLE III: PRINCIPAL COMPOUND ATTACKS WITH FEINTS OPPOSED TO CIRCULAR PARRIES (CONTINUED)

NO.	OFFENSIVE ACTION	NUMBER OF MOVEMENTS COMPRISING ACTION	INVITATION OR ENGAGEMENT FROM WHICH THE ACTION IS EXECUTED	PARRY OR PARRIES ELUDED	FINAL LINE OF ATTACK
77.	1) Feint by glide to the inside low line and double deceive	Three	From one's own engagement in first	Double counter of second	Inside low line
	2) Feint by glide to the outside low line and double deceive	Three	From one's own engagement in second	Double counter of first	Outside low line
	3) Feint by glide to the outside high line and double deceive	Three	From one's own engagement in third	Double counter of fourth	Outside high line
	4) Feint by glide to the inside high line and double deceive	Three	From one's own engagement in fourth	Double counter of third	Inside high line
	Feint by flanconade in fourth and double deceive	Three	From one's own engagement in fourth	Double counter of first	Outside low line

FINAL PARRY THAT MAY BE USED IN OPPOSITION TO THE ACTION	RIPOSTE THAT MAY FOLLOW THE FINAL PARRY	COUNTERATTACKS THAT MAY BE OPPOSED TO THE ACTION IN FIRST MOVEMENT	COUNTERATTACKS THAT MAY BE OPPOSED TO THE ACTION IN SECOND MOVEMENT	COUNTERATTACKS THAT MAY BE OPPOSED TO THE ACTION IN THIRD MOVEMENT
First or Counter of second	To the inside low line (detached or contact) To the high line (detached) or outside low line (contact)	Arrest to the inside	Arrest to the low line	Time thrust
Second or Counter of first	To the high line (detached) or outside low line (contact) To the inside low line (detached or contact)	Arrest to the high line	Arrest to the high line	Time thrust
Third or Counter of fourth	To the low line (detached) or outside high line (contact) To the inside high line (detached or contact) or outside low line (flanconade in fourth)	Arrest to the low line	Arrest to the low line	Time thrust or Passata sotto
Fourth or Counter of third	To the inside high line (detached or contact) or outside low line (flanconade in fourth) To the low line (detached) or outside high line (contact)	Arrest to the high line	Arrest to the high line	Time thrust or Inquartata
Second or Counter of first	To the high line (detached) or outside low line (contact) To the inside low line (detached or contact)	Arrest by disengagement to the high line	Arrest to the high line	Time thrust

TABLE IV: PRINCIPAL COMPOUND ATTACKS WITH ACTIONS ON THE BLADE					
NO.	OFFENSIVE ACTION	NUMBER OF MOVEMENTS COMPRISING ACTION	INVITATION OR ENGAGEMENT FROM WHICH THE ACTION IS EXECUTED	PARRY OR PARRIES ELUDED	FINAL LINE OF ATTACK
97.	1) Blade seizure and glide to the inside low line	Two	Adversary's blade in line		Inside low line
	2) Blade seizure and glide to the outside low line	Two	Opponent's steel in line		Outside low line
	3) Blade seizure and glide to the outside high line	Two	Adversary's blade in line		Outside high line
	4) Blade seizure and glide to the inside high line	Two	Opponent's steel in line		Inside high line
	Blade seizure and flanconade in fourth	Two	Adversary's blade in line		Outside low line
98.	1) Single change of engagement and glide to the outside low line	Two	From one's own engagement in first		Outside low line
	2) Single change of engagement and glide to the inside low line	Two	From one's own engagement in second		Inside low line
	3) Single change of engagement and glide to the inside high line	Two	From one's own engagement in third		Inside high line

FINAL PARRY THAT MAY BE USED IN OPPOSITION TO THE ACTION	RIPOSTE THAT MAY FOLLOW THE FINAL PARRY	COUNTERATTACKS THAT MAY BE OPPOSED TO THE ACTION IN FIRST MOVEMENT	COUNTERATTACKS THAT MAY BE OPPOSED TO THE ACTION IN SECOND MOVEMENT	COUNTERATTACKS THAT MAY BE OPPOSED TO THE ACTION IN THIRD MOVEMENT
First or Ceding third or Counter of second	To the inside low line (detached or contact) To the low line (detached) or outside high line (contact) To the high line (detached) or outside low line (contact)	Disengagement in time to the outside low line	Inquartata	
Second or Ceding fourth or Counter of first	To the high line (detached) or outside low line (contact) To the inside high line (detached or contact) or outside low line (flanconade in fourth) To the inside low line (detached or contact)	Disengagement in time to the high line	Time thrust	
Third or Counter of fourth	To the low line (detached) or outside high line (contact) To the inside high line (detached or contact) or outside low line (flanconade in fourth)	Disengagement in time to the inside	Time thrust or Passata sotto	
Fourth or Counter of third	To the inside high line (detached or contact) or outside low line (flanconade in fourth) To the low line (detached) or outside high line (contact)	Disengagement in time to the outside	Inquartata	
Second or Ceding fourth or Counter of first	To the high line (detached) or outside low line (contact) To the inside high line (detached or contact) or outside low line (flanconade in fourth) To the inside low line (detached or contact)	Disengagement in time to the outside	Imbroccata	
Second or Ceding fourth or Counter of first	To the high line (detached) or outside low line (contact) To the inside high line (detached or contact) or outside low line (flanconade in fourth) To the inside low line (detached or contact)	Disengagement in time to the high line	Time thrust	
First or Ceding third or Counter of second	To the inside low line (detached or contact) To the low line (detached) or outside high line (contact) To the high line (detached) or outside low line (contact)	Disengagement in time to the outside low line	Inquartata	
Fourth or Counter of third	To the inside high line (detached or contact) or outside low line (flanconade in fourth) To the low line (detached) or outside high line (contact)	Disengagement in time to the outside	Inquartata	

		NUMBER OF MOVEMENTS COMPRISING	INVITATION OR ENGAGEMENT FROM WHICH THE ACTION IS	PARRY OR PARRIES	
NO.	OFFENSIVE ACTION	ACTION	EXECUTED	ELUDED	FINAL LINE OF ATTACK
98.	4) Single change of engagement and glide to the outside high line	Two	From one's own engagement in fourth		Outside high line
	Single change of engagement and flanconade in fourth	Two	From one's own engagement in third		Outside low line
99.	1) Transport to third and glide to the outside high line	Two	From one's own engagement in first		Outside high line
	2) Transport to fourth and glide to the inside high line	Two	From one's own engagement in second		Inside high line
	3) Transport to first and glide to the inside low line (internal flanconade)	Two	From one's own engagement in third		Inside low line
	4) Transport to second and glide to the outside low line (flanconade in second)	Two	From one's own engagement in fourth		Outside low line
103,	1) Simple beat in first and straight thrust to the inside low line	Two	Adversary's blade in line or from one's own engagement in first		Inside low line
	2) Simple beat in second and straight thrust to the high line or outside low line	Two	Opponent's steel in line or from one's own engagement in second		a) High line
					b) Outside low line

TABLE IV: PRINCIPAL COMPOUND ATTACKS WITH ACTIONS ON THE BLADE (CONTINUED)

FINAL PARRY THAT MAY BE USED IN OPPOSITION TO THE ACTION	RIPOSTE THAT MAY FOLLOW THE FINAL PARRY	COUNTERATTACKS THAT MAY BE OPPOSED TO THE ACTION IN FIRST MOVEMENT	COUNTERATTACKS THAT MAY BE OPPOSED TO THE ACTION IN SECOND MOVEMENT	COUNTERATTACKS THAT MAY BE OPPOSED TO THE ACTION IN THIRD MOVEMENT
Third or Counter of fourth	To the low line (detached) or outside high line (contact) To the inside high line (detached or contact) or outside low line (flanconade in fourth)	Disengagement in time to the inside	Time thrust or Passata sotto	
Second or Ceding fourth or Counter of first	To the high line (detached) or outside low line (contact) To the inside high line (detached or contact) or outside low line (flanconade in fourth) To the inside low line (detached or contact)	Disengagement in time to the outside	Imbroccata	
Third or Counter of fourth	To the low line (detached) or outside high line (contact) To the inside high line (detached or contact) or outside low line (flanconade in fourth)	Disengagement in time to the inside	Time thrust or Passata sotto	
Fourth or Counter of third	To the inside high line (detached or contact) or outside low line (flanconade in fourth) To the low line (detached) or outside high line (contact)	Disengagement in time to the outside	Inquartata	
First or Ceding third or Counter of second	To the inside low line (detached or contact) To the low line (detached) or outside high line (contact) To the high line (detached) or outside low line (contact)	Disengagement in time to the low line	Inquartata	
Second or Ceding fourth or Counter of first	To the high line (detached) or outside low line (contact) To the inside high line (detached or contact) or outside low line (flanconade in fourth) To the inside low line (detached or contact)	Disengagement in time to the high line	Imbroccata	
First or Counter of second	To the inside low line (detached or contact) To the high line (detached) or outside low line (contact)	Disengagement in time to the outside low line	Inquartata	
First or Third or Fourth Second or Counter of first	To the inside low line (detached or contact) To the low line (detached) or outside high line (contact) To the inside high line (detached or contact) or outside low line (flanconade in fourth) To the high line (detached) or outside low line (contact) To the inside low line (detached or contact)	Disengagement in time to the high line	Time thrust or Passata sotto	

NO.	OFFENSIVE ACTION	NUMBER OF MOVEMENTS COMPRISING ACTION	INVITATION OR ENGAGEMENT FROM WHICH THE ACTION IS EXECUTED	PARRY OR PARRIES ELUDED	FINAL LINE OF ATTACK
	TABLE IV: PRINCIPAL COMPOUND ATTACKS WITH ACTIONS ON THE BLADE (CONTINUED)				
103.	3) Simple beat in third and straight thrust to the outside high line or low line	Two	Adversary's blade in line or from one's own engagement in third		a) Outside high line b) Low line
	4) Simple beat in fourth and straight thrust to the inside high line	Two	Opponent's steel in line or from one's own engagement in fourth		Inside high line
106.	1) Change beat in first and straight thrust to the inside low line	Two	From one's own or from the adversary's engagement in second		Inside low line
	2) Change beat in second and straight thrust to the high line or outside low line	Two	From one's own or from the opponent's engagement in first		a) High line b) Outside low line
	3) Change beat in third and straight thrust to the outside high line or low line	Two	From one's own or from the adversary's engagement in fourth		a) Outside high line b) Low line
	4) Change beat in fourth and straight thrust to the inside high line	Two	From one's own or from the opponent's engagement in third		Inside high line
110.	1) Expulsion in third and straight thrust to the outside high line	Two	From one's own engagement in third		Outside high line
	2) Expulsion in fourth and straight thrust to the inside high line	Two	From one's own engagement in fourth		Inside high line

FINAL PARRY THAT MAY BE USED IN OPPOSITION TO THE ACTION	RIPOSTE THAT MAY FOLLOW THE FINAL PARRY	COUNTERATTACKS THAT MAY BE OPPOSED TO THE ACTION IN FIRST MOVEMENT	COUNTERATTACKS THAT MAY BE OPPOSED TO THE ACTION IN SECOND MOVEMENT	COUNTERATTACKS THAT MAY BE OPPOSED TO THE ACTION IN THIRD MOVEMENT
Third or Counter of fourth Second	To the low line (detached) or outside high line (contact) To the inside high line (detached or contact) or outside low line (flanconade in fourth) To the high line (detached) or outside low line (contact)	Disengagement in time to the inside	Time thrust or Passata sotto Time thrust	
Fourth or Counter of third	To the inside high line (detached or contact) or outside low line (flanconade in fourth) To the low line (detached) or outside high line (contact)	Disengagement in time to the outside	Time thrust or Inquartata	
First or Counter of second	To the inside low line (detached or contact) To the high line (detached) or outside low line (contact)	Disengagement in time to the outside low line	Inquartata	
First or Third or Fourth Second or Counter of first	To the inside low line (detached or contact) To the low line (detached) or outside high line (contact) To the inside high line (detached or contact) or outside low line (flanconade in fourth) To the high line (detached) or outside low line (contact) To the inside low line (detached or contact)	Disengagement in time to the high line	Time thrust or Passata sotto	
Third or Counter of fourth Second	To the low line (detached) or outside high line (contact) To the inside high line (detached or contact) or outside low line (flanconade in fourth) To the high line (detached) or outside low line (contact)	Disengagement in time to the inside	Time thrust or Passata sotto Time thrust	
Fourth or Counter of third	To the inside high line (detached or contact) or outside low line (flanconade in fourth) To the low line (detached) or outside high line (contact)	Disengagement in time to the outside	Time thrust or Inquartata	
Third or Counter of fourth	To the low line (detached) or outside high line (contact) To the inside high line (detached or contact) or outside low line (flanconade in fourth)		Passata sotto	
Fourth or Counter of third	To the inside high line (detached or contact) or outside low line (flanconade in fourth) To the low line (detached) or outside high line (contact)		Inquartata	

TABLE IV: PRINCIPAL COMPOUND ATTACKS WITH ACTIONS ON THE BLADE (CONTINUED)					
NO.	OFFENSIVE ACTION	NUMBER OF MOVEMENTS COMPRISING ACTION	INVITATION OR ENGAGEMENT FROM WHICH THE ACTION IS EXECUTED	PARRY OR PARRIES ELUDED	FINAL LINE OF ATTACK
111.	1) Pressure in first and straight thrust to the inside low line	Two	Adversary's blade in line		Inside low line
	2) Pressure in second and straight thrust to the high line or outside low line	Two	Opponent's steel in line		a) High line
					b) Outside low line
	3) Pressure in third and straight thrust to the outside high line or low line	Two	Adversary's blade in line		a) Outside high line
					b) Low line
	4) Pressure in fourth and straight thrust to the inside high line	Two	Opponent's steel in line		Inside high line
112.	Blade cover and straight thrust to the inside high line	Two	Adversary's blade in line		Inside high line
113.	1) Spiral disarmament to the left and straight thrust to the inside high line	Two	Opponent's steel in line or from one's own engagement in third		Inside high line
	2) Spiral disarmament to the right and straight thrust to the low line	Two	Adversary's blade in line or from one's own engagement in fourth		Low line

FINAL PARRY THAT MAY BE USED IN OPPOSITION TO THE ACTION	RIPOSTE THAT MAY FOLLOW THE FINAL PARRY	COUNTERATTACKS THAT MAY BE OPPOSED TO THE ACTION IN FIRST MOVEMENT	COUNTERATTACKS THAT MAY BE OPPOSED TO THE ACTION IN SECOND MOVEMENT	COUNTERATTACKS THAT MAY BE OPPOSED TO THE ACTION IN THIRD MOVEMENT
First or Counter of second	To the inside low line (detached or contact) To the high line (detached) or outside low line (contact)	Disengagement in time to the outside low line	Inquartata	
First or Third or Fourth	To the inside low line (detached or contact) To the low line (detached) or outside high line (contact) To the inside high line (detached or contact) or outside low line (flanconade in fourth)	Disengagement in time to the high line	Time thrust or Passata sotto	
Second or Counter of first	To the high line (detached) or outside low line (contact) To the inside low line (detached or contact)		Time thrust	
Third or Counter of fourth	To the low line (detached) or outside high line (contact) To the inside high line (detached or contact) or outside low line (flanconade in fourth)	Disengagement in time to the inside	Time thrust or Passata sotto	
Second	To the high line (detached) or outside low line (contact)		Time thrust	
Fourth or Counter of third	To the inside high line (detached or contact) or outside low line (flanconade in fourth) To the low line (detached) or outside high line (contact)	Disengagement in time to the outside	Time thrust or Inquartata	
Fourth or Counter of third	To the inside high line (detached or contact) or outside low line (flanconade in fourth) To the low line (detached) or outside high line (contact)	Disengagement in time to the outside	Inquartata	
First or Fourth	To the inside low line (detached or contact) To the inside high line (detached or contact) or outside low line (flanconade in fourth)	Disengagement in time to the inside [1]		
Second or Counter of first	To the high line (detached) or outside low line (contact) To the inside low line (detached or contact)	Disengagement in time to the outside [2]		

1 Disengagement in time is possible only when the disarmament is executed in opposition to the weapon line.
2 As above.

TABLE V: PRINCIPAL COMPOUND ATTACKS WITH ACTIONS ON THE BLADE & FEINTS OPPOSED TO SIMPLE PARRIES					
NO.	OFFENSIVE ACTION	NUMBER OF MOVEMENTS COMPRISING ACTION	INVITATION OR ENGAGEMENT FROM WHICH THE ACTION IS EXECUTED	PARRY OR PARRIES ELUDED	FINAL LINE OF ATTACK
114.	1) Single change of engagement and feint direct to the high line	Three	From one's own engagement in first	First	Outside low line
	2) Single change of engagement and feint direct to the inside low line	Three	From one's own engagement in second	First	Outside low line
	3) Single change of engagement and feint direct to the inside high line	Three	From one's own engagement in third	Fourth	Outside high line
	4) Single change of engagement and feint direct to the outside high line	Three	From one's own engagement in fourth	Third	Inside high line
	Single change of engagement and feint by flanconade in fourth	Three	From one's own engagement in third	Second	High line
115.	1) Transport to third and feint by glide to the outside high line	Three	From one's own engagement in first	Third	a) Low line b) Inside high line
	2) Transport to fourth and feint by glide to the inside high line	Three	From one's own engagement in second	Fourth	Outside high line
	3) Transport to first and feint by glide to the inside low line (feint by internal flanconade)	Three	From one's own engagement in third	First	Outside low line

FINAL PARRY THAT MAY BE USED IN OPPOSITION TO THE ACTION	RIPOSTE THAT MAY FOLLOW THE FINAL PARRY	COUNTERATTACKS THAT MAY BE OPPOSED TO THE ACTION IN FIRST MOVEMENT	COUNTERATTACKS THAT MAY BE OPPOSED TO THE ACTION IN SECOND MOVEMENT	COUNTERATTACKS THAT MAY BE OPPOSED TO THE ACTION IN THIRD MOVEMENT
Second or Counter of first	To the high line (detached) or outside low line (contact) To the inside low line (detached or contact)	Disengagement in time to the high line	Arrest to the low line	Time thrust
Second or Counter of first	To the high line (detached) or outside low line (contact) To the inside low line (detached or contact)	Disengagement in time to the outside low line	Arrest to the high line	Time thrust
Third or Counter of fourth	To the low line (detached) or outside high line (contact) To the inside high line (detached or contact) or outside low line (flanconade in fourth)	Disengagement in time to the outside	Arrest to the inside	Time thrust or Passata sotto
Fourth or Counter of third	To the inside high line (detached or contact) or outside low line (flanconade in fourth) To the low line (detached) or outside high line (contact)	Disengagement in time to the inside	Arrest to the low line	Inquartata
First or Third or Fourth	To the inside low line (detached or contact) To the low line (detached) or outside high line (contact) To the inside high line (detached or contact) or outside low line (flanconade in fourth)	Disengagement in time to the outside	Arrest by disengagement to the high line	Time thrust or Passata sotto
Second Fourth or Counter of third	To the high line (detached) or outside low line (contact) To the inside high line (detached or contact) or outside low line (flanconade in fourth) To the low line (detached) or outside high line (contact)	Disengagement in time to the low line	Arrest to the low line	Time thrust Inquartata
Third or Counter of fourth	To the low line (detached) or outside high line (contact) To the inside high line (detached or contact) or outside low line (flanconade in fourth)	Disengagement in time to the outside	Arrest to the inside	Time thrust or Passata sotto
Second or Counter of first	To the high line (detached) or outside low line (contact) To the inside low line (detached or contact)	Disengagement in time to the low line	Arrest to the low line	Time thrust

		NUMBER OF MOVEMENTS COMPRISING ACTION	INVITATION OR ENGAGEMENT FROM WHICH THE ACTION IS EXECUTED	PARRY OR PARRIES ELUDED	
NO.	OFFENSIVE ACTION				FINAL LINE OF ATTACK
115.	4) Transport to second and feint by glide to the outside low line (feint by flanconade in second)	Three	From one's own engagement in fourth	Second	High line
117.	1) Simple beat in first and feint direct to the inside low line	Three	Adversary's blade in line or from one's own engagement in first	First	Outside low line
	2) Simple beat in second and feint direct to the high line or outside low line	Three	Opponent's steel in line or from one's own engagement in second	First or Second	a) Outside low line (feint direct to the high line) b) High line (feint direct to the outside low line)
	3) Simple beat in third and feint direct to the outside high line or low line	Three	Adversary's blade in line or from one's own engagement in third	Third or Second	a) Low line (feint direct to the outside high line) b) Inside high line (feint direct to the outside high line) High line (feint direct to the low line)
	4) Simple beat in fourth and feint direct to the inside high line	Three	Opponent's steel in line or from one's own engagement in fourth	Fourth	Outside high line
120.	1) Pressure in first and feint direct to the inside low line	Three	Adversary's blade in line	First	Outside low line

TABLE V: PRINCIPAL COMPOUND ATTACKS WITH ACTIONS ON THE BLADE & FEINTS OPPOSED TO SIMPLE PARRIES (CONT.)

FINAL PARRY THAT MAY BE USED IN OPPOSITION TO THE ACTION	RIPOSTE THAT MAY FOLLOW THE FINAL PARRY	COUNTERATTACKS THAT MAY BE OPPOSED TO THE ACTION IN FIRST MOVEMENT	COUNTERATTACKS THAT MAY BE OPPOSED TO THE ACTION IN SECOND MOVEMENT	COUNTERATTACKS THAT MAY BE OPPOSED TO THE ACTION IN THIRD MOVEMENT
First or Third or Fourth	To the inside low line (detached or contact) To the low line (detached) or outside high line (contact) To the inside high line (detached or contact) or outside low line (flanconade in fourth)	Disengagement in time to the high line	Arrest to the high line	Time thrust or Passata sotto
Second or Counter of first	To the high line (detached) or outside low line (contact) To the inside low line (detached or contact)	Disengagement in time to the outside low line	Arrest to the inside	Time thrust
Second or Counter of first	To the high line (detached) or outside low line (contact) To the inside low line (detached or contact)	Disengagement in time to the high line	Arrest to the low line	Time thrust
First or Third or Fourth	To the inside low line (detached or contact) To the low line (detached) or outside high line (contact) To the inside high line (detached or contact) or outside low line (flanconade in fourth)		Arrest to the high line	Passata sotto
Second	To the high line (detached) or outside low line (contact)	Disengagement in time to the inside	Arrest to the low line	Time thrust
Fourth or Counter of third	To the inside high line (detached or contact) or outside low line (flanconade in fourth) To the low line (detached) or outside high line (contact)			Inquartata
First or Third or Fourth	To the inside low line (detached or contact) To the low line (detached) or outside high line (contact) To the inside high line (detached or contact) or outside low line (flanconade in fourth)		Arrest to the high line	Passata sotto
Third or Counter of fourth	To the low line (detached) or outside high line (contact) To the inside high line (detached or contact) or outside low line (flanconade in fourth)	Disengagement in time to the outside	Arrest to the inside	Time thrust or Passata sotto
Second or Counter of first	To the high line (detached) or outside low line (contact) To the inside low line (detached or contact)	Disengagement in time to the outside low line	Arrest to the inside	Time thrust

TABLE V: PRINCIPAL COMPOUND ATTACKS WITH ACTIONS ON THE BLADE & FEINTS OPPOSED TO SIMPLE PARRIES (CONT.)					
NO.	OFFENSIVE ACTION	NUMBER OF MOVEMENTS COMPRISING ACTION	INVITATION OR ENGAGEMENT FROM WHICH THE ACTION IS EXECUTED	PARRY OR PARRIES ELUDED	FINAL LINE OF ATTACK
120.	2) Pressure in second and feint direct to the high line or outside low line	Three	Opponent's steel in line	First or	a) Outside low line (feint direct to the high line)
				Second	b) High line (feint direct to the outside low line)
	3) Pressure in third and feint direct to the outside high line or low line	Three	Adversary's blade in line	Third or	a) Low line (feint direct to the outside high line) b) Inside high line (feint direct to the outside high line)
				Second	High line (feint direct to the low line)
	4) Pressure in fourth and feint direct to the inside high line	Three	Opponent's steel in line	Fourth	Outside high line
122.	Blade cover and feint direct to the inside high line	Three	Adversary's blade in line	Fourth	Outside high line

FINAL PARRY THAT MAY BE USED IN OPPOSITION TO THE ACTION	RIPOSTE THAT MAY FOLLOW THE FINAL PARRY	COUNTERATTACKS THAT MAY BE OPPOSED TO THE ACTION IN FIRST MOVEMENT	COUNTERATTACKS THAT MAY BE OPPOSED TO THE ACTION IN SECOND MOVEMENT	COUNTERATTACKS THAT MAY BE OPPOSED TO THE ACTION IN THIRD MOVEMENT
Second or Counter of first First or Third or Fourth	To the high line (detached) or outside low line (contact) To the inside low line (detached or contact) To the inside low line (detached or contact) To the low line (detached) or outside high line (contact) To the inside high line (detached or contact) or outside low line (flanconade in fourth)	Disengagement in time to the high line	Arrest to the low line Arrest to the high line	Time thrust Passata sotto
Second Fourth or Counter of third First or Third or Fourth	To the high line (detached) or outside low line (contact) To the inside high line (detached or contact) or outside low line (flanconade in fourth) To the low line (detached) or outside high line (contact) To the inside low line (detached or contact) To the low line (detached) or outside high line (contact) To the inside high line (detached or contact) or outside low line (flanconade in fourth)	Disengagement in time to the inside	Arrest to the low line Arrest to the high line	Time thrust Inquartata Passata sotto
Third or Counter of fourth	To the low line (detached) or outside high line (contact) To the inside high line (detached or contact) or outside low line (flanconade in fourth)	Disengagement in time to the outside	Arrest to the inside	Time thrust or Passata sotto
Third or Counter of fourth	To the low line (detached) or outside high line (contact) To the inside high line (detached or contact) or outside low line (flanconade in fourth)	Disengagement in time to the outside	Arrest to the inside	Time thrust or Passata sotto

TABLE VI: PRINCIPAL COMPOUND ATTACKS WITH ACTIONS ON THE BLADE & FEINTS OPPOSED TO CIRCULAR PARRIES					
NO.	OFFENSIVE ACTION	NUMBER OF MOVEMENTS COMPRISING ACTION	INVITATION OR ENGAGEMENT FROM WHICH THE ACTION IS EXECUTED	PARRY OR PARRIES ELUDED	FINAL LINE OF ATTACK
118.	1) Simple beat in first, feint direct to the inside low line and deceive	Three	Adversary's blade in line or from one's own engagement in first	Counter of second	Inside low line
	2) Simple beat in second, feint direct to the outside low line and deceive	Three	Opponent's steel in line or from one's own engagement in second	Counter of first	Outside low line
	3) Simple beat in third, feint direct to the outside high line and deceive	Three	Adversary's blade in line or from one's own engagement in third	Counter of fourth	Outside high line
	4) Simple beat in fourth, feint direct to the inside high line and deceive	Three	Opponent's steel in line or from one's own engagement in fourth	Counter of third	Inside high line
120.	1) Pressure in first, feint direct to the inside low line and deceive	Three	Adversary's blade in line	Counter of second	Inside low line
	2) Pressure in second, feint direct to the outside low line and deceive	Three	Opponent's steel in line	Counter of first	Outside low line
	3) Pressure in third, feint direct to the outside high line and deceive	Three	Adversary's blade in line	Counter of fourth	Outside high line
	4) Pressure in fourth, feint direct to the inside high line and deceive	Three	Opponent's steel in line	Counter of third	Inside high line
123.	Blade cover, feint direct to the inside high line and deceive	Three	Adversary's blade in line	Counter of third	Inside high line

FINAL PARRY THAT MAY BE USED IN OPPOSITION TO THE ACTION	RIPOSTE THAT MAY FOLLOW THE FINAL PARRY	COUNTERATTACKS THAT MAY BE OPPOSED TO THE ACTION IN FIRST MOVEMENT	COUNTERATTACKS THAT MAY BE OPPOSED TO THE ACTION IN SECOND MOVEMENT	COUNTERATTACKS THAT MAY BE OPPOSED TO THE ACTION IN THIRD MOVEMENT
First or Counter of second	To the inside low line (detached or contact) To the high line (detached) or outside low line (contact)	Disengagement in time to the outside low line	Arrest to the inside	Time thrust
Second or Counter of first	To the high line (detached) or outside low line (contact) To the inside low line (detached or contact)	Disengagement in time to the high line	Arrest to the high line	Time thrust
Third or Counter of fourth	To the low line (detached) or outside high line (contact) To the inside high line (detached or contact) or outside low line (flanconade in fourth)	Disengagement in time to the inside	Arrest to the low line	Time thrust or Passata sotto
Fourth or Counter of third	To the inside high line (detached or contact) or outside low line (flanconade in fourth) To the low line (detached) or outside high line (contact)	Disengagement in time to the outside	Arrest to the inside	Time thrust or Inquartata
First or Counter of second	To the inside low line (detached or contact) To the high line (detached) or outside low line (contact)	Disengagement in time to the outside low line	Arrest to the inside	Time thrust
Second or Counter of first	To the high line (detached) or outside low line (contact) To the inside low line (detached or contact)	Disengagement in time to the high line	Arrest to the high line	Time thrust
Third or Counter of fourth	To the low line (detached) or outside high line (contact) To the inside high line (detached or contact) or outside low line (flanconade in fourth)	Disengagement in time to the inside	Arrest to the low line	Time thrust or Passata sotto
Fourth or Counter of third	To the inside high line (detached or contact) or outside low line (flanconade in fourth) To the low line (detached) or outside high line (contact)	Disengagement in time to the outside	Arrest to the inside	Time thrust or Inquartata
Fourth or Counter of third	To the inside high line (detached or contact) or outside low line (flanconade in fourth) To the low line (detached) or outside high line (contact)	Disengagement in time to the outside	Arrest to the inside	Time thrust or Inquartata

PART II

THE SABRE

CHAPTER 1

ESSENTIAL ELEMENTS

1. PARTS OF THE SABRE

The sabre, like the foil, is divided into two major parts: the guard, and the blade.

The guard is comprised of four elements: guard, cushion, grip, and nut (Fig. 56).

1) The guard is an oval-shaped metal shield, less than 15 x 14 centimeters in diameter, with two openings for the tang, one in the guard, the other at the small end of the knuckle-bow.

2) The cushion is a leather, fabric, or rubber pad, perforated at the center, and fitted behind the guard.

3) The grip is a hollow wooden or plastic handle, with two metal rings, one on each end, through which the tang passes.

4) The nut is a metal fastening device that holds the threaded end of the tang.

Figure 56. Parts of the sabre.

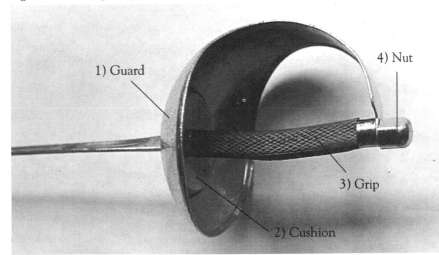

1) Guard

4) Nut

3) Grip

2) Cushion

The blade consists of seven elements: blunted end, counter-cut, back, cut, grooves, heel, and tang.

1) The blunted end is an enlargement at the point of the blade.

2) The counter-cut is a third of the back edge of the blade, beginning at the tip and extending to the grooves.

3) The back is a part of the blade that opposes the cut, commencing where the counter-cut ends, and extending to the guard.

4) The cut is a thin edge of the blade that begins at the point and extends about two-thirds the length of the blade.

5) The grooves are channels that run the length of the blade, commencing a third of the way back from the tip, and terminating at the heel.

6) The heel is a sturdy portion of the blade without grooves that rests against the guard.

7) The tang is a part of the blade that passes through the grip and screws into the nut.

The blade is made of tempered steel. It must not exceed 88 centimeters in length from the convex side of the guard to the blunted end.

Again, degrees of strength are distinguished by dividing the blade into three equal sections: strong, medium, and weak.

2. BALANCE, WEIGHT, AND LENGTH OF THE SABRE

The sabre is properly balanced when its center of gravity is at the strong of the blade, about four fingers from the guard.

By regulation, the sabre must be under 500 grams in weight, and must not exceed 105 centimeters in length, measuring from the tip of the blade to the end of the nut.

3. HOLDING THE SABRE

The sabre is grasped by putting the first phalanx of the index finger under the grip, near the cushion, and setting the ball of the thumb on top of the grip, in opposition to the index finger; the middle, ring, and little fingers

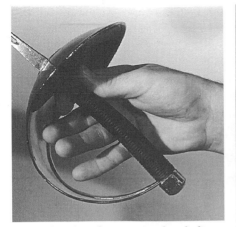 

Figure 57 The sabre is grasped with the index finger and thumb in opposition.   *Figure 58. The grip extends along the base of the fingers, leaving the palm of the hand empty.*

are curled around the grip, with the bottom of the grip resting on the second phalanx of each finger. Correctly seated, the grip extends along the base of the fingers, leaving the palm of the hand empty (Figs. 57-58).

Observation: Against heavy-handed opponents it is advisable to place the thumb and index finger about a centimeter away from the cushion, so that violent blows will not force the guard against the thumb.

4. HAND POSITIONS

In sabre fencing there are seven hand positions. Four of these are termed principal positions, and three, intermediate positions. The principal positions are first, second, third, and fourth; and the intermediate positions, first in second, second in third, and third in fourth.

With the weapon in hand, the positions are effected by rotating the hand one quarter turn for the principal positions, and one eighth turn for the intermediate positions. In first position the back of the hand faces left, cutting edge of the blade up (Fig. 59); in second position the back of the hand faces up, cutting edge of the blade to the right (Fig. 60); in third position the back of the hand faces right, cutting edge of the blade down (Fig. 61); in fourth position the back of the hand faces down, cutting edge of the blade to the left (Fig. 62); in first in second position the back of the hand faces obliquely up toward the left, cutting edge of the blade diagonal

and up toward the right (Fig. 63); in second in third position the back of
the hand faces obliquely up toward the right, cutting edge of the blade
diagonal and down toward the right (Fig. 64); and in third in fourth position the back of the hand faces obliquely down toward the right, cutting
edge of the blade diagonal and down toward the left (Fig. 65).

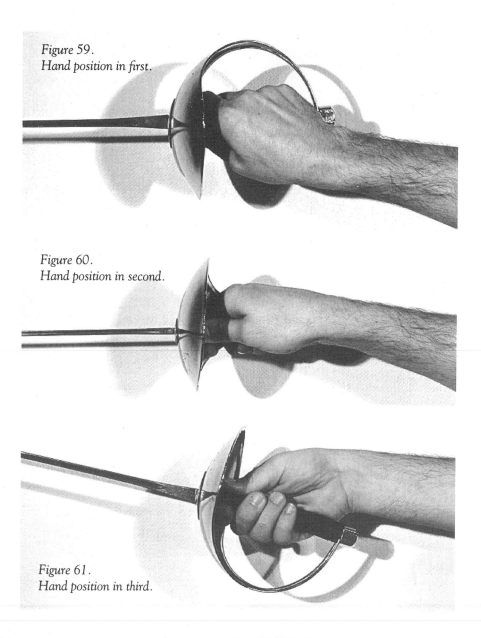

Figure 59.
Hand position in first.

Figure 60.
Hand position in second.

Figure 61.
Hand position in third.

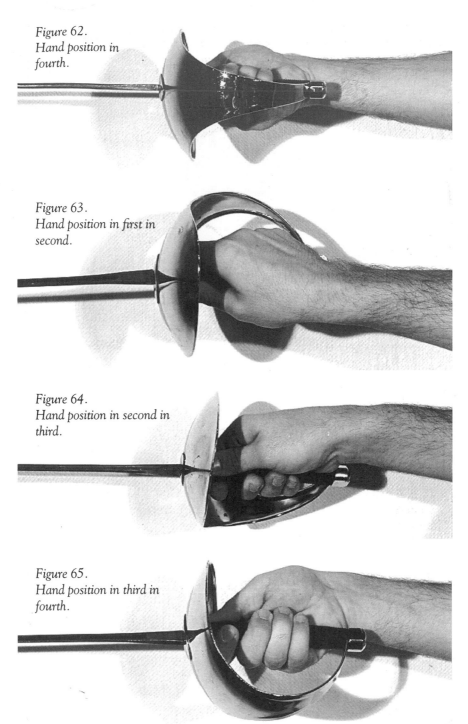

Figure 62.
Hand position in
fourth.

Figure 63.
Hand position in first in
second.

Figure 64.
Hand position in second in
third.

Figure 65.
Hand position in third in
fourth.

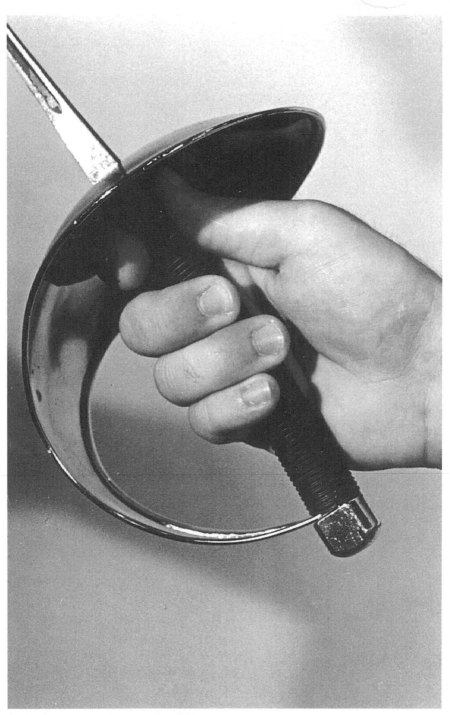

Plate XVI. Holding the Sabre.

CHAPTER 2

THE GUARD AND THE LUNGE

5. FIRST POSITION

The posture assumed by the fencer with his body and weapon before the salute and during periods of rest is called first position (Fig. 66).

6. WEAPON IN LINE

The weapon is in line when it forms, with the extended right arm, a straight line parallel with the floor.

From first position the sabre is lifted into line, arm shoulder high, and fully extended, hand in second position, cutting edge to the right, and point aimed at the adversary's chest (Figs. 67-68).

Figure 66. First position.

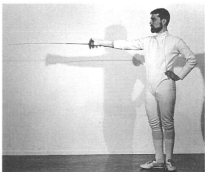

Figure 67. Weapon in line. From first position…

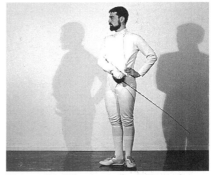

Figure 68. …the sabre is lifted into line.

Figure 69.
First movement.

Figure 70.
Second movement.

Figure 71.
Third movement.

Figure 72.
Fourth movement.

The Salute

Figure 73.
Fifth movement.

Figure 74.
Sixth movement.

Figure 75.
Seventh movement.

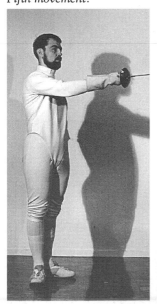

7. The Salute

The salute is a traditional act of courtesy directed to the adversary and spectators, and must always be observed at the beginning and end of the lesson and combat. It is performed in the same way as the foil salute, with one minor difference: in the first movement the sabre is raised directly into line (Figs. 69-75).

8. The Line of Direction

The imaginary line connecting two fencers, beginning at the left heel of one, passing through the axis of his right foot, and continuing until it encounters the same points in his adversary's feet, is called the line of direction. This is the normal route the feet must travel in the lesson, in exercise, and in combat.

9. The Guard

The position taken by the fencer with his body and weapon to be ready for the offense, defense, or counteroffense is called the guard.

The sabre guard, like the foil guard, is taken from first position in two movements:

1) The sabre is raised into line (Fig. 76).

2) Same procedure as in foil except that the right hand is turned to second in third position, and slightly below chest level, point of the

Figure 76. First movement of the guard.   *Figure 77. Second movement of the guard.*

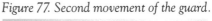

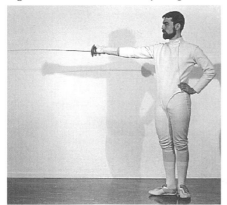

weapon at the height of the adversary's eyes, sabre, hand, forearm, and elbow to the right of the flank, left hand closed in a fist, and set on the hip, knuckles down, back of the hand facing left (Fig. 77).

This is called the guard in third, and is the most commonly used guard in contemporary fencing.

Observation: There are, in fact, five sabre guards, each corresponding to the invitation of the same number. However, other than the sabre guard in third, the only guard occasionally encountered today is the guard in second. In this the hand is rotated to first in second position, and nearly level with the flank, point of the weapon aimed to the right of the opponent's abdomen, and sabre hand, forearm, and elbow to the right of the flank. It should be noted that the weakness of this guard, as well as the guards in first, fourth, and fifth, is that the sword arm is exposed to counterattacks.

10. THE LINE OF OFFENSE

The weapon is considered in the line of offense when its point, with the arm naturally extended, menaces some part of the adversary's valid target.

11. THE LUNGE

The lunge is the position the fencer assumes with his body at the end of an offensive action executed from the guard. The passage from guard to lunge must be effected in a single movement. Its manner of execution is the same in sabre as in foil except that the left hand is kept on the hip throughout the action.

From the guard (Fig. 78), in a single, coordinated movement, the right arm is extended fully (Fig. 79), right foot advanced, and left leg straightened (Fig. 80).

12. THE RETURN ON GUARD

The recovery from the lunge back to the guard position is called the return on guard. The recovery in sabre is the same as in foil except that the left hand remains on the hip.

Figure 78. From the guard…

Figure 79. …the right arm is
extended fully…

Figure 80. …right foot advanced,
and left leg straightened.

13. Foot Movements

For foot movements see pages 15 through 18.

Observation: Since sabre fencing requires considerable movement, the student must be given intensive training in footwork. For example, he might be directed to advance, retreat, lunge, recover backward, jump backward, gain on the lunge, recover forward, advance lunge, recover backward, jump lunge, recover forward, retreat lunge, recover backward, and execute a running attack.

At the completion of this exercise he should be permitted a brief rest; then he must be asked to perform further drills, using the same foot movements as above, but in a revised order.

14. Fencing Measure

Fencing measure is the distance that separates two fencers placed on guard. There are three measures: out of distance, correct distance, and close distance. Since the sword arm is valid target in sabre, the three fencing measures must be modified to read:

1) From out of distance the opponent's trunk can be touched by taking a step forward and lunging, and his arm by lunging directly.

2) From correct distance the adversary's torso can be hit by lunging, and his arm by remaining in the guard position.

3) From close distance the opponent's trunk or arm can be reached without lunging.

Observation: Because the sword arm is valid target, sabre fencers tend to keep a greater distance between themselves than foilsmen.

CHAPTER 3

PLACEMENT OF THE WEAPON

15. PLACEMENT OF THE WEAPON

Placement of the weapon refers to the position the fencer on guard adopts with his armed hand in relation to his adversary. There are three such positions, and they are designated invitation, engagement, and blade in line.

16. THE SABRE TARGET

The sabre target comprises the head, arms, and torso above a line extending through the highest points where thighs and trunk meet.

Again, the target is divided into four quarters; each represents a line of attack: 1) inside (head, left cheek, chest, abdomen, and internal arm), 2) outside (head, right cheek, chest, flank, and external arm), 3) high (head, right and left cheeks, chest, and top of arm), and 4) low (flank, abdomen, and bottom of arm).

17. INVITATIONS

Invitations are positions taken with the weapon, exposing a specific line, to induce the opponent to attack. There are five sabre invitations: first, second, third, fourth, and fifth.

1) In the invitation in first the weapon is carried to the left of the line of offense, elbow bent, and raised, hand in first position, and at chin level, blade, cutting edge up, directed forward from high to low diagonally to the left (Fig. 81). The invitation in first exposes the flank.

2) In the invitation in second the sabre is shifted to the right of the line of offense, elbow flexed, and to the right, hand in first in second position, and almost level with the flank, blade, cutting edge obliquely up toward the right, point directed to the right of the adversary's abdomen (Fig. 82). The invitation in second uncovers the right or outside cheek.

Figure 81. In first.

Figure 82. In second.

Figure 83. In third.

Invitations

Figure 84. In fourth.

Figure 85. In fifth.

3) In the invitation in third the weapon is brought to the right of the line of offense, elbow bent, and to the right, hand in second in third position, and chest high, blade, cutting edge obliquely down to the right, point directed to the right of the opponent's face (Fig. 83). The invitation in third reveals the abdomen and left or inside cheek.

4) In the invitation in fourth the sabre is moved to the left of the line of offense, elbow flexed, and to the left, hand in third in fourth position, and chest high, blade, cutting edge obliquely down toward the left, point directed to the left of the adversary's face (Fig. 84). The invitation in fourth opens the right or outside cheek.

5) In the invitation in fifth the weapon is elevated to the height of the forehead, elbow bent, and to the right, hand in first position, and level with the right temple, blade, cutting edge up, directed forward from low to high diagonally to the left (Fig. 85). The invitation in fifth exposes the flank and abdomen.

18. ENGAGEMENTS

Engagements are contact invitations in which the opposing steel is dominated and deviated from the line of offense. There are five engagements: first, second, third, fourth, and fifth. In these the hand and weapon occupy precisely the same position they did in the invitations.

Observation: In modern sabre fencing engagements are generally effected only in second and third. Engagements in first, fourth, and fifth tend to be avoided because they expose the sword arm.

19. CHANGES OF ENGAGEMENT

Changes of engagement are used to shift from one engagement to another. These movements are accomplished by passing the point over or under the opposing steel and carrying it to an opposite line of engagement. If the engagement is in the low line, the point passes over the hostile blade; if it is in the high line, it passes under. In sabre, changes may be made from second to first or fifth and vice versa, or from third to fourth and vice versa.

Movement is centered at the elbow, with the weapon, hand, and forearm functioning as a single unit. Wrist motion must be excluded.

Observation: In sabre, as in foil, changes of engagement from second to third and vice versa are also possible; but those changes of engagement are rarely employed because they are more difficult to effect.

20. TRANSPORTS

Transports carry the blade, strong against weak, without a break in contact, from one line of engagement to another. They may be executed from first to third and vice versa, from second to fourth and vice versa, or from third to fifth.

Again, the elbow serves as a pivot for the forearm.

21. PRELIMINARY EXERCISES

The exercises described below are designed to develop blade control. They should be executed slowly at first, and then with increasing speed, moving progressively from large to small motions. With the exception of the fourth exercise in which movement is centered at the shoulder, all the other exercises must be effected from the elbow, with the weapon, hand, and forearm moving together as a unit. Each of the exercises should begin with the sabre in line; the hand is then rotated to the correct initial position, and the exercise performed in two motions. To avoid excessive strain, the legs may be extended, feet comfortably apart, and at right angles.

Observation: During the following exercises, and in all subsequent work with the sabre, particular stress must be placed on gripping the weapon correctly; it should never be allowed to move around loosely in the hand, rather, it must be held firmly, though with a light grip.

FIRST EXERCISE

The hand is turned from second to third position.

1) The hand is brought back near the right temple, elbow flexed, and at shoulder height (Fig. 86).

2) The motion is reversed; the hand is carried forward and down, arm fully extended, hand in third position, and level with the shoulder (Fig. 87).

First Exercise

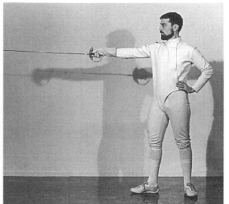

Figure 86. First movement.   Figure 87. Second movement.

Second Exercise

Figure 88. First movement.   Figure 89. Second movement.

SECOND EXERCISE

The hand is kept in second position.

1) The hand is drawn back along a horizontal plane to the chin, elbow bent, and at shoulder height (Fig. 88).

2) The movement is reversed; the hand is brought forward, arm completely extended, hand in second position, and level with the shoulder (Fig. 89).

THIRD EXERCISE

The hand is rotated from second to first in second position.

1) The hand is carried back in an arc from high to low, past the left temple, and down to chin level, elbow flexed, and at shoulder height (Fig. 90).

2) The hand is brought forward in an arc from low to high, arm fully extended, hand in first in second position, and level with the shoulder (Fig. 91).

FOURTH EXERCISE

The hand is turned from second to third position.

1) The hand is raised a little higher than an imagined adversary's head, arm straight, and movement centered at the shoulder (Fig. 92).

2) The hand is lowered to shoulder level, arm still extended, and fingers tightening progressively on the grip as the movement nears completion (Fig. 93).

FIFTH EXERCISE

The hand is rotated from second to third in fourth position.

1) The hand is brought back near the right temple, elbow bent, and at shoulder height.

2) The hand is carried forward and downward to shoulder level in a diagonal motion from right to left, and then turned, with a circular movement, to the guard in third.

SIXTH EXERCISE

The hand is turned from second to second in third position.

1) The hand is carried back near the left temple, elbow flexed, and at shoulder height.

Third Exercise

 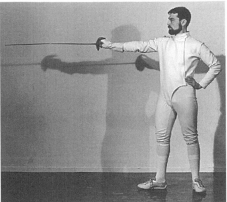

Figure 90. First movement.   Figure 91. Second movement.

Fourth Exercise

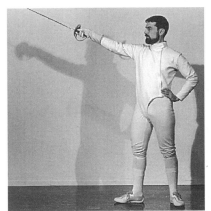 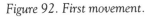

Figure 92. First movement.   Figure 93. Second movement.

2) The hand is brought forward and downward to shoulder level in a diagonal motion from left to right, and then rotated, with a circular movement, to the guard in third.

22. EXERCISES WITH CIRCULAR CUTS

Exercises with circular cuts develop loose and elastic arm motions, and impart precision to the direction and placement of cuts. Movement is

Figure 94. First movement of the circular cut to the head from the left (the weapon is rotated in a clockwise circular motion forward, past the left shoulder).

Figure 95. Second movement of the circular cut to the head from the left (the action is completed).

centered at the elbow, with slight assistance from the wrist. The weapon, hand, and forearm must function as a single unit, with the fingers tightening progressively as the action nears completion.

In the initial phase of instruction, circular cuts should be executed in two motions; and when these are mastered, in one movement.

Circular cuts may be vertical (to the head from the left and right), horizontal (to the right and left cheeks), and ascending (to the flank and abdomen).

THE CIRCULAR CUT TO THE HEAD FROM THE LEFT

The circular cut to the head from the left is performed with the weapon in line, or from the guard position in third, in two motions:

1) The sabre is carried to the left to a position approximating the invitation in first, arm raised and bent, hand at the height of the left temple, so that the line of vision passes under it.

2) With the elbow serving as a pivot, the weapon is rotated rapidly in a clockwise circular movement forward, past the left shoulder (Fig. 94), arm extending, hand in third position, fingers tightening progressively, with the cut delivered vertically to the supposed adversary's head (Fig. 95).

Figure 96. First movement of the circular cut to the head from the right.

Figure 97. Second movement of the circular cut to the head from the right.

THE CIRCULAR CUT TO THE HEAD FROM THE RIGHT

The circular cut to the head from the right is accomplished with the sabre in line, or from the guard position in third, in two motions:

1) Turning the cutting edge of the weapon to the left, the arm is lifted and flexed, hand at the height of the right temple, elbow up, cutting edge to the right (Fig. 96).

2) With the elbow functioning as a pivot, the sabre is rotated swiftly in a counterclockwise circular movement forward, past the right shoulder, arm extending, hand in third position, fingers tightening progressively, with the cut delivered vertically to the imagined opponent's head (Fig. 97).

THE CIRCULAR CUT TO THE RIGHT CHEEK

The circular cut to the right or outside cheek is made with the weapon in line, or from the guard position in third, in two motions:

1) The hand is turned to first in second position, arm raised and bent at the elbow, sabre brought to the left, with the point describing a counterclockwise arc toward the rear, hand at the height of the left shoulder, and the forearm and weapon forming a single line, cutting edge to the left (Fig. 98).

Figure 98. First movement of
the circular cut to the right
cheek.

Figure 99. Second movement of the circular cut to
the right cheek.

2) With the elbow serving as a pivot, the arm is extended quickly forward, fingers tightening progressively, with the cut delivered horizontally to the supposed adversary's right cheek, hand at chin level, cutting edge diagonally up toward the right (Fig. 99).

THE CIRCULAR CUT TO THE LEFT CHEEK

The circular cut to the left or inside cheek is effected with the sabre in line, or from the guard position in third, in two motions:

1) The hand is turned to fourth position, arm lifted and flexed at the elbow, weapon carried to the right, with the point describing a clockwise arc toward the rear, hand at the height of the right temple, and the forearm and sabre forming a single line, cutting edge to the right (Fig. 100).

2) With the elbow functioning as a pivot, the arm is extended rapidly forward, fingers tightening progressively, with the cut delivered horizontally to the imagined opponent's left cheek, hand at chin level, cutting edge diagonally up toward the left (Fig. 101).

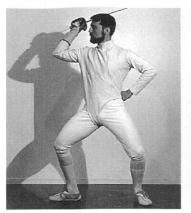 

Figure 100. First movement of the   *Figure 101. Second movement of the circular cut*
circular cut to the left cheek.   *to the left cheek.*

THE CIRCULAR CUT TO THE FLANK

The circular cut to the flank is executed with the weapon in line, or from the guard position in third, in two motions:

1) Same as the first movement of the circular cut to the right cheek.

2) With the elbow serving as a pivot, the arm is extended swiftly forward, fingers tightening progressively, with the cut delivered horizontally in an ascending motion to the supposed adversary's flank, hand at chest level, cutting edge diagonally up toward the right.

THE CIRCULAR CUT TO THE ABDOMEN

The circular cut to the abdomen is performed with the sabre in line, or from the guard position in third, in two motions:

1) Same as the first movement of the circular cut to the left cheek.

2) With the elbow functioning as a pivot, the arm is extended quickly forward, fingers tightening progressively, with the cut delivered horizontally in an ascending motion to the imagined opponent's abdomen, hand at chest level, cutting edge diagonally up toward the left.

Observation: With each circular cut, movement of the hand must be arrested at the exact point where the action terminates, so that the momentum of the cutting motion does not carry the hand and weapon beyond their specified limit.

Although at the beginning of the exercises the cutting actions should be large, they must be reduced gradually until they can be accomplished in one tight movement with a simple rotation of the hand and slight flexing of the wrist accompanied by a smooth extension of the arm. Once this is achieved, a step forward, retreat, and lunge may be added. It is important to note, however, that in every case, precedence should be given to the point; the feet must not be permitted to move before the arm is well extended.

CHAPTER 4

OFFENSE

23. THE OFFENSE

The offense is the act of attacking the adversary.

24. SIMPLE ATTACKS

Offensive actions consisting of a single blade movement are called simple attacks.

In sabre fencing simple attacks are effected with the point, the cut, and the counter-cut.

Point thrusts may be: 1) direct, 2) by disengagement, and 3) by glide.

Cuts may be: 1) direct, 2) circular, and 3) descending.

25. THE DIRECT POINT THRUST

The direct point thrust is an action, without blade contact, in which the point of the sabre follows a straight line to the exposed target; it is a direct attack in one movement, and may be used in opposition to any of the adversary's invitations.

From the guard in third, or from another placement of the weapon, the sword arm is extended smoothly, hand rotated to first in second position, opposition to the right, point directed to the chest or flank. The action is completed with a rapid lunge.

Observation: Coordination between arm extension and lunge is of paramount importance: the sword arm must be straightened before the right foot moves. Care should be taken that the arm and blade form an obtuse angle, so that the external arm is well protected.

In sabre it must also be noted that the point or cut should reach the target a fraction of a second before the right heel touches the floor for the completion of the lunge.

26. THE DISENGAGEMENT WITH THE POINT

The disengagement with the point is an action in which the blade, with a spiral motion of the point, is detached from the opponent's engagement, and directed to the exposed target; it is an indirect attack in one movement, and may be employed when the adversary engages blades.

To disengage the blade from the opponent's engagement, a small, semicircular motion of the point is effected with the fingers and wrist, assisted by the forearm, sword arm extending smoothly, and hand turning to first in second position, opposition to the right. The action is completed with a quick lunge.

In opposition to engagements in first, second, third, fourth, and fifth, the disengagements end respectively in the flank, chest, inside chest, outside chest, and flank.

27. THE GLIDE WITH THE POINT

The glide with the point is an action in which the blade slides along the opposing steel to the exposed target; it is an attack in one movement that may be used when the adversary's blade is engaged in second and third. ·

To accomplish the action the sword arm is extended smoothly, blades touching, cut opposed to cut, hand in first in second position (engagement in second), opposition to the right, or rotated to first in second position (engagement in third), opposition to the right. The movement is completed with a fast lunge. As the steel slips along the hostile blade it maintains constant contact, dominating and forcing it progressively to one side.

The glides in second and third terminate respectively in the flank and outside chest.

Observation: Glides employed in opposition to the opponent's imperfect or weak engagements are designated forced glides. Their function is to regain opposition.

Forced glides resemble, in execution, glides in second and third. For instance, if the adversary engages blades in second without closing the line sufficiently, the forced glide in second can be accomplished with strong opposition to the right.

28. Direct Cuts

Direct cuts are made in one motion and reach the target via the shortest route. As in the preceding actions, the arm must be fully extended before the right foot is advanced for the lunge.

Observation: All cutting actions must be executed with a light touch; the blade should glide over the target in a slicing motion. Cuts are effected with the first third of the cutting edge of the blade or with the counter-cut.

It is particularly important that hand placement during the cutting movements be correct, since even the slightest exposure can result in a time thrust or cut to the arm.

The Direct Cut to the Head

From the guard in second or third, or from one's own invitation, the direct cut to the head is performed by rotating the hand to third position, extending the arm simultaneously, and, with a tight downward snap of the wrist, directing a vertical cut to the top of the head, blade moving forward in a slicing action. The movement is completed with a swift lunge.

At the end of the action the sword arm should be fully extended, hand in line with the right shoulder, point of the weapon a little higher than the hand (Fig. 102).

The direct cut to the head may be effected in opposition to the opponent's invitations in second, third, and fourth, and from one's own engagements in third or fourth.

Figure 102. The direct cut to the head.

Observation: Cuts to the head, right cheek, and flank are pushed forward across the target in a slicing action.

THE DIRECT CUT TO THE RIGHT CHEEK

From the guard in second or third, or from one's own invitation, the direct cut to the right or outside cheek is accomplished by turning or keeping the hand in second position, extending the arm contemporaneously, and, with a tight flick of the wrist to the right, delivering a horizontal cut to the right cheek. The blade must glide forward in a slicing motion.

At the termination of the action the sword arm should be completely extended, hand at chin level and to the right (Fig. 103).

The direct cut to the right cheek may be made in opposition to the adversary's invitations in second and fourth, and from one's own engagements in second or fourth.

THE DIRECT CUT TO THE LEFT CHEEK

From the guard in second or third, or from one's own invitation, the direct cut to the left or inside cheek is executed by rotating the hand to fourth position, extending the arm simultaneously, and, with a tight snap of the wrist to the left, delivering a horizontal cut to the left cheek. The blade must be drawn backward in a slicing movement.

At the completion of the action the sword arm should be fully extended, hand at chin level and to the right (Fig. 104).

The direct cut to the left cheek may be performed in opposition to the opponent's invitations in second, third, and fifth, and from one's own engagement in fourth.

Observation: Cuts to the left cheek, chest, and abdomen are pulled back across the target with the hand progressively rotated, and the elbow flexed in coordination, so that the weapon, hand, and arm are returned in one continuous motion to the guard in third.

Figure 103.
The direct cut to the
right cheek.

Figure 104.
The direct cut to the
left cheek.

THE DIRECT CUT TO THE CHEST

From the guard in second or third, or from one's own invitation, the direct cut to the chest is effected by turning the hand to third in fourth position, extending the arm contemporaneously, and, with a tight downward flick of the wrist, delivering a diagonal cut to the chest. The blade must be drawn from high to low in a slicing motion.

The direct cut to the chest may be accomplished in opposition to the adversary's invitations in second, third, and fifth, and from one's own engagement in fourth.

Observation: The diagonal cut must be delivered in a tight motion so that the forearm is not exposed during the action.

Figure 105. The direct cut to the abdomen.

Figure 106. The direct cut to the flank.

THE DIRECT CUT TO THE ABDOMEN

The direct cut to the abdomen is made in the same way as the direct cut to the left cheek, except that the cut is lower and directed to the abdomen instead of the left cheek (Fig. 105).

Like the direct cut to the left cheek, this action may be executed in opposition to the opponent's invitations in second, third, and fifth, and from one's own engagement in fourth.

THE DIRECT CUT TO THE FLANK

The direct cut to the flank is performed in the same manner as the direct cut to the right cheek, except that the cut is lower and directed to the flank instead of the right cheek (Fig. 106).

This movement may be effected in opposition to the adversary's invitations in first, fourth, and fifth, and from one's own engagements in first, third, or fifth.

29. CIRCULAR CUTS

Circular cuts are made in one movement and reach the target via a circular route. In every case the point of the weapon must travel around the opposing steel in as tight a circle as possible.

For execution of circular cuts see pages 199 through 204.

Observation: In both circular and descending cuts the lunge must be delayed until the sword arm is well extended, and the cutting edge of the blade close to its objective.

THE CIRCULAR CUT TO THE HEAD FROM THE LEFT

The circular cut to the head from the left is accomplished from one's own engagements in first and fifth.

THE CIRCULAR CUT TO THE HEAD FROM THE RIGHT

The circular cut to the head from the right is made from one's own engagement and from the opponent's engagement in second.

THE CIRCULAR CUT TO THE RIGHT CHEEK

The circular cut to the right cheek is executed from one's own engagement in first, and from the adversary's engagement in fourth.

THE CIRCULAR CUT TO THE LEFT CHEEK

The circular cut to the left cheek is performed from one's own engagements in first, second, third, and fifth, and from the opponent's engagements in second, third, and fifth.

THE CIRCULAR CUT TO THE FLANK

The circular cut to the flank is effected from one's own engagement in fourth, and from the adversary's engagements in first, fourth, and fifth.

THE CIRCULAR CUT TO THE ABDOMEN

The circular cut to the abdomen is accomplished from the same engage-ments as the circular cut to the left cheek.

Observation: Since sabre fencers today maintain a wide distance between themselves, and rarely engage blades, circular cuts tend to be used chiefly as riposting actions.

30. DESCENDING CUTS

Descending cuts are made in one motion and reach the target by passing over the point of the opposing steel.

From the adversary's engagements in third and fourth the hand is ro-tated to third position, elbow flexed, and point passed over the hostile blade; the arm is then extended, and a vertical cut delivered to the top of the head.

If the opponent's engagement is in third, the descending cut is di-rected to the inside; if his engagement is in fourth, the descending cut is aimed at the outside.

Observation: Descending cuts may also be employed in opposition to the adversary's pressures against one's own engagements in third and fourth.

31. CUTS TO THE ARM

Direct, circular, and descending cuts can be delivered to the arm in the same way that they are to the head and torso. Depending upon fencing measure, the cut is executed from the guard, or with a lunge.

Cuts to the internal arm are performed with the cut and counter-cut, hand respectively in third in fourth, and in second in third position; cuts to the external arm are effected with the cut, hand in first in second posi-tion; cuts to the top of the arm are accomplished with the cut, hand in third or third in fourth position; and cuts to the bottom of the arm are made with the cut and counter-cut, hand respectively in first in second, and in second in third position.

*The Descending
Cut to the Head*

Plate VI.

Plate VII.

Plate VIII.

Plate IX.

CHAPTER 5

DEFENSE

32. THE DEFENSE

Blade motions that deviate the adversary's point before it reaches the target, or foot movements that remove the body from the range of attack, are called the defense.

33. PARRIES

Defensive movements of the blade that deflect the incoming steel are termed parries. In sabre, as in foil, these may be simple, circular, half circular, or ceding.

34. SIMPLE PARRIES

Simple parries are protective displacements of the blade that cover exposed target areas by traveling the shortest route from one invitation or engagement to another.

In sabre fencing there are six simple parries, each covering certain parts of the valid target: thus, the parry of first protects the left cheek, inside chest, abdomen, and internal arm (Fig. 107); the parry of second, the flank, and bottom of arm (Fig. 108); the parry of third, the right cheek, outside chest, flank, and external arm (Fig. 109); the parry of fourth, the left cheek, inside chest, abdomen, and internal arm (Fig. 110); the parry of fifth, the head, and top of arm (Fig. 111); and the parry of sixth, the head, and top of arm (Fig. 112).

Placement of the hand and weapon is the same as in invitations and engagements designated by the same number. See pages 193 through 195.

Since there is no invitation or engagement in sixth, the parry of sixth remains to be described: it is executed by reversing the position of the parry of fifth, with the elbow flexed, and to the left, hand in first position, and level with the left temple, blade, cutting edge up, directed forward from low to high diagonally to the right.

Parries must be effected with the cutting edge, medium strong opposed to medium weak of the attacking steel.

Figure 107. Parry of first.

Figure 108. Parry of second.

Figure 109. Parry of third.

Figure 110. Parry of fourth.

Figure 111. Parry of fifth.

Figure 112. Parry of sixth.

Observation: It should be noted that the parry of sixth is rarely used today.

Older works on sabre fencing also mention parries of low third and low fourth. These are nothing more than lowered parries of third and fourth which serve as alternate parries for second and first to defend, respectively, the flank and abdomen.

35. Passage from One Simple Parry to Another

From the parry, invitation, or engagement in first, it is possible to execute the simple parry of second, third, fourth, or fifth.

From the parry, invitation, or engagement in second, it is possible to effect the simple parry of first, third, or fifth.

From the parry, invitation, or engagement in third, it is possible to accomplish the simple parry of second, fourth, or sixth.

From the parry, invitation, or engagement in fourth, it is possible to perform the simple parry of third or fifth.

From the parry or invitation in fifth, it is possible to make the simple parry of second, third, or fourth.

From the parry of sixth, it is possible to execute the simple parry of third or fourth.

Observation: The passage from one parry to another must be accomplished in one movement, with a loose arm, and without interference of the shoulder; the grip should be tightened gradually as the parry is effected.

In the passage from second to first or fifth and vice versa, controlled movement of the forearm must guide the blade along a curved path, so that it catches the incoming steel.

36. Ceding Parries

Ceding parries are employed against gliding actions. Rather than resisting the attack, it is yielded to, blades in continuous contact, wrist flexed, so that the parry is taken, and the incoming steel deflected, the moment before the point reaches the target.

There are two ceding parries in sabre fencing: the ceding parry of first, and the ceding parry of fourth. These are used, respectively, in opposition to the glide in third, and the glide in second.

37. PARRY EXERCISES

The exercises that follow are designed to develop precision in placement of the parry. Movement of the arm must be controlled and smooth.

FIRST PARRY EXERCISE

From the position with the sabre in line, parries in first, second, and fifth are assumed. As each parry is achieved, the forearm, with the elbow serving as a pivot, is flexed and extended three times, so that the weapon is drawn back toward the body, and then returned to its exact parry position.

SECOND PARRY EXERCISE

From the position with the sabre in line, parries in first, second, and fifth are assumed. As each parry is attained, the forearm, with the elbow functioning as a pivot, is rotated three times in a counterclockwise motion that grows progressively smaller, and brings the weapon back to its original parry position.

THIRD PARRY EXERCISE

The first and second parry exercises are combined, with the flexing and extending movements followed by the circular motions. Each of the actions should move from large to small, and from slow to fast.

Observation: It should be noted that the circular movements in the second and third parry exercises, for the sake of uniformity, all move counterclockwise. This is the reverse of the direction normally taken by counter of first and counter of fifth.

38. THE RIPOSTE

The riposte is the thrust or cut delivered immediately after the adversary's attack has been parried. Ripostes may be simple or compound, and they may be executed with the point, cut, and counter-cut.

Parries can be followed by ripostes in which the blade is detached, or kept in contact (glide with the point). In ripostes made with the cut, the blade is always detached.

39. Simple Ripostes

After the parry of first the riposte may be performed with a point thrust to the chest, or direct cut to the flank or bottom of the arm, or circular cut to the head, right or left cheek, chest, abdomen, or top of the arm.

After the parry of second the riposte may be effected with a glide with the point to the flank, or point thrust above to the chest, or direct cut to the right cheek, head, top of the arm or external arm, or abdomen under the opposing steel with the cut or counter-cut, or circular cut to the head or left cheek.

After the parry of third the riposte may be accomplished with a glide with the point to the outside chest or point thrust below to the flank, or direct cut to the head, flank, top of the arm, or left cheek with the cut or counter-cut, or circular cut to the chest, abdomen, or internal arm, or ascending cut to the bottom of the arm.

After the parry of fourth the riposte may be made with a point thrust to the inside chest, or direct cut to the right or left cheeks, head, chest, abdomen, top of the arm or internal arm, or circular cut to the flank.

After the parry of fifth the riposte may be achieved with a point thrust to the chest, or direct cut to the flank or bottom of the arm, or circular cut to the head, left cheek, chest, abdomen, or internal arm.

After the parry of sixth the riposte may be executed with a point thrust to the chest, or direct cut to the left cheek, chest, abdomen, or internal arm, or circular cut to the head or flank.

Observation: During the initial period of training, it is customary to have the student riposte with the cut to a designated target. For example, the parry of first is generally followed with a circular cut to the head; the parry of second with a direct cut to the right cheek; the parry of third with a direct cut to the head; the parry of fourth with a direct cut to the right cheek; the parry of fifth with a direct cut to the flank; and the parry of sixth with a direct cut to the abdomen.

CHAPTER 6

COMPOUND ATTACKS

40. COMPOUND ATTACKS

Offensive actions consisting of two or more blade movements are called compound or composed attacks.

41. THE FEINT

The feint is a simulated thrust or menace that resembles so closely a genuine assault that the adversary is forced to parry.

In sabre fencing the feint can be effected with either a simulated point thrust or cut (Figs. 113-116).

Observation: In sabre, as in foil, point motion must be kept as tight as possible. Correct placement of the hand during the feinting movement is of cardinal importance, since exposure of the arm will invite a time thrust or cut to the arm.

42. SINGLE FEINTS

Single or simple feints elude one parry; they are used in opposition to the invitation and engagement.

43. THE FEINT WITH THE DIRECT POINT THRUST OR DIRECT CUT

1) In opposition to the invitation in first:

Master	Pupil
Invites in first.	First movement: simulates a point thrust or a direct cut to the flank.
Parries second.	Second movement: eludes the parry of second with a disengagement clockwise with the point to the chest above, or cut to the right or left cheek, head, chest, or arm.
Receives the touch.	

Observation: The feint must be placed with precision, and held long enough to draw the parry. The tighter the movement is, the more efficient the action will be.

Feint Point Thrust

Figure 113.

Figure 114.

Feint Head Cut

Figure 115.

Figure 116.

Plate X. The
Feint Direct Cut
to the Head

Plate XI. The
Feint Direct Cut
to the Flank

2) In opposition to the invitation in second:

Master	Pupil
Invites in second.	First movement: simulates a point thrust to the chest above, or a direct cut to the right cheek, arm, or head.
Parries first, third, or fifth.	Second movement: eludes the parry of first with a disengagement counterclockwise with the point to the flank, or cut to the flank or arm; or eludes the parry of third with a disengagement counterclockwise with the point to the inside chest, or circular cut to the left cheek, chest, abdomen, arm, or head (also descending); or eludes the parry of fifth with a disengagement counterclockwise with the point, or cut to the flank, or circular cut to the left cheek, chest, abdomen, or arm.
Receives the touch.	

3) In opposition to the invitation in third:

Master	Pupil
Invites in third.	First movement: simulates a point thrust to the inside chest, or a direct cut to the left cheek, chest, abdomen, arm, or head.
Parries first, fourth or fifth.	Second movement: eludes the parry of first with a disengagement counterclockwise with the point to the flank, or cut to the flank, or arm; or eludes the parry of fourth with a disengagement clockwise with the point to the outside chest, or cut to the right cheek (also circular), arm, or head (also descending); or eludes the parry of fifth with a disengagement counterclockwise with the point, or cut to the flank, or circular cut to the left cheek, chest, abdomen, or arm.
Receives the touch.	

4) In opposition to the invitation in fourth:

Master	Pupil
Invites in fourth.	First movement: simulates a point thrust to the outside chest, or a direct cut to the right cheek, arm, or head.
Parries third or fifth.	Second movement: eludes the parry of third with a disengagement counterclockwise with the point to the inside chest, or circular cut to the left cheek, chest, abdomen, arm, or head (also descending); or eludes the parry of fifth with a disengagement counterclockwise with the point, or cut to the flank, or circular cut to the left cheek, chest, abdomen, or arm.
Receives the touch.	

5) In opposition to the invitation in fifth:

Master	Pupil
Invites in fifth.	First movement: simulates a point thrust to the flank, or a direct cut to the flank, left cheek, chest, or abdomen.
Parries second or fourth.	Second movement: eludes the parry of second with a disengagement clockwise with the point to the chest above, or cut to the right or left cheek, head, chest, or arm; or eludes the parry of fourth with a disengagement clockwise with the point to the outside chest, or cut to the right cheek (also circular), arm, or head (also descending).
Receives the touch.	

44. THE FEINT BY DISENGAGEMENT WITH THE POINT

The feint by disengagement with the point is similar in execution to the feint with the direct point thrust except that it is initiated from the adversary's engagement.

45. THE FEINT BY GLIDE WITH THE POINT

1) From engagement in second:

Master	Pupil
	First movement: from his own engagement in second simulates a glide with the point to the flank.
Parries second.	Second movement: eludes the parry of second with a disengagement clockwise with the point to the chest above, or cut to the right or left cheek, head, chest, or arm.
Receives the touch.	

2) From engagement in third:

Master	Pupil
	First movement: from his own engagement in third simulates a glide with the point to the outside chest.
Parries third.	Second movement: eludes the parry of third with a disengagement counterclockwise with the point to the inside chest, or circular cut to the left cheek, chest, abdomen, arm, or head (also descending).
Receives the touch.	

Observation: If the adversary effects weak engagements, his engagements are opposed with the feint by forced glide with the point.

46. COMPOUND RIPOSTES

Ripostes consisting of two or more blade motions are termed compound ripostes; their function is to elude one or more counterparries, that is, parries opposed to the riposte.

47. RIPOSTES WITH FEINTS

In sabre fencing ripostes with feints may be accomplished with either the point or cut.

48. DOUBLE FEINTS

Double feints elude two parries; they are employed in opposition to the invitation and engagement.

Observation: When the double feint is combined with a step forward, it should be remembered that the first feint must coincide with the movement of the right foot, the second with the motion of the left foot, and the final point thrust or cut with the lunge.

49. The Double Feint with the Direct Point Thrust or Direct Cut

1) In opposition to the invitation in first:

Master	Pupil
Invites in first.	First movement: simulates a point thrust or a direct cut to the flank.
Parries second.	Second movement: eludes the parry of second with a feint by disengagement clockwise with the point to the chest above, or cut to the right or left cheek, head, chest, or arm.
Parries first, third, or fifth.	Third movement: eludes the parry of first with a disengagement counterclockwise with the point to the flank, or cut to the flank, or arm; or eludes the parry of third with a disengagement counterclockwise with the point to the inside chest, or circular cut to the left cheek, chest, abdomen, arm, or head (also descending); or eludes the parry of fifth with a disengagement counterclockwise with the point, or cut to the flank, or circular cut to the left cheek, chest, abdomen, or arm.
Receives the touch.	

2) In opposition to the invitation in second:

Master	Pupil
Invites in second.	First movement: simulates a point thrust to the chest above, or a direct cut to the right cheek, arm, or head.
Parries first, third, or fifth.	Second movement: eludes the parry of first with a feint by disengagement counterclockwise with the point to the flank, or cut to the flank, or arm; or eludes the parry of third with a feint by disengagement counterclockwise with the point to the inside chest, or circular cut to the left cheek, chest,

abdomen, arm, or head (also descending); or eludes the parry of fifth with a feint by disengagement counterclockwise with the point, or cut to the flank, or circular cut to the left cheek, chest, abdomen, or arm.

Parries second, fourth, or fifth.

Third movement: eludes the parry of second with a disengagement clockwise with the point to the chest above, or cut to the right or left cheek, head, chest, or arm; or eludes the parry of fourth with a disengagement clockwise with the point to the outside chest, or cut to the right cheek (also circular), arm, or head (also descending); or eludes the parry of fifth with a disengagement counterclockwise with the point, or cut to the flank, or circular cut to the left cheek, chest, abdomen, or arm.

Receives the touch.

3) In opposition to the invitation in third:

Master	Pupil
Invites in third.	First movement: simulates a point thrust to the inside chest, or a direct cut to the left cheek, chest, abdomen, arm, or head.
Parries first, fourth, or fifth.	Second movement: eludes the parry of first with a feint by disengagement counterclockwise with the point to the flank, or cut to the flank, or arm; or eludes the parry of fourth with a feint by disengagement clockwise with the point to the outside chest, or cut to the right cheek (also circular), arm or head (also descending); or eludes the parry of fifth with a feint by disengagement counterclockwise with the point, or cut to the flank, or circular cut to the left cheek, chest, abdomen, or arm.
Parries second, third, fourth or fifth.	Third movement: eludes the parry of second with a disengagement clockwise with the point to the chest above, or cut to the right or left cheek, head, chest, or arm; or eludes

the parry of third with a disengagement counterclockwise with the point to the inside chest, or circular cut to the left cheek, chest, abdomen, arm, or head (also descending); or eludes the parry of fourth with a disengagement clockwise with the point to the outside chest, or cut to the right cheek (also circular), arm or head (also descending); or eludes the parry of fifth with a disengagement counterclockwise with the point, or cut to the flank, or circular cut to the left cheek, chest, abdomen, or arm.

Receives the touch.

4) In opposition to the invitation in fourth:

Master	Pupil
Invites in fourth.	First movement: simulates a point thrust to the outside chest, or a direct cut to the right cheek, arm, or head.
Parries third or fifth.	Second movement: eludes the parry of third with a feint by disengagement counterclockwise with the point to the inside chest, or circular cut to the left cheek, chest, abdomen, arm, or head (also descending); or eludes the parry of fifth with a feint by disengagement counterclockwise with the point, or cut to the flank, or circular cut to the left cheek, chest, abdomen, or arm.
Parries first, second or fifth.	Third movement: eludes the parry of first with a disengagement counterclockwise with the point to the flank, or cut to the flank, or arm; or eludes the parry of second with a disengagement clockwise with the point to the chest above, or cut to the right or left cheek, head, chest, or arm; or eludes the parry of fifth with a disengagement counterclockwise with the point, or cut to the flank, or circular cut to the left cheek, chest, abdomen, or arm.
Receives the touch.	

5) In opposition to the invitation in fifth:

Master	Pupil
Invites in fifth.	First movement: simulates a point thrust to the flank, or a direct cut to the flank, left cheek, chest, or abdomen.
Parries second or fourth.	Second movement: eludes the parry of second with a feint by disengagement clockwise with the point to the chest above, or cut to the right or left cheek, head, chest, or arm; or eludes the parry of fourth with a feint by disengagement clockwise with the point to the outside chest, or cut to the right cheek (also circular), arm, or head (also descending).
Parries first, third or fifth.	Third movement: eludes the parry of first with a disengagement counterclockwise with the point to the flank, or cut to the flank, or arm; or eludes the parry of third with a disengagement counterclockwise with the point to the inside chest, or circular cut to the left cheek, chest, abdomen, arm, or head (also descending); or eludes the parry of fifth with a disengagement counterclockwise with the point, or cut to the flank, or circular cut to the left cheek, chest, abdomen, or arm.
Receives the touch.	

50. THE DOUBLE FEINT BY DISENGAGEMENT WITH THE POINT

The double feint by disengagement with the point is similar in execution to the double feint with the direct point thrust except that it is initiated from the opponent's engagement.

51. The Double Feint by Glide with the Point

1) From engagement in second:

Master	Pupil
	First movement: from his own engagement in second simulates a glide with the point to the flank.
Parries second.	Second movement: eludes the parry of second with a feint by disengagement clockwise with the point to the chest above, or cut to the right or left cheek, head, chest, or arm.
Parries first, third or fifth.	Third movement: eludes the parry of first with a disengagement counterclockwise with the point to the flank, or cut to the flank, or arm; or eludes the parry of third with a disengagement counterclockwise with the point to the inside chest, or circular cut to the left cheek, chest, abdomen, arm or head (also descending); or eludes the parry of fifth with a disengagement counterclockwise with the point, or cut to the flank, or circular cut to the left cheek, chest, abdomen, or arm.
Receives the touch.	

2) From engagement in third:

Master	Pupil
	First movement: from his own engagement in third simulates a glide with the point to the outside chest.
Parries third.	Second movement: eludes the parry of third with a feint by disengagement counterclockwise with the point to the inside chest, or circular cut to the left cheek, chest, abdomen, arm, or head (also descending).
Parries fourth or fifth.	Third movement: eludes the parry of fourth with a disengagement clockwise with the

point to the outside chest, or cut to the right cheek (also circular), arm, or head (also descending); or eludes the parry of fifth with a disengagement counterclockwise with the point, or cut to the flank, or circular cut to the left cheek, chest, abdomen, or arm.

Receives the touch.

Observation: If the opponent effects imperfect engagements, his engagements are opposed with the double feint by forced glide with the point.

52. CONVENTIONAL EXERCISES

Conventional exercises consist of pre-established actions executed by two fencers alternately assuming the role of attacker and defender.

EXERCISES WITH SIMPLE PARRIES

FIRST EXERCISE

The direct point thrust or direct cut in opposition to the five invitations:

A	B
Invites.	Aims a direct point thrust or direct cut at the exposed target.
Executes a simple parry and ripostes with the point or cut.	Receives the touch.

SECOND EXERCISE

The disengagement with the point in opposition to the five engagements:

A	B
Engages.	Directs a disengagement with the point to the exposed target.
Executes a simple parry and ripostes with the point or cut.	Receives the touch.

Third Exercise

The direct point thrust or direct cut, or the feint with the direct point thrust or direct cut in opposition to the five invitations:

A	B
Invites.	Aims a direct point thrust or direct cut, or a feint with the direct point thrust or direct cut at the exposed target.
Executes one simple parry if the attack is a direct point thrust or direct cut, or two simple parries if it is a feint with the direct point thrust or direct cut and disengagement with the point or cut, and ripostes with the point or cut.	Receives the touch or opposes the riposte with the counterparry riposte.

Fourth Exercise

The single or double feint with the direct point thrust or direct cut is opposed to the five invitations, first from correct, or lunging distance, then from out of distance, with a step forward and lunge; the single feint is countered with two simple parries, the double feint with three simple parries.

CHAPTER 7

CIRCULAR ATTACKS

53. CIRCULAR PARRIES

Circular parries are defensive blade movements in which the point describes a tight, complete circle around the incoming steel, intercepting and transferring it to the opposite line.

The circular parry in sabre is accomplished with the hand and forearm.

In sabre fencing there are five circular parries, each protecting particular areas of the valid target: thus, the parry of counter of first defends the flank, and bottom of the arm; the parry of counter of second, the chest, abdomen, and internal arm; the parry of counter of third, the left cheek, inside chest, and internal arm; the parry of counter of fourth, the right cheek, outside chest, and external arm; and the parry of counter of fifth, the chest, and bottom of the arm.

As in the preceding parries, the medium strong of the defending blade must encounter the medium weak of the attacking steel.

From the invitation or engagement in first, the parry of counter of first is made in one motion, with the point moving clockwise over the adversary's blade.

From the invitation or engagement in second, the parry of counter of second is achieved in one movement, with the point traveling counterclockwise over the opponent's steel.

From the invitation or engagement in third, the parry of counter of third is effected in one motion, with the point moving clockwise under the adversary's blade.

From the invitation or engagement in fourth, the parry of counter of fourth is accomplished in one movement, with the point traveling counterclockwise under the opponent's steel.

From the invitation or engagement in fifth, the parry of counter of fifth is executed in one motion, with the point moving clockwise under the adversary's blade.

Observation: It is important to note that circular parries are used in sabre in opposition to actions with the point.

54. HALF CIRCULAR PARRIES

Half circular parries are defensive displacements of the blade along a diagonal semicircular route from a high to a low line and vice versa.

In sabre fencing half circular parries are formed by moving from second to fourth, from third to first and to fifth, and from fifth to first.

55. CIRCULAR ATTACKS

Circular attacks are used in opposition to circular parries. In these compound offensive actions the feint provokes a circular parry, which is then deceived by a circular thrust moving in the same direction as the parry.

The circular point thrust or deceive may be preceded by a feint with the point thrust, feint by disengagement with the point, or feint by glide with the point, depending upon placement of the adversary's weapon.

56. THE FEINT WITH THE DIRECT POINT THRUST AND DECEIVE

1) In opposition to the invitation in first:

Master	Pupil
Invites in first.	First movement: simulates a point thrust to the flank.
Parries counter of first.	Second movement: eludes the parry of counter of first with a deceive counterclockwise to the flank.
Receives the touch.	

2) In opposition to the invitation in second:

Master	Pupil
Invites in second.	First movement: simulates a point thrust to the chest above.
Parries counter of second.	Second movement: eludes the parry of counter of second with a deceive clockwise to the chest above.
Receives the touch.	

3) In opposition to the invitation in third:

Master	Pupil
Invites in third.	First movement: simulates a point thrust to the inside chest.
Parries counter of third.	Second movement: eludes the parry of counter of third with a deceive counter-clockwise to the inside chest.
Receives the touch.	

4) In opposition to the invitation in fourth:

Master	Pupil
Invites in fourth.	First movement: simulates a point thrust to the outside chest.
Parries counter of fourth.	Second movement: eludes the parry of counter of fourth with a deceive clockwise to the outside chest.
Receives the touch.	

5) In opposition to the invitation in fifth:

Master	Pupil
Invites in fifth.	First movement: simulates a point thrust to the flank.
Parries counter of fifth.	Second movement: eludes the parry of counter of fifth with a deceive counter-clockwise to the flank.
Receives the touch.	

57. THE FEINT BY DISENGAGEMENT WITH THE POINT AND DECEIVE

The feint by disengagement with the point and deceive is similar in execution to the feint with the direct point thrust and deceive except that it is initiated from the adversary's engagement.

58. The Feint by Glide with the Point and Deceive

1) From engagement in second:

Master	Pupil
	First movement: from his own engagement in second simulates a glide with the point to the flank.
Parries counter of first.	Second movement: eludes the parry of counter of first with a deceive counterclockwise to the flank.
Receives the touch.	

2) From engagement in third:

Master	Pupil
	First movement: from his own engagement in third simulates a glide with the point to the outside chest.
Parries counter of fourth.	Second movement: eludes the parry of counter of fourth with a deceive clockwise to the outside chest.
Receives the touch.	

Observation: If the adversary effects weak engagements, his engagements are opposed with the feint by forced glide with the point and deceive.

59. The Feint with the Direct Point Thrust, Deceive, and Disengagement with the Point

1) In opposition to the invitation in first:

Master	Pupil
Invites in first.	First movement: simulates a point thrust to the flank.
Parries counter of first.	Second movement: eludes the parry of counter of first with a feint by deceive counterclockwise to the flank.
Parries second.	Third movement: eludes the parry of sec-

ond with a disengagement clockwise with the point to the chest above.

Receives the touch.

2) In opposition to the invitation in second:

Master	Pupil
Invites in second.	First movement: simulates a point thrust to the chest above.
Parries counter of second.	Second movement: eludes the parry of counter of second with a feint by deceive clockwise to the chest above.
Parries third.	Third movement: eludes the parry of third with a disengagement counterclockwise with the point to the inside chest.
Receives the touch.	

3) In opposition to the invitation in third:

Master	Pupil
Invites in third.	First movement: simulates a point thrust to the inside chest.
Parries counter of third.	Second movement: eludes the parry of counter of third with a feint by deceive counterclockwise to the inside chest.
Parries fourth.	Third movement: eludes the parry of fourth with a disengagement clockwise with the point to the outside chest.
Receives the touch.	

4) In opposition to the invitation in fourth:

Master	Pupil
Invites in fourth.	First movement: simulates a point thrust to the outside chest.
Parries counter of fourth.	Second movement: eludes the parry of counter of fourth with a feint by deceive clockwise to the outside chest.

Parries third.

Receives the touch.

Third movement: eludes the parry of third with a disengagement counterclockwise with the point to the inside chest.

5) In opposition to the invitation in fifth:

Master	Pupil
Invites in fifth.	First movement: simulates a point thrust to the flank.
Parries counter of fifth.	Second movement: eludes the parry of counter of fifth with a feint by deceive counterclockwise to the flank.
Parries second.	Third movement: eludes the parry of second with a disengagement clockwise with the point to the chest above.
Receives the touch.	

60. THE FEINT BY DISENGAGEMENT WITH THE POINT, DECEIVE, AND DISENGAGEMENT WITH THE POINT

The feint by disengagement with the point, deceive, and disengagement with the point is similar in execution to the feint with the direct point thrust, deceive, and disengagement with the point except that it is initiated from the opponent's engagement.

61. THE FEINT BY GLIDE WITH THE POINT, DECEIVE, AND DISENGAGEMENT WITH THE POINT

1) From engagement in second:

Master	Pupil
	First movement: from his own engagement in second simulates a glide with the point to the flank.
Parries counter of first.	Second movement: eludes the parry of counter of first with a feint by deceive counterclockwise to the flank.

Parries second.	Third movement: eludes the parry of second with a disengagement clockwise with the point to the chest above.
Receives the touch.	

2) From engagement in third:

Master	Pupil
	First movement: from his own engagement in third simulates a glide with the point to the outside chest.
Parries counter of fourth.	Second movement: eludes the parry of counter of fourth with a feint by deceive clockwise to the outside chest.
Parries third.	Third movement: eludes the parry of third with a disengagement counterclockwise with the point to the inside chest.
Receives the touch.	

Observation: If the opponent effects imperfect engagements, his engagements are opposed with the feint by forced glide with the point, deceive, and disengagement with the point.

62. THE DOUBLE FEINT WITH THE DIRECT POINT THRUST AND DECEIVE

1) In opposition to the invitation in first:

Master	Pupil
Invites in first.	First movement: simulates a point thrust to the flank.
Parries second.	Second movement: eludes the parry of second with a feint by disengagement clockwise with the point to the chest above.
Parries counter of second.	Third movement: eludes the parry of counter of second with a deceive clockwise to the chest above.
Receives the touch.	

2) In opposition to the invitation in second:

Master	Pupil
Invites in second.	First movement: simulates a point thrust to the chest above.
Parries first or third.	Second movement: eludes the parry of first with a feint by disengagement counterclockwise with the point to the flank; or eludes the parry of third with a feint by disengagement counterclockwise with the point to the inside chest.
Parries counter of first or counter of third.	Third movement: eludes the parry of counter of first with a deceive counterclockwise to the flank; or eludes the parry of counter of third with a deceive counterclockwise to the inside chest.
Receives the touch.	

3) In opposition to the invitation in third:

Master	Pupil
Invites in third.	First movement: simulates a point thrust to the inside chest.
Parries fourth.	Second movement: eludes the parry of fourth with a feint by disengagement clockwise with the point to the outside chest.
Parries counter of fourth.	Third movement: eludes the parry of counter of fourth with a deceive clockwise to the outside chest.
Receives the touch.	

4) In opposition to the invitation in fourth:

Master	Pupil
Invites in fourth.	First movement: simulates a point thrust to the outside chest.
Parries third.	Second movement: eludes the parry of third with a feint by disengagement counterclockwise with the point to the inside chest.

Parries counter of third.	Third movement: eludes the parry of counter of third with a deceive counter-clockwise to the inside chest.
Receives the touch.	

5) In opposition to the invitation in fifth:

Master	Pupil
Invites in fifth.	First movement: simulates a point thrust to the flank.
Parries second.	Second movement: eludes the parry of second with a feint by disengagement clock-wise with the point to the chest above.
Parries counter of second.	Third movement: eludes the parry of counter of second with a deceive clockwise to the chest above.
Receives the touch.	

63. THE DOUBLE FEINT BY DISENGAGEMENT WITH THE POINT AND DECEIVE

The double feint by disengagement with the point and deceive is similar in execution to the double feint with the direct point thrust and deceive except that it is initiated from the adversary's engagement.

64. THE DOUBLE FEINT BY GLIDE WITH THE POINT AND DECEIVE

1) From engagement in second:

Master	Pupil
	First movement: from his own engagement in second simulates a glide with the point to the flank.
Parries second.	Second movement: eludes the parry of second with a feint by disengagement clock-wise with the point to the chest above.
Parries counter of second.	Third movement: eludes the parry of counter of second with a deceive clockwise to the chest above.
Receives the touch.	

2) From engagement in third:

Master	Pupil
	First movement: from his own engagement in third simulates a glide with the point to the outside chest.
Parries third.	Second movement: eludes the parry of third with a feint by disengagement counter-clockwise with the point to the inside chest.
Parries counter of third.	Third movement: eludes the parry of counter of third with a deceive counter-clockwise to the inside chest.
Receives the touch.	

Observation: If the adversary effects weak engagements, his engagements are opposed with the double feint by forced glide with the point and deceive.

It should also be noted that in addition to the defensive systems already cited consisting of a simple parry, a circular parry, a circular and simple parry, and a simple and circular parry, the opponent could employ two circular parries, as in foil. This defense may, in turn, be countered with a feint with the direct point thrust, feint by disengagement with the point, or feint by glide with the point, depending upon placement of the adversary's weapon, followed by two deceives. While these point attacks are rarely encountered in combat, they are, nevertheless, highly useful during the lesson in developing point control.

65. Exercises with Circular Parries

First Exercise

The direct point thrust or disengagement with the point in opposition to the five invitations or engagements:

A	B
Invites or engages.	Aims a direct point thrust or disengagement with the point at the exposed target.
Executes a circular parry and ripostes with the point or cut.	Receives the touch.

Second Exercise

The direct point thrust or disengagement with the point, or the feint with the direct point thrust or disengagement with the point in opposition to the five invitations or engagements:

A	B
Invites or engages.	Aims a direct point thrust or disengagement with the point, or feint with the direct point thrust or disengagement with the point at the exposed target.
Executes one circular parry if the attack is a direct point thrust or disengagement with the point, or one circular and one simple parry if it is a feint with the direct point thrust or disengagement with the point and deceive, and ripostes with the point or cut.	Receives the touch or opposes the riposte with the counterparry riposte.

THIRD EXERCISE

The single or double feint with the direct point thrust or disengagement with the point is opposed to the five invitations or engagements, first from correct, or lunging distance, then from out of distance, with a step forward and lunge; the single feint is countered with one circular and one simple parry, the double feint with one simple, one circular, and one simple parry.

66. CIRCULAR RIPOSTES

Circular ripostes, like circular attacks, are used in opposition to circular parries.

ACTIONS ON THE BLADE

67. ACTIONS ON THE BLADE

Actions on the blade are movements that deviate or deflect the opposing steel during the attack.

The glide with the point is an action on the blade effected in one motion.

Blade seizure, changes of engagement, transports, beats, expulsions, and pressures are actions on the blade used in attacks of two or more blade movements to deviate or deflect the opposing steel so that a point thrust, cut, or feint may be executed.

68. BLADE SEIZURE

Blade seizure is an action on the blade opposed to the adversary's weapon in line; it consists of an engagement usually combined with an advance, and followed by a point thrust, glide with the point, cut, or feint.

69. BLADE SEIZURE FOLLOWED BY POINT THRUSTS OR CUTS

1) Blade seizure in second:

First movement: from the guard in third, invitation, or blade in line, engagement is taken in second, strong against weak, and without interrupting the flow of motion, or breaking contact, the blade is pressed along the weak and medium of the opposing steel, until it has been gradually shifted downward to the right.

Second movement: a glide with the point is directed to the flank or point thrust above to the chest, or direct cut to the flank, right cheek, head, top of the arm or external arm, or abdomen under the opposing steel with the cut or counter-cut, or circular cut to the head or left cheek.

2) Blade seizure in third:

First movement: from the guard in third, invitation, or blade in line, engagement is taken in third, strong against weak, and without interrupting the flow of motion, or breaking contact, the blade is pressed along the weak and medium of the opposing steel, until it has been gradually transferred to the right.

Second movement: a glide with the point is directed to the outside chest or point thrust below to the flank, or direct cut to the head, flank, top of the arm, right or left cheek (the latter with the cut or counter-cut), or circular cut to the chest, abdomen, or internal arm, or ascending cut to the bottom of the arm.

3) Blade seizure in fourth:

First movement: from the guard in third, invitation, or blade in line, engagement is taken in fourth, strong against weak, and without interrupting the flow of motion, or breaking contact, the blade is pressed along the weak and medium of the opposing steel, until it has been gradually moved to the left.

Second movement: a point thrust is directed to the inside chest, or direct cut to the right or left cheek, head, chest, abdomen, top of the arm or internal arm, or circular cut to the flank.

Observation: While it is possible to effect blade seizure in first and fifth, these actions tend to be risky, and should therefore be avoided in combat.

70. CHANGES OF ENGAGEMENT FOLLOWED BY POINT THRUSTS OR CUTS

Changes of engagement followed by point thrusts or cuts may be used when the adversary's blade is engaged. At the completion of the change of engagement a point thrust, cut, or feint can be directed to the exposed target.

71. TRANSPORTS FOLLOWED BY POINT THRUSTS OR CUTS

Transports followed by point thrusts or cuts may be used when the opponent's steel is engaged.

These actions on the blade are executed from engagement in two movements, without a break in blade contact: with the first motion the opposing steel is transported, strong against weak, to a new line of engagement; with the second movement a point thrust, cut, or feint is directed to the target.

1) Transport to first or fifth:

First movement: from engagement in third, strong against weak, and without breaking contact, the opposing steel is moved from right to left to the position of engagement in first, or upward to the position of engagement in fifth.

Second movement: from first a point thrust is directed to the chest, or direct cut to the flank or bottom of the arm, or circular cut to the head, right or left cheek, chest, abdomen, or top of the arm; from fifth a point thrust is aimed at the chest, or direct cut at the flank or bottom of the arm, or circular cut to the head, left cheek, chest, abdomen, or internal arm.

2) Transport to second:

First movement: from engagement in fourth, strong against weak, and without breaking contact, the hostile blade is shifted downward from left to right to the position of engagement in second.

Second movement: a glide with the point is directed to the flank or point thrust above to the chest, or direct cut to the flank, right cheek, head, top of the arm or external arm, or abdomen under the opposing steel with the cut or counter-cut, or circular cut to the head or left cheek.

3) Transport to third:

First movement: from engagement in first, strong against weak, and without breaking contact, the opposing steel is transferred from left to right to the position of engagement in third.

Second movement: a glide with the point is directed to the outside chest or point thrust below to the flank, or direct cut to the head, flank, top of the arm, right or left cheek (the latter with the cut or counter-cut), or circular cut to the chest, abdomen, or internal arm, or ascending cut to the bottom of the arm.

4) Transport to fourth:

First movement: from engagement in second, strong against weak, and without breaking contact, the hostile blade is carried upward from right to left to the position of engagement in fourth.

Second movement: a point thrust is directed to the inside chest, or direct cut to the right or left cheek, head, chest, abdomen, top of the arm or internal arm, or circular cut to the flank.

Observation: The transport from fourth to second followed by the glide with the point to the flank is also known, in sabre as in foil, as the flanconade in second.

72. BEATS

Beats are blows of measured violence delivered with the strong of the blade against the medium of the adversary's steel to dislodge it from engagement or its position in line. In sabre fencing beats may be effected in first, second, third, fourth, and fifth.

Beats can be classified as simple beats, change beats, circular beats, and grazing beats. With the exception of grazing beats, beats are accomplished by striking the adversary's blade at one point only.

In sabre the beats may be executed with either the cutting edge or the back edge of the blade. Beats with the back edge are preferable when the beat is succeeded by a point thrust to the inside chest, or a cut to the right cheek.

Attacks with beats are performed in two or more movements, with the beat representing the first motion, and the point thrust, cut, or feint, the second.

Beats are made with the sword arm flexed; the weapon, hand, and forearm must function as a single unit. Movement of the blade and forearm should be kept as tight as possible, with the steel stopping dead on contact, and then moving forward promptly for the point thrust or cut.

73. Simple Beats

Simple beats are effected by moving the blade the shortest distance necessary to encounter the opposing steel.

74. The Simple Beat and Point Thrust or Cut

1) The simple beat in first:

   First movement: from the guard in second or third, or blade in line, the hand is rotated to first position, and, without flexing the wrist, the opposing steel is deflected with a blow diagonally upward to the left.

   Second movement: the sword arm is extended immediately, and a point thrust delivered to the chest, or direct cut to the flank or bottom of the arm, or circular cut to the head, right or left cheek, chest, abdomen, or top of the arm.

2) The simple beat in second:

   First movement: from the guard in second or third, or blade in line, and the adversary's weapon directed to the flank, or from the guard in fifth, and the opposing steel aimed at the chest, the hand is turned to first in second position, and the hostile blade deviated with a blow downward to the right.

   Second movement: the sword arm is straightened promptly, and a point thrust delivered to the flank or above to the chest, or direct cut to the flank, right cheek, head, top of the arm or external arm, or circular cut to the head or left cheek.

3) The simple beat in third:

   First movement: from the guard in second, third, or fourth, or blade in line, the hand is rotated to second in third position, and the opposing steel is deflected with a blow diagonally downward to the right.

   Second movement: the sword arm is extended immediately, and a point thrust delivered to the outside chest or below to the flank, or direct cut to the head, flank, top of the arm, right or left cheek (the latter with the cut or counter-cut), or circular cut to the chest or abdomen.

4) The simple beat in fourth:

First movement: from the guard in second, third, or fifth, or blade in line, the hand is turned to third in fourth position, and the hostile blade is deviated with a blow diagonally downward to the left.

Second movement: the sword arm is straightened promptly, and a point thrust delivered to the inside chest, or direct cut to the right or left cheek, head, chest, abdomen, top of the arm or internal arm, or circular cut to the flank.

5) The simple beat in fifth:

First movement: from the guard in second or third, or blade in line, and the opposing steel directed to the chest, the hand is rotated to first position, and, without flexing the wrist, the hostile blade is deflected with a blow upward.

Second movement: the sword arm is extended immediately, and a point thrust delivered to the chest, or direct cut to the flank or bottom of the arm, or circular cut to the head, left cheek, chest, abdomen, or internal arm.

Observation: The simple beat in fourth must be executed with both the cutting edge and back edge of the blade. It should be noted that the beat with the back edge has the advantage of being faster, since the hand does not have to be turned to first in second position for the point thrust to the inside chest, or second position for the direct cut to the right cheek.

75. Change Beats

Change beats are made from one's own or the adversary's engagement by carrying the point over or under the opposing steel, and striking it on the opposite side.

76. The Change Beat and Point Thrust or Cut

1) The change beat in first:

First movement: from engagement in second the point is brought clock-wise over the hostile blade, hand rotated to first position, and the opposing steel deflected with a blow diagonally upward to the left.

Second movement: the sword arm is extended immediately, and a point thrust delivered to the chest, or direct cut to the flank or bottom of the arm, or circular cut to the head, right or left cheek, chest, abdo-men, or top of the arm.

2) The change beat in second:

First movement: from engagement in first the point is shifted counter-clockwise over the hostile blade, hand turned to first in second posi-tion, and the opposing steel deviated with a blow diagonally down-ward to the right.

Second movement: the sword arm is straightened promptly, and a point thrust delivered to the flank or above to the chest, or direct cut to the flank, right cheek, head, top of the arm or external arm, or circular cut to the head or left cheek.

3) The change beat in third:

First movement: from engagement in fourth the point is transferred clockwise under the hostile blade, hand rotated to second in third position, and the opposing steel deflected with a blow diagonally down-ward to the right.

Second movement: the sword arm is extended immediately, and a point thrust delivered to the outside chest or below to the flank, or direct cut to the head, flank, top of the arm, right or left cheek (the latter with the cut or counter-cut), or circular cut to the chest or abdomen.

4) The change beat in fourth:

First movement: from engagement in third the point is carried coun-terclockwise under the hostile blade, hand turned to third in fourth position, and the opposing steel deviated with a blow diagonally downward to the left.

Second movement: the sword arm is straightened promptly, and a point thrust delivered to the inside chest, or direct cut to the right or left cheek, head, chest, abdomen, top of the arm or internal arm, or circular cut to the flank.

77. CIRCULAR BEATS

Circular beats are effected in exactly the same way as circular parries: the elbow remains fixed in its position of invitation or engagement, and serves as a pivot, while the point, set in motion by the hand and forearm, describes a tight, complete circle around the opponent's extended blade, beating it in the direction of the invitation or engagement.

78. GRAZING BEATS

Grazing beats are sliding beats in which the point is withdrawn, and the line changed by passing over the opposing steel.

In sabre, grazing beats are effected with the back edge of the blade. The elbow and wrist are slightly flexed, and the blade brought back in a circular movement, striking the opposing steel, and passing over and under it in a continuous motion. The beat and point thrust or cut must fuse into one another so smoothly that the two movements of the action appear to be a single, rapid motion.

The grazing beat in third is followed by a cut to the abdomen or internal arm; the grazing beat in fourth is succeeded by a point thrust or cut to the flank, or cut to the external arm.

Observation: Grazing beats are particularly effective in attacks directed to the arm.

79. EXPULSIONS

Expulsions are powerful sliding beats in which the strong of the attacking weapon is forced along the opposing steel, expelling it from its position in engagement or line.

In sabre, expulsions are generally accomplished from engagements in third and fourth.

The expulsion in third is followed by a point thrust to the outside chest, or direct cut to the head, top of the arm, right or left cheek (the latter with the cut or counter-cut); the expulsion in fourth is succeeded by a point thrust to the inside chest, or direct cut to the right or left cheek, head, chest, abdomen, top of the arm or internal arm.

80. PRESSURES

Pressures are gradual applications of force with the strong or medium of the blade against the adversary's weak to deviate it from its position in line.

In sabre fencing pressures are made from engagement in second, third, and fourth. The action is executed from the forearm, sword arm extending, with the strong of the blade pressing against the weak of the opposing steel, deviating it from its position in line.

The pressure in second is followed by a glide with the point to the flank or point thrust above to the chest, or direct cut to the flank, right cheek, head, top of the arm or external arm, or abdomen under the opposing steel with the cut or counter-cut, or circular cut to the head or left cheek; the pressure in third is succeeded by a glide with the point to the outside chest or point thrust below to the flank, or direct cut to the head, flank, top of the arm, right or left cheek (the latter with the cut or counter-cut), or circular cut to the chest, abdomen, or internal arm, or ascending cut to the bottom of the arm; and the pressure in fourth is followed by a point thrust to the inside chest, or direct cut to the right or left cheek, head, chest, abdomen, top of the arm or internal arm, or circular cut to the flank.

81. ACTIONS ON THE BLADE FOLLOWED BY FEINTS

All of the actions on the blade described above may be followed by feints. In every case the simulated point thrust or cut is intended to draw the parry, thus exposing a part of the valid target to the real point thrust or cut.

With a single feint the action is performed in three movements; with a double feint it is effected in four motions.

82. Exercises with Simple Parries

First Exercise

The simple beat and direct point thrust or direct cut in opposition to the blade in line:

A	B
Places the weapon in line.	Beats the opposing steel and aims a direct point thrust or direct cut at the exposed target.
Executes a simple parry and ripostes with the point or cut.	Receives the touch.

Second Exercise

The simple beat and direct point thrust or direct cut, or the feint with the direct point thrust or direct cut in opposition to the blade in line:

A	B
Places the weapon in line.	Beats the opposing steel and aims a direct point thrust or direct cut, or a feint with the direct point thrust or direct cut at the exposed target.
Executes one simple parry if the attack is a simple beat and direct point thrust or direct cut, or two simple parries if it is a simple beat and feint with the direct point thrust or direct cut and disengagement with the point or cut, and ripostes with the point or cut.	Receives the touch or opposes the riposte with the counterparry riposte.

Third Exercise

The simple beat followed by the single or double feint with the direct point thrust or direct cut is opposed to the blade in line, first from correct, or lunging distance, then from out of distance, with a step forward and lunge; the single feint is countered with two simple parries, the double feint with three simple parries.

Observation: The above exercises should be repeated substituting the beats with seizures of the blade, transports, expulsions, and pressures.

83. EXERCISES WITH CIRCULAR PARRIES

FIRST EXERCISE

The simple beat and direct point thrust in opposition to the blade in line:

A	B
Places the weapon in line.	Beats the opposing steel and aims a direct point thrust at the exposed target.
Executes a circular parry and ripostes with the point or cut.	Receives the touch.

SECOND EXERCISE

The simple beat and direct point thrust, or feint with the direct point thrust in opposition to the blade in line:

A	B
Places the weapon in line.	Beats the opposing steel and aims a direct point thrust or feint with the direct point thrust at the exposed target.
Executes one circular parry if the attack is a simple beat and direct point thrust, or one circular and one simple parry if it is a simple beat and feint with the direct point thrust and deceive, and ripostes with the point or cut.	Receives the touch or opposes the riposte with the counterparry riposte.

Third Exercise

The simple beat followed by the single or double feint with the direct point thrust is opposed to the blade in line, first from correct, or lunging distance, then from out of distance, with a step forward and lunge; the single feint is countered with one circular and one simple parry, the double feint with one simple, one circular, and one simple parry.

Observation: The above exercises should be repeated substituting the beats with seizures of the blade, transports, expulsions, and pressures.

84. Renewed Attacks

Renewed attacks are second offensive actions launched against an opponent who, having parried the initial assault, either hesitates or fails to respond.

Observation: As in foil, for the advanced student the most profitable drills with renewed attacks are those consisting of a recovery forward and second lunge or running attack. Again, such movements are performed in opposition to the master's parry with a retreat and delay in the riposte. For instance, in opposition to the invitation in third the pupil can be instructed to execute a direct point thrust to the inside chest; on the teacher's parry of fourth in retreat and hesitation, the student recovers forward rapidly with a tight feint by disengagement with the point to the outside chest. The instructor's parry of third is then eluded with a disengagement with the point to the inside chest and second lunge or running attack.

When the pupil has mastered this action using the point, the final disengagement with the point may be substituted with a descending cut to the head. In other words, the teacher's parry of third is eluded with a descending cut.

Care must be exercised that the student, in executing a running attack, always passes on the opposite side of the hostile blade. In the examples cited above, he should pass on the master's inside.

CHAPTER 9

COUNTEROFFENSE

85. TIME, VELOCITY, AND MEASURE

The three fundamental elements of fencing are time, velocity, and measure.

Time in fencing signifies the favorable moment at which an offensive action will catch the adversary off guard.

Velocity refers to the minimum time necessary to complete an offensive, defensive, or counteroffensive movement.

Measure is the distance that must be covered to reach the target with a point thrust or cut. See page 192.

86. FENCING TIME

Each fencing movement represents one unit of fencing time.

87. COUNTERATTACKS

Counterattacks are offensive actions opposed to attacks.

There are six counterattacks in sabre fencing: 1) the arrest, 2) the disengagement in time, 3) the time thrust or cut to the arm, 4) the appuntata, 5) the inquartata, and 6) the time thrust.

88. THE ARREST

The arrest is a counterattack that interrupts completion of a compound attack with feints.

The arrest must prevent the opposing steel from passing to an opposite line.

If the adversary's feint is aimed at the chest, the arrest is directed to the flank; if the opponent's feint is aimed at the flank, the arrest is directed to the chest.

89. THE DISENGAGEMENT IN TIME

The disengagement in time is a counterattack against actions on the blade.

In sabre fencing the disengagement in time may be effected with either the point or cut. For instance, if the adversary attempts an attack with the simple beat in fourth and point thrust or cut, his beat can be avoided by a disengagement in time with the point to the outside chest, or cut to the right cheek.

90. THE TIME THRUST OR CUT TO THE ARM

The time thrust or cut to the arm is a counterattack directed to the advanced target (Fig. 117). It can be executed with the point, cut, or countercut during the first, second, or third movement of the attack, and may be aimed at the top of the arm, bottom of the arm, internal arm, or external arm, depending upon the line of assault.

While the time thrust or cut to the arm is most successful against attacks initiated from out of distance, it may also be employed in opposition to attacks made from lunging distance. In the latter instance it is usual to follow the counterattack with a parry in retreat, thus providing a defense against the completion of the attack should the time thrust or cut fail. For example, if the opponent feints to the head, the time cut can be delivered to the bottom of the arm or external arm. Immediately following the counterattack, the parry of third is performed with a step backward or a jump backward; the opposing steel, if it has penetrated, is deflected to the right, and a riposte is directed to the adversary's exposed target.

Figure 117. The time cut to the bottom of the arm.

Observation: The time thrust or cut to the arm must only be used in opposition to simple attacks if the opponent's arm is well exposed; similarly, it should only be employed against running attacks if the distance is excessively large, or the attacker withdraws his arm as he begins the action.

The Time Cut to the Bottom of the Arm

Plate XII.

Plate XIII.

Plate XIV.

91. THE APPUNTATA

The appuntata is a counterattack in opposition to the compound riposte.
If the attack against the adversary consists of a feint to the head and cut to the flank, and he parries fifth and second and ripostes with a feint to the right cheek and point thrust to the flank, his second movement can be anticipated with the appuntata or point thrust to his flank. In other words, the appuntata is accomplished from the lunge position, and is aimed at the same target as the original assault, that is to say, at the flank. To give the counterattack impetus, it should be accompanied by an appel.

92. THE INQUARTATA

The inquartata is a counterattack in opposition to both simple and com-pound attacks terminating in the inside.
In sabre fencing the inquartata is used in opposition to the opponent's point thrust to the inside chest, or cut to the head, or left cheek. The inquartata is effected with either a point thrust to the antagonist's chest (Fig. 118), or a cut to his left cheek, while simultaneously extending the left leg, and shifting the left foot to the right of the line of direction. Throughout the action the left hand remains on the hip.

Figure 118. The inquartata.

93. THE TIME THRUST

The time thrust is a counterattack that precedes the final movement of the attack.

In sabre fencing the time thrust can be executed only in second and third. The action is performed without a lunge, and with the line closed to the right, so that the incoming steel is deflected to the outside.

The time thrust in second is effected from one's own invitation or engagement in first, third, and fifth. As the adversary attacks, the sword arm is straightened rapidly, and a point thrust directed to the flank (Fig. 119).

The time thrust in third is accomplished from one's own invitation or engagement in second and fourth. As the opponent attacks, the sword arm is extended and raised quickly, and a point thrust aimed at the chest (Fig. 120).

Figure 119.
The time thrust
in second.

Figure 120.
The time thrust
in third.

94. COUNTERTIME

Actions in countertime are movements used in opposition to counterattacks.

The counterattack is generally prompted by a feint coordinated with a short step forward. The moment the adversary reacts, his movement is opposed with the rapid parry and riposte in countertime.

If the opponent, in opposition to the feint to the head with an advance and cut to the flank, executes an arrest to the flank, the counterattack is parried in second, and a riposte, from the guard position, is directed immediately to the exposed target.

If the adversary, in opposition to the simple beat in fourth with an advance and cut to the right cheek, effects a disengagement in time with the point or cut to the outside line, the counterattack is parried in third, and a riposte, from the guard position, is directed instantly to the exposed target.

If the opponent, in opposition to the feint to the head with an advance and cut to the flank, performs a time thrust or cut to the arm, the counterattack is parried in third, and a riposte, with a lunge or running attack, is aimed promptly at the exposed target, catching the adversary as he retreats.

95. THE FEINT IN TIME

The feint in time is a movement opposed to actions in countertime.

96. THE ARREST IN COUNTERTIME

The arrest in countertime is an action opposed to the single or double feint in time.

CHAPTER 10

ACTIONS IN TIME

97. PROBING ACTIONS

Probing actions are feigned attacks that test the adversary's defensive and counteroffensive responses.

98. ACTIONS OF CONCEALMENT

Actions of concealment are movements used to confuse the opponent and hide one's own intentions.

In sabre fencing these consist of changes in placement of the weapon, beats, and pressures combined with small forward and backward steps.

99. INITIATIVE FOR THE ATTACK

Attacks may be executed on one's own initiative, or on the adversary's.

100. ATTACKS IN TIME

Attacks in time are offensive actions effected while the adversary is in the act of changing the placement of his weapon.

101. FIRST AND SECOND INTENTION

Every simple and compound offensive action may be accomplished in first or second intention. In first intention the movement is executed with the intent of reaching the target directly through the action itself. In second intention the movement is performed with the express purpose of provoking defensive responses against which counteractions can be applied.

CHAPTER 11

PEDAGOGY

102. METHOD OF INSTRUCTION

For the method of instruction see page 124.

Observation: A typical lesson commences with the orders: "First position!"; "Salute!"; "Mask on!"; "On guard!" (Fig. 121); "Point thrust, via!"; "Hup!" (Fig. 122); "On guard!"; "Disengagement with the point, via!"; "Hup!"; "On guard!"; "Glide with the point, via!" (if the attack is parried and a riposte delivered); "Remain in the lunge position!"; "Counterparry fifth and riposte with cut to the flank, via!" "Hup!"; "On guard!" (Fig. 123); "Head cut, via!"; "Hup!" (Fig. 124); "On guard!"; "First position, rest!"; etc.

For the advanced sabre fencer, parry riposte exercises should play an important role in the composition of the lesson. One of the most useful of these drills consists of having the student execute the simple parry of fifth in retreat, and riposte with the direct cut to the flank, followed by the counterparry of fifth in retreat, and riposte with the circular cut to the abdomen. When he has mastered this combination, an additional counterparry of fifth in retreat, and riposte with the direct cut to the flank, may be added to the exercise. Occasionally, the teacher should retreat on the final counterparry riposte so that the pupil must lunge.

103. ORGANIZATION OF THE LESSON

For the organization of the lesson see page 127.

104. PREPARATION FOR COMBAT

Concerning the preparation for combat see page 128.

105. FREE FENCING

For free fencing see pages 128 and 129.

Figure 121. "On guard!"

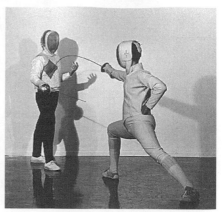

Figure 122. "Point thrust, via!" "Hup!"

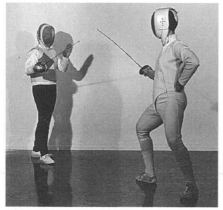

Figure 123. "On guard!"

Figure 124. "Head cut, via!" "Hup!"

106. THE ASSAULT

Combat between two fencers is called an assault or bout.

107. DOUBLE HITS

The rules governing double hits in foil are also applicable to sabre. See page 130.

108. The Left-Handed Opponent

The left-handed adversary does not, in general, present problems for the sabre fencer. Although the target is reversed, it should still be viewed as if it were on a right-handed opponent.

109. Fencing Tactics

For fencing tactics see page 133.

Observation: In sabre, as in foil, the adversary should be attacked vigorously, so that he is forced on the defensive.

When using feints, point feints are especially recommended because they can be executed with a minimum of exposure.

During the course of the assault, particular attention must be paid to the opponent's hand placement; the instant he feints with his hand too high, too low, too far to the right, or too far to the left, his action should be opposed with a time thrust or cut to the arm. He must be intimidated to such an extent that he loses his self-confidence.

Plate XV. The direct cut to the head with a runnig attack.

PART III

THE ÉPÉE

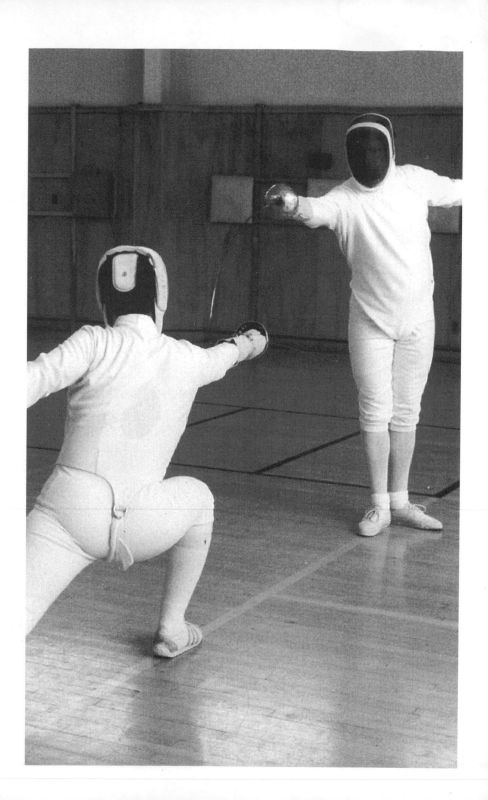

CHAPTER 1

ESSENTIAL ELEMENTS

1. PARTS OF THE ÉPÉE

The épée, like the foil and sabre, is divided into two principal parts: the guard, and the blade.

The guard is composed of five elements: bell guard, cushion, crossbar, grip, and pommel (Fig. 125).

1) The bell guard is a circular metal shield, less than 13.5 centimeters in diameter, and 5.5 centimeters in depth, with a rectangular opening off center for the tang and ricasso.

2) The cushion is a leather, fabric, or rubber pad, perforated at the center, and fitted behind the bell guard.

3) The crossbar is a metal rod, equal in length to the diameter of the bell guard, with a hole off center for the tang.

4) The grip is a hollow wooden or plastic handle through which the tang passes.

Figure 125. Parts of the épée.

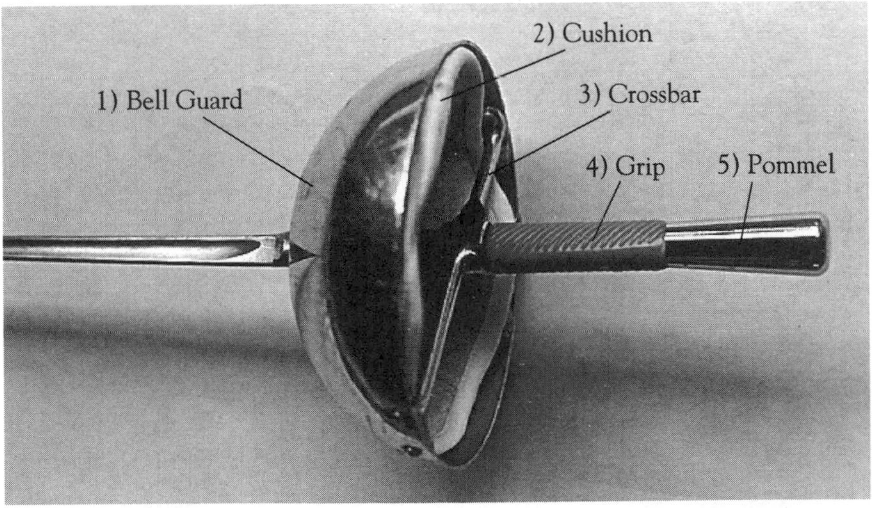

2) Cushion

1) Bell Guard

3) Crossbar

4) Grip

5) Pommel

5) The pommel is a cylindrical metal counterbalance that receives the threaded end of the tang.

The épée blade consists of the same three elements as the foil blade: button, ricasso, and tang.

The blade is made of tempered steel. It is triangular in cross section, and must not exceed 90 centimeters in length from the convex side of the bell guard to the button.

While both the foil and sabre blades are flexible, the épée blade is semirigid; it is the stiff blade that was used for dueling. As with the other blades, degrees of strength are distinguished by dividing the blade into three equal sections: strong, medium, and weak.

2. BALANCE, WEIGHT, AND LENGTH OF THE ÉPÉE

The épée is properly balanced when its center of gravity is at the strong of the blade, approximately four fingers from the bell guard.

By regulation, the épée must be under 770 grams in weight, and must not exceed 110 centimeters in length, measuring from the tip of the blade to the end of the pommel.

3. HOLDING THE ÉPÉE

The Italian épée is gripped in the same manner as the Italian foil; however, since the ricasso is off center, the middle finger must be placed on the shorter of the two arms of the crossbar.

4. HAND POSITIONS

Hand positions in foil and épée are the same. See pages 6 and 7.

CHAPTER 2

THE GUARD AND THE LUNGE

5. FIRST POSITION

The posture assumed by the fencer with his body and weapon before the salute and during periods of rest is called first position.

6. WEAPON IN LINE

The weapon is in line when it forms, with the extended right arm, a straight line parallel with the floor.

7. THE SALUTE

The salute is a traditional act of courtesy directed to the adversary and spectators, and must always be observed at the beginning and end of the lesson and combat.

8. THE LINE OF DIRECTION

The imaginary line connecting two fencers, beginning at the left heel of one, passing through the axis of his right foot, and continuing until it encounters the same points in his adversary's feet, is called the line of direction. This is the normal route the feet must travel in the lesson, in exercise, and in combat.

9. THE GUARD

The position taken by the fencer with his body and weapon to be ready for the offense, defense, or counteroffense is called the guard.

The épée guard is taken in two movements, and resembles the foil guard in all particulars except one: the point of the weapon is directed toward the adversary's wrist, so that the blade and forearm form a straight line parallel with the floor (Fig. 126). In this way the opponent's advanced target is menaced, while one's own arm is protected behind the bell guard. Seen from in front, the lower arm should be hidden from sight (Fig. 127).

Figure 126. The guard.

Figure 127. The lower arm
should be hidden from sight.

10. THE LINE OF OFFENSE

The weapon is considered in the line of offense when its point, with the arm naturally extended, menaces some part of the adversary's valid target.

11. THE LUNGE

The lunge is the position the fencer assumes with his body at the end of an offensive action executed from the guard. The passage from guard to lunge must be effected in a single movement.

12. THE RETURN ON GUARD

The recovery from the lunge back to the guard position is called the return on guard.

13. FOOT MOVEMENTS

For foot movements see pages 15 through 18.

14. FENCING MEASURE

Fencing measure is the distance that separates two fencers placed on guard. There are three measures: out of distance, correct distance, and close distance. Since the sword arm is a valid target in épée, as in sabre, the three fencing measures must be modified in similar fashion.

1) From out of distance the opponent's trunk can be touched by taking a step forward and lunging, and his arm by lunging directly.

2) From correct distance the adversary's torso can be hit by lunging, and his arm by remaining in the guard position.

3) From close distance the opponent's trunk or arm can be reached without lunging.

Observation: Because the sword arm is valid target, épée fencers tend to keep a greater distance between themselves than foilsmen.

CHAPTER 3

PLACEMENT OF THE WEAPON

15. PLACEMENT OF THE WEAPON

Placement of the weapon refers to the position the fencer on guard adopts with his armed hand in relation to his adversary. There are three such positions, and they are designated: invitation, engagement, and blade in line.

16. THE ÉPÉE TARGET

In épée fencing the entire body from head to foot is valid target. Touches to the advanced target are directed, as in sabre, to the top of the arm, bottom of the arm, internal arm, and external arm.

17. INVITATIONS

Invitations are positions taken with the weapon, exposing a specific line, to induce the opponent to attack. There are four épée invitations: first, second, third, and fourth.

18. ENGAGEMENTS

Engagements are contact invitations in which the opposing steel is dominated and deviated from the line of offense. There are four engagements: first, second, third, and fourth. In these the hand and weapon assume exactly the same position they did in the invitations.

19. CHANGES OF ENGAGEMENT

Changes of engagement are used to shift from one engagement to another. These movements are accomplished by passing the point over or under the opposing steel and carrying it to an opposite line of engagement. If the engagement is in the low line, the point passes over the hostile blade; if it is in the high line, it passes under.

20. Transports

Transports carry the blade, strong against weak, without a break in contact, from one line of engagement to another.

21. Envelopments

Envelopments are movements that encircle the opposing steel, so that the blade, in a continuous motion and without a loss of contact, returns to the original line of engagement.

CHAPTER 4

OFFENSE

22. THE OFFENSE

The offense is the act of attacking the adversary.

23. SIMPLE ATTACKS

Offensive actions consisting of a single blade movement are called simple attacks.

In épée fencing there are four simple attacks: 1) the straight thrust, 2) the disengagement, 3) the glide, and 4) the angulation.

24. THE ANGULATION

The angulation is a thrust, effected with a flexed wrist, that passes over, under, or on either side of the adversary's bell guard to the advanced target. It may be directed to the top of the arm (Fig. 128), bottom of the arm (Fig. 129), internal arm (Fig. 130), and external arm (Fig. 131).

Observation: In épée fencing straight thrusts can be opposed with angulations, and angulations with straight thrusts.

Figure 128.
The angulation to the
top of the arm.

Figure 129.
The angulation to the
bottom of the arm.

Figure 130.
The angulation to the
internal arm.

Figure 131.
The angulation to the
external arm.

CHAPTER 5

DEFENSE

25. THE DEFENSE

Blade motions that deviate the adversary's point before it reaches the target, or foot movements that remove the body from the range of attack, are called the defense.

26. PARRIES

Defensive movements of the blade that deflect the incoming steel are termed parries. In épée, as in foil and sabre, these may be simple, circular, half circular, or ceding.

27. SIMPLE PARRIES

Simple parries are protective displacements of the blade that cover exposed target areas by traveling the shortest route from one invitation or engagement to another.

Simple parries in épée and foil are the same.

Observation: Since the simple parries of first and fourth expose the external arm, they should be used with caution in épée fencing.

It must also be noted that the bell guard of the épée provides ample protection against attacks to the advanced target; in many cases it suffices to shift the hand slightly up, down, or to the right or left, to deflect the incoming steel, without actually taking the point from its offensive position.

28. PASSAGE FROM ONE SIMPLE PARRY TO ANOTHER

Concerning passage from one simple parry to another, see pages 35 and 36.

29. Ceding Parries

Ceding parries are used in opposition to gliding actions in the low lines. Instead of resisting the attack, it is yielded to, blades in constant contact, hand lowered, wrist flexed, and point raised, so that the parry is assumed, and the incoming steel deviated, just before the point reaches its destination.

30. The Riposte

The riposte is the thrust delivered immediately after the adversary's attack has been parried. Ripostes may be simple or compound.

Observation: In épée fencing ripostes along the blade tend to be the most secure and effective. If possible, the parry and riposte should be executed as a continuous action.

31. Simple Ripostes

After the parry of first the riposte may be directed to the inside low line by detaching the blade, or by maintaining contact.

After the parry of second the riposte may be aimed at the high line by detaching the blade, or at the outside low line by maintaining contact.

After the parry of third the riposte may be directed to the low line by detaching the blade, or to the outside high line by maintaining contact.

After the parry of fourth the riposte may be aimed at the inside high line by detaching the blade, or by maintaining contact, or it can be directed to the outside low line with the flanconade in fourth.

Observation: In épée fencing the riposte may be aimed at any part of the adversary's body; during the lesson, however, it is usually directed to the sword arm (Figs. 132-133).

Figure 132.
Parry of third.

Figure 133.
Simple riposte to the
arm by detaching the
blade.

COMPOUND ATTACKS

32. COMPOUND ATTACKS

Offensive actions consisting of two or more blade movements are called compound or composed attacks.

33. THE FEINT

The feint is a simulated thrust or menace that resembles so closely a genuine assault that the adversary is forced to parry.

Observation: During the feint the forearm must remain covered

Feints may be aimed at any part of the opponent's body, but in the lesson, they are generally directed to the torso or forearm.

34. SINGLE FEINTS

Single or simple feints elude one parry; they are used in opposition to the invitation and engagement.

Observation: Single feints may be employed with considerable effect in épée fencing, particularly when they are used to open the adversary's outside line. For example, the feint direct or feint by disengagement may be aimed at the opponent's internal arm, so that he will be tempted to react with the simple parry of fourth, thus exposing his external arm to the second movement of the attack.

35. COMPOUND RIPOSTES

Ripostes consisting of two or more blade motions are termed compound ripostes; their function is to elude one or more counterparries, that is, parries opposed to the riposte.

Observation: Compound ripostes expose the defender to the counterattack; the student should therefore be warned to use them sparingly.

36. Ripostes with Feints

For ripostes with feints see page 44.

Observation: In épée fencing ripostes with feints are generally aimed at the arm. For example, after the parry of third the feint may be directed to the bottom of the arm, and the counterparry of second eluded with a dis-engagement traveling clockwise to the top of the arm.

37. Double Feints

Double feints elude two parries; they are employed in opposition to the invitation and engagement.

Observation: Double feints should be avoided since they expose the at-tacker to a counterattack.

38. Conventional Exercises

Conventional exercises consist of pre-established actions executed by two fencers alternately assuming the role of attacker and defender.

Exercises with Simple Parries

First Exercise

The straight thrust in opposition to the four invitations:

A	B
Invites.	Directs a straight thrust to the ex-posed target.
Executes a simple parry and ripostes to the arm by detach-ing the blade, or by maintain-ing contact.	Receives the touch.

SECOND EXERCISE

The disengagement in opposition to the four engagements:

A	B
Engages.	Directs a disengagement to the exposed target.
Executes a simple parry and ripostes to the arm by detaching the blade, or by maintaining contact.	Receives the touch.

THIRD EXERCISE

The straight thrust or feint direct and disengagement in opposition to the four invitations:

A	B
Invites.	Directs a straight thrust or feint direct and disengagement to the exposed target.
Executes one simple parry if the attack is a straight thrust, or two simple parries if it is a feint direct and disengagement, and ripostes to the arm by detaching the blade, or by maintaining contact.	Receives the touch or opposes the riposte with the counterparry riposte.

FOURTH EXERCISE

The disengagement or feint by disengagement and disengagement in opposition to the four engagements:

A	B
Engages.	Directs a disengagement or feint by disengagement and disengagement to the exposed target.
Executes one simple parry if the attack is a disengagement,	Receives the touch or opposes the riposte with the counterparry riposte.

or two simple parries if it is a
feint by disengagement and
disengagement, and ripostes to
the arm by detaching the blade,
or by maintaining contact.

FIFTH EXERCISE

The feint direct and disengagement is opposed to the four invitations,
first from correct, or lunging distance, then from out of distance, with a
step forward and lunge; the feint direct is countered with two simple parries.

SIXTH EXERCISE

The feint by disengagement and disengagement is opposed to the four
engagements, first from correct, or lunging distance, then from out of distance, with a step forward and lunge; the feint by disengagement is countered with two simple parries.

CIRCULAR ATTACKS

39. CIRCULAR PARRIES

Circular parries are defensive blade movements in which the point describes a tight, complete circle around the incoming steel, intercepting and transferring it to the opposite line.

Observation: Circular parries of first and fourth expose the external arm and should therefore be employed with caution in épée fencing.

40. HALF CIRCULAR PARRIES

Half circular parries are defensive displacements of the blade along a diagonal semicircular route from a high to a low line and vice versa.
Half circular parries in épée and foil are the same.

41. CIRCULAR ATTACKS

Circular attacks are used in opposition to circular parries. In these compound offensive actions the feint provokes a circular parry, which is then deceived by a circular thrust moving in the same direction as the parry.

Observation: Again, the feint should be employed to open the opponent's outside line. For instance, the feint direct or feint by disengagement may be directed to the adversary's external arm, so that he will be prompted to react with the parry of counter of fourth, thus exposing his external arm to the second movement of the attack.

42. Exercises with Circular Parries

First Exercise

The straight thrust in opposition to the four invitations:

A	B
Invites.	Directs a straight thrust to the exposed target.
Executes a circular parry and ripostes to the arm by detaching the blade, or by maintaining contact.	Receives the touch.

Second Exercise

The disengagement in opposition to the four engagements:

A	B
Engages.	Directs a disengagement to the exposed target.
Executes a circular parry and ripostes to the arm by detaching the blade, or by maintaining contact.	Receives the touch.

Third Exercise

The straight thrust or feint direct and deceive in opposition to the four invitations:

A	B
Invites.	Directs a straight thrust or feint direct and deceive to the exposed target.
Executes one circular parry if the attack is a straight thrust, or two circular parries if it is a feint direct and deceive, and ri-	Receives the touch or opposes the riposte with the counterparry riposte.

postes to the arm by detaching
the blade, or by maintaining
contact.

FOURTH EXERCISE

The disengagement or feint by disengagement and deceive in opposition
to the four engagements:

A	B
Engages.	Directs a disengagement or feint by disengagement and deceive to the exposed target.
Executes one circular parry if the attack is a disengagement, or two circular parries if it is a feint by disengagement and deceive, and ripostes to the arm by detaching the blade, or by maintaining contact.	Receives the touch or opposes the riposte with the counterparry riposte.

43. CIRCULAR RIPOSTES

Circular ripostes, like circular attacks, are used in opposition to circular
parries.

CHAPTER 8

ACTIONS ON THE BLADE

44. ACTIONS ON THE BLADE

Actions on the blade are movements that deviate or deflect the opposing steel during the attack.

Observation: In épée fencing actions terminating with a thrust to the outside line are particularly effective: for example, the change of engagement from fourth to third and glide to the arm, the transport from fourth to second and glide to the flank, the envelopment in third and glide to the arm, the beat in fourth and disengagement to the arm, and the pressure in fourth and disengagement to the arm.

Although actions on the blade followed by feints should, as a rule, be avoided, there are a few exceptions. These include the change of engagement from fourth to third, simple beat in third, and pressure in third succeeded by a feint direct to the low line. Correctly placed, the feint is just under the adversary's wrist; as he parries second, the disengagement, moving clockwise, is directed to the top of the arm. If the action is sufficiently tight, there is little opportunity for the opponent to launch a counterattack.

45. RENEWED ATTACKS

Renewed attacks are second offensive actions launched against an opponent who, having parried the initial assault, either hesitates or fails to respond.

Observation: Renewed attacks are common in épée fencing. Generally, the second thrust is delivered from the lunge.

CHAPTER 9

COUNTEROFFENSE

46. TIME, VELOCITY, AND MEASURE

The three fundamental elements of fencing are time, velocity, and measure.

Time in fencing signifies the favorable moment at which an offensive action will catch the adversary off guard.

Velocity refers to the minimum time necessary to complete an offensive, defensive, or counteroffensive movement.

Measure is the distance that must be covered to reach the target with a point thrust or cut. See page 273.

47. FENCING TIME

There are no conventions in épée fencing concerning priority of hits: if the attack and counterattack arrive simultaneously, both fencers are considered touched.

48. COUNTERATTACKS

Counterattacks are offensive actions opposed to attacks.

The seven counterattacks employed in foil are also used in épée.

Observation: Counterattacks are characteristic of épée fencing. The most common of these is the arrest to the arm (Fig. 134) or mask; this may be accomplished from the guard, or by reassembling backward, that is to say, withdrawing the right foot until it touches the left heel, straightening the legs, and throwing back the left arm.

During the épée lesson the master should occasionally parry the attack and riposte to the leg, so that the student can practice the arrest to the top of the arm while reassembling backward. And when he has mastered this, he must be instructed to direct his arrest to the mask.

Figure 134.
The arrest to the top
of the arm while
reassembling
backward.

49. COUNTERTIME

Actions in countertime are movements used in opposition to counterattacks.

50. THE FEINT IN TIME

The feint in time is a movement opposed to actions in countertime.

51. THE ARREST IN COUNTERTIME

The arrest in countertime is an action opposed to the single or double feint in time.

CHAPTER 10

ACTIONS IN TIME

52. PROBING ACTIONS

Probing actions are feigned attacks that test the adversary's defensive and counteroffensive responses.

53. ACTIONS OF CONCEALMENT

Actions of concealment are movements used to confuse the opponent and hide one's own intentions.

54. INITIATIVE FOR THE ATTACK

Attacks may be executed on one's own initiative, or on the adversary's.

55. ATTACKS IN TIME

Attacks in time are offensive actions effected while the adversary is in the act of changing the placement of his weapon.

56. THE COUNTER-DISENGAGEMENT

The counter-disengagement is an action in time opposed to the disengagement.

57. FIRST AND SECOND INTENTION

Every simple and compound offensive attack may be accomplished in first or second intention. In first intention the movement is executed with the intent of reaching the target directly through the action itself. In second intention the movement is performed with the express purpose of provoking defensive responses against which counteractions can be applied.

CHAPTER 11

PEDAGOGY

58. METHOD OF INSTRUCTION

For the method of instruction see page 124.

Observation: The épée lesson should be devoted principally to actions against the arm.

A typical lesson begins with the commands: "First position!"; "Salute!"; "Mask on!"; "On guard!"; "Straight thrust to the top of the arm, via!"; "Hup!"; "On guard!"; "Disengagement to the external arm, via!"; "Hup!"; "On guard!"; "Glide, via!" (if the attack is parried and a riposte delivered to the leg); "Reassemble backward with an arrest to the top of the arm, via!"; "Hup!"; "On guard!"; "First position, rest!", etc.

To develop in the student a sense of épée fencing measure, it is useful at the beginning of the lesson to have him direct his first straight thrusts to the body, his second, to the crook of the arm, and his third, to the top of the wrist.

If the lesson is to be the mirror of combat, then, obviously, one thrust suffices to injure the opponent. But because some attacks will miss or may be deflected, it is wise to train the pupil to follow his first thrust immediately with a second, thus hitting two targets in rapid succession. For example, the student can be instructed to execute a feint direct to the internal arm and disengagement to the external arm with a lunge. After making his first touch, and without rising from the lunge, he should be directed to rotate his hand from fourth to second position and aim a second thrust to an exposed target area in the low line. As a variation on this combination of actions, the pupil can be instructed to follow the feint direct and disengagement to the external arm with a second hit by angulation to the bottom of the arm during recovery on guard, or an arrest to the top of the arm while reassembling backward.

In the advanced épée lesson the student's speed and accuracy in placing multiple touches should be developed. For instance, he can be directed to disengage in time to the internal arm with an advance, disengage in time to the external arm with another advance, and then parry third and riposte along the blade to the body (outside high line) with a lunge, followed immediately by an arrest to the top of the arm while reassembling backward. With this combination of actions the pupil scores four hits.

59. ORGANIZATION OF THE LESSON

For the organization of the lesson see page 127.

60. PREPARATION FOR COMBAT

Concerning the preparation for combat see page 128.

61. FREE FENCING

For free fencing see pages 128 and 129.

62. THE ASSAULT

Combat between two fencers is called an assault or bout.

63. DOUBLE HITS

Since fencing is based on the principles of the duel, it is apparent that double hits must be avoided because in actual combat they would result in both swordsmen being wounded.

64. THE LEFT-HANDED OPPONENT

In épée fencing the left-handed adversary does not present special problems, as long as his reversed target is viewed as though it were on a right-handed opponent.

65. FENCING TACTICS

For fencing tactics see page 133.

Observation: Because of the extended target, and the fact that right of way does not exist in épée fencing, the adversary should be approached with extreme caution. He must be forced with feints to open some part of the target. Once a parry or counterattack can be drawn, the opponent becomes vulnerable; if he parries, his parry can be eluded with a disengagement or deceive; if he counterattacks, his counterattack may be opposed with countertime.

Among the attacks directed to the body, the flanconade in second is especially recommended, since this action provides excellent cover, and offers little opportunity for a double hit.

Finally, it should be noted that in épée fencing, emphasis is generally placed on renewed attacks, counterattacks, countertime, and second intention.

APPENDICES

SAMPLE LESSONS

INTRODUCTION

The lessons that follow are intended to serve the teacher as models for developing his own lessons. The length of the lesson will depend, of course, upon the individual student's level of concentration and his physical condition. Each of the actions in these lessons should be repeated five or six times, or approximately one length of the fencing strip. To keep the text as brief as possible the actions in the foil and épée lessons are generally executed only in opposition to invitations and engagements in third; the same actions should, naturally, also be performed from invitations and engagements in first, second, and fourth. All commands must be loud, clear, and concise. The phrases in parentheses are included only for clarity; they are not spoken.

Lessons are usually classified according to degree of complexity as beginning, intermediate, and advanced. Beginning lessons introduce the basic elements of fencing; intermediate lessons refine fencing technique; and advanced lessons develop tactical skills. The training program of every accomplished fencer must include both intermediate and advanced lessons, and these should be alternated.

The lessons below do not represent a complete, progressive series of fencing exercises commencing with the first day's instruction; they are merely examples of the three types of lessons. Foil Lesson 1 must be preceded by one or more preliminary lessons in which the pupil learns the hand positions, how to salute, how to go on guard, and how to lunge. During this initial period he must also be instructed in fencing safety. He should be taught how to carry his weapon safely, and he must be cautioned never to fence without a mask and protective clothing.

Foil Lessons

Foil Lesson 1 (beginning) – Master's Commands

First position! Salute! Mask on! With the order "On!" place your weapon in line, and with the command "Guard!" assume the guard position, feet properly spaced, legs flexed, torso profiled, head up, shoulders down, right arm slightly bent and relaxed, elbow in, left arm up, hand bent forward at the wrist, thumb out, and fingers together. On! Guard!

(Master invites in third) Straight thrust (to the inside high line) in two movements, opposition to the inside! Blade in line! Lunge slowly at first until your legs are warmed up. Via! Hup! Remain in the lunge until I tell you to return on guard! Steady! On guard! Now in one motion!

(Master invites in third) Straight thrust (to the inside high line)! The sword arm must be completely extended before the foot moves! Keep the shoulders relaxed, and extend the arm smoothly, bringing the right hand gradually up to shoulder level! As the arm straightens, feel yourself drawn to the target, as though by a magnet. Keep the point directed to the target, but close the line, progressively moving the hand to the left! Halfway through the lunge, throw the left hand straight back, giving impetus to the thrust! The right foot should almost graze the surface of the floor as it moves forward along the line of direction. Keep the left foot flat against the floor, so that it can act as a brake! The force of the lunge will cause the foot to slide forward; press down to counteract this movement! Once your legs are warmed up the lunge should be explosive! Via! Hup! On guard!

(Master engages in third) Disengage (to the inside high line), opposition to the inside! Disengagement must be effected with the fingers alone, so that the point describes a tiny, semicircular movement, penetrating forward! There should be no hand, arm, or shoulder motion! Via! Hup! On guard!

Engage in third! Glide (to the outside high line), opposition to the outside! Extend the arm smoothly, maintaining constant blade contact, and slide along the opposing steel! Via! Hup! On guard!

Engage in third! Parry fourth and riposte by detaching the blade (to the inside high line)! In parrying, move the hand just far enough to the inside to close the line, and catch the incoming steel! Sink with the parry, and lean into the riposte! Drive the point home! During the parry and riposte the rear arm remains elevated! Hup!

Engage in third! Parry fourth and riposte by disengagement (to the out-side high line), opposition to the outside! Wait until you feel the pressure from my blade before disengaging! Hup!

Engage in third! Parry fourth and riposte along the blade (to the inside high line)! This is simply a riposte by glide; after parrying, maintain blade contact and slide along the opposing steel! Hup!

Engage in third! Parry fourth and riposte by flanconade in fourth, crossbar flat, opposition to the inside! Hup!

(Master invites in third) Straight thrust (to the inside high line), opposition to the inside! Via! Hup! Remain in the lunge until I tell you to return on guard! Steady! On guard!

(Master invites in third) Straight thrust (to the inside high line), opposition to the inside! More slowly! Via! Hup! On guard!

(Master invites in third) Straight thrust (to the inside high line), opposition to the inside! Even more slowly! Via! Hup! On guard! First position! Mask off! Salute! Shake hands!

Observation: When the student is on guard the master must check to see that the weapon is properly gripped; he should examine the pupil's shoulders to be certain that they are relaxed; and he must make adjustments, if necessary, to bring the torso, arms, and legs into correct guard position. During the lunge stress should be placed on precedence of point: the sword arm must be completely extended before the right foot is allowed to move. At the end of the lunge, the position of the torso, arms, and legs should again be checked, and corrections made.

FOIL LESSON 2 (BEGINNING) – MASTER'S COMMANDS

First position! Salute! Mask on! On! Guard!

(Master invites in third) Blade in line! Straight thrust (to the inside high line)! Via! Hup! On guard! Now in one motion!

(Master invites in third) Straight thrust (to the inside high line)! Via! Hup! On guard!

(Master engages in third) Disengage (to the inside high line)! Via! Hup! On guard!

Engage in third! Glide (to the outside high line)! Via! Hup! On guard!

Engage in third! Parry fourth and riposte by detaching the blade (to the inside high line)! Hup!

Engage in third! Parry fourth and riposte by disengagement (to the outside high line)! Wait for the pressure against your blade before riposting. Hup!

(Master invites in third) Feint direct and disengage (to the outside high line), opposition to the outside! The arm must be fully extended for the feint direct, and remain extended for the disengagement! Disengagement is effected solely with the fingers; there should be no motion in the hand, arm, and shoulder! Wait until the feint has provoked the parry, and then disengage just before your blade is caught! Make the disengagement as tiny as possible! Via! Hup! On guard!

(Master invites in third) Double feint direct and disengage (to the inside high line)! There is slight reserve in the arm with the feint direct, and full extension for the feint by disengagement and disengagement! Again, point motion must be accomplished with the fingers alone, and should be as tight as possible! Keep the point moving progressively forward! Via! Hup! On guard!

Engage in third! Parry fourth and third and riposte by feint direct to the low line and disengagement (to the high line)! Hup!

Engage in third! Parry fourth, third, and fourth and riposte by double feint direct and disengagement (to the inside high line)! Hup!

(Master invites in third) Straight thrust (to the inside high line)! Via! Hup! On guard!

(Master invites in third) Straight thrust (to the inside high line)! More slowly! Via! Hup! On guard!

(Master invites in third) Straight thrust (to the inside high line)! Even more slowly! Via! Hup! On guard! First position! Mask off! Salute! Shake hands!

Observation: Point motion in the feints must be kept as tight as possible. Parries should be precise, and ripostes must be immediate. The student should be alerted that the riposte by disengagement is triggered by pressure from the opposing blade. Although three simple parries are used as an exercise in this and the two following lessons, three or more simple parries must be avoided in combat; two simple parries and a circular parry provide a more secure defense.

FOIL LESSON 3 (BEGINNING) – MASTER'S COMMANDS

First position! Salute! Mask on! On! Guard!

(Master invites in third) Blade in line! Straight thrust (to the inside high line)! Via! Hup! On guard! Now in one motion!

(Master invites in third) Straight thrust (to the inside high line)! Via! Hup! On guard!

(Master engages in third) Disengage (to the inside high line)! Via! Hup! On guard!

Engage in third! Glide (to the outside high line)! Via! Hup! On guard!

Engage in third! Parry fourth and riposte along the blade (to the inside high line)! Hup!

(Master engages in third) Feint by disengagement and disengage (to the outside high line)! Via! Hup! On guard!

(Master engages in third) Double feint by disengagement and disengage (to the inside high line)! Via! Hup! On guard!

Engage in third! Parry fourth and third and riposte by feint by disengagement and disengagement (to the outside high line)!

Engage in third! Parry fourth, third, and fourth and riposte by double feint by disengagement and disengagement (to the outside high line)! Hup!

(Master invites in third) Straight thrust (to the inside high line)! Via! Hup! On guard!

(Master invites in third) Straight thrust (to the inside high line)! More slowly! Via! Hup! On guard!

(Master invites in third) Straight thrust (to the inside high line)! Even more slowly! Via! Hup! On guard! First position! Mask off! Salute! Shake hands!

FOIL LESSON 4 (BEGINNING) – MASTER'S COMMANDS

First position! Salute! Mask on! On! Guard!

(Master invites in third) Blade in line! Straight thrust (to the inside high line)! Via! Hup! On guard! Now in one motion!

(Master invites in third) Blade in line! Straight thrust (to the inside high line)! Via! Hup! On guard!

(Master engages in third) Disengage (to the inside high line)! Via! Hup! On guard!

Engage in third! Glide (to the outside high line)! Via! Hup! On guard!

Engage in third! Parry fourth and riposte along the blade (to the inside high line)! Hup!

Engage in third! Feint by glide and disengage (to the inside high line)! During the feint by glide maintain opposition to the right and blade contact! The blade must slide along the opposing steel! Wait until you feel pressure before disengaging! Via! Hup! On guard!

Engage in third! Double feint by glide and disengage (to the outside high line)! Via! Hup! On guard!

Engage in third! Parry fourth and third and riposte by feint along the blade and disengage (to the inside high line)! Hold the feint! Hup!

Engage in third! Parry fourth, third, and fourth and riposte by double feint along the blade and disengage (to the inside high line)! Hup!

(Master invites in third) Straight thrust (to the inside high line)! Via!
Hup! On guard!

(Master invites in third) Straight thrust (to the inside high line)! More
slowly! Via! Hup! On guard!

(Master invites in third) Straight thrust (to the inside high line)! Even
more slowly! Via! Hup! On guard! First position! Mask off! Salute!
Shake hands!

Lessons 2-4 should be repeated adding a retreat to the parry-riposte exercises, and an advance to the compound attacks with single and double
feints. With movement of the feet, care must be taken that the armed
hand always moves first, whether in the parrying action as the student
steps back, or in the attack as he steps forward. In the advance lunge, the
length of the step forward is critical: it must be short. To emphasize this,
the teacher should follow his commands for compound attacks with an
advance with the words, "short step, long lunge!" Particular attention must
be paid to the coordinated step.

During the course of the lesson the master should advance and retreat
periodically so that the student learns to maintain correct fencing measure. Occasionally, the teacher must parry the pupil's attack, so that he
will be forced to counterparry riposte from the lunge. In the parry-riposte
exercises the master should, every now and then, step back so that the
student must lunge with his riposte.

FOIL LESSON 5 (INTERMEDIATE) – MASTER'S COMMANDS

First position! Salute! Mask on! On! Guard!

(Master invites in third) Blade in line! Straight thrust (to the inside high
line)! Via! Hup! On guard! Now in one motion!

(Master invites in third) Straight thrust (to the inside high line)! Via!
Hup! On guard!

(Master engages in third) Disengage (to the inside high line)! Via! Hup!
On guard!

Engage in third! Glide (to the outside high line)! Via! Hup! On guard!

Engage in third! Parry fourth with a retreat and riposte along the blade (to the inside high line)! Hup!

Engage in third! Parry fourth and third with a retreat and riposte along the blade (to the outside high line)! Hup!

(Master invites in third) Feint direct and disengage (to the outside high line)! Via! Hup! On guard!

(Master invites in third) Double feint direct and disengage (to the inside high line)! Via! Hup! On guard!

Engage in third! Parry counter of third with a retreat and riposte along the blade (to the outside high line)! Hup!

(Master invites in third) Feint direct and deceive (to the inside high line)! Wait until the feint has provoked the circular parry, and then elude the parry with a tiny, circular motion of the point! The point must advance in a tight, spiral movement! Via! Hup! On guard!

(Master invites in third) Feint direct, deceive, and disengage (to the outside high line)! Via! Hup! On guard!

Engage in third! Parry counter of third with a retreat and riposte along the blade (to the outside high line)! Hup!

Engage in third! Parry double counter of third with a retreat and riposte along the blade (to the outside high line)! Hup!

Engage in third! Parry double counter of third with a retreat and riposte by disengagement (to the inside high line)! Hup!

Engage in third! Parry double counter of third with a retreat and riposte by feint by disengagement and disengagement (to the outside high line)! Hup!

Engage in third! Parry double counter of third with a retreat and riposte by feint by disengagement and deceive (to the inside high line)! Hup!

(Master invites in third) Straight thrust (to the inside high line)! Via! Hup! On guard!

(Master invites in third) Straight thrust (to the inside high line)! More slowly! Via! Hup! On guard!

(Master invites in third) Straight thrust (to the inside high line)! Even more slowly! Via! Hup! On guard! First position! Mask off! Salute! Shake hands!

FOIL LESSON 6 (INTERMEDIATE)

Lesson 5 is repeated with an advance added to the compound attacks with single and double feints.

FOIL LESSON 7 (INTERMEDIATE) – MASTER'S COMMANDS

First position! Salute! Mask on! On! Guard!

(Master invites in third) Blade in line! Straight thrust (to the inside high line)! Via! Hup! On guard! Now in one motion!

(Master invites in third) Straight thrust (to the inside high line)! Via! Hup! On guard!

(Master engages in third) Disengage (to the inside high line)! Via! Hup! On guard!

Engage in third! Glide (to the outside high line)! Via! Hup! On guard!

Engage in third! Parry fourth with a retreat and riposte along the blade (to the inside high line)! Hup!

Engage in third! Parry fourth and third with a retreat and riposte along the blade (to the outside high line)! Hup!

(Master invites in third) Feint direct and disengage (to the outside high line)! Via! Hup! On guard!

(Master invites in third) Double feint direct and disengage (to the inside high line)! Via! Hup! On guard!

Engage in third! Parry counter of third with a retreat and riposte along the blade (to the outside high line)! Hup!

Engage in third! Parry counter of third and fourth with a retreat and riposte along the blade (to the inside high line)! Hup!

Engage in third! Parry fourth and counter of fourth with a retreat and riposte along the blade (to the inside high line)! Hup!

(Master invites in third) Feint direct and deceive (to the inside high line)! Via! Hup! On guard!

(Master invites in third) Feint direct, deceive, and disengage (to the outside high line)! Via! Hup! On guard!

(Master invites in third) Double feint direct and deceive (to the outside high line)! Via! Hup! On guard!

(Master invites in third) Feint direct and double deceive (to the inside high line)! Via! Hup! On guard!

(Master invites in third) Straight thrust (to the inside high line)! Via! Hup! On guard!

(Master invites in third) Straight thrust (to the inside high line)! More slowly! Via! Hup! On guard!

(Master invites in third) Straight thrust (to the inside high line)! Even more slowly! Via! Hup! On guard! First position! Mask off! Salute! Shake hands!

Foil Lesson 8 (intermediate)

Lesson 7 is repeated with an advance added to the compound attacks with single and double feints.

Foil Lesson 9 (intermediate) – Master's Commands

First position! Salute! Mask on! On! Guard!

(Master invites in third) Blade in line! Straight thrust (to the inside high line)! Via! Hup! On guard! Now in one motion!

(Master invites in third) Straight thrust (to the inside high line)! Via! Hup! On guard!

(Master engages in third) Disengage (to the inside high line)! Via! Hup! On guard!

Engage in third! Glide (to the outside high line)! Via! Hup! On guard!

Engage in third! Parry fourth with a retreat and riposte along the blade (to the inside high line)! Hup!

Engage in third! Parry counter of third with a retreat and riposte along the blade (to the outside high line)! Hup!

(Master engages in third) Cut-over (to the inside high line)! Lunge late! Via! Hup! On guard!

(Master invites in third) Feint direct and cut-over (to the outside high line)! Via! Hup! On guard!

(Master invites in third) Feint direct and cut-over (to the low line)! Via! Hup! On guard!

(Master engages in third) Feint by cut-over and disengage (to the outside high line)! Via! Hup! On guard!

Engage in third! Parry fourth with a retreat and riposte by cut-over (to the outside high line)! Hup!

Engage in third! Parry counter of third with a retreat and riposte by cut-over (to the inside high line)! Hup!

(Master invites in third) Straight thrust (to the inside high line)! Via! Hup! On guard!

(Master invites in third) Straight thrust (to the inside high line)! More slowly! Via! Hup! On guard!

(Master invites in third) Straight thrust (to the inside high line)! Even more slowly! Via! Hup! On guard! First position! Mask off! Salute! Shake hands!

Observation: In executing the cut-over, movement should be centered primarily at the wrist, and the lunge must be delayed until the sword arm is fully extended. As a riposte, the cut-over, like the disengagement, is triggered by blade pressure; the parry and riposte by cut-over flow together in a continuous motion.

FOIL LESSON 10 (INTERMEDIATE)

Lesson 9 is repeated with an advance added to the compound attacks with a feint.

FOIL LESSON 11 (INTERMEDIATE) – MASTER'S COMMANDS

First position! Salute! Mask on! On! Guard!

(Master invites in third) Blade in line! Straight thrust (to the inside high line)! Via! Hup! On guard! Now in one motion!

(Master invites in third) Straight thrust (to the inside high line)! Via! Hup! On guard!

(Master engages in third) Disengage (to the inside high line)! Via! Hup! On guard!

Engage in third! Glide (to the outside high line)! Via! Hup! On guard!

Engage in third! Parry fourth with a retreat and riposte along the blade (to the inside high line)! Hup!

Engage in third! Parry fourth with a retreat and riposte by flanconade in fourth! Hup!

Engage in third! Change engagement and glide (to the inside high line)! Via! Hup! On guard!

Engage in third! Double change of engagement and glide (to the outside high line)! Via! Hup! On guard!

Engage in third! Transport to first and glide (to the inside low line)! Via! Hup! On guard!

Engage in third! Envelopment in third and glide (to the outside high line)! Via! Hup! On guard!

(Master engages in first) Parry ceding parry of third and riposte (to the outside high line)! Relax the arm and lower the hand! Hup!

(Master engages in second) Parry ceding parry of fourth and riposte (to the inside high line)! Yield, hand low, and point high! Hup!

(Master invites in third) Straight thrust (to the inside high line)! Via! Hup! On guard!

(Master invites in third) Straight thrust (to the inside high line)! More slowly! Via! Hup! On guard!

(Master invites in third) Straight thrust (to the inside high line)! Even more slowly! Via! Hup! On guard! First position! Mask off! Salute! Shake hands!

Observation: Changes of engagement, transports, and envelopments must be effected with the strong against the weak. Each action should be tightly controlled, with the point of the blade close to the opposing steel.

FOIL LESSON 12 (INTERMEDIATE) – MASTER'S COMMANDS

First position! Salute! Mask on! On! Guard!

(Master invites in third) Blade in line! Straight thrust (to the inside high line)! Via! Hup! On guard! Now in one motion!

(Master invites in third) Straight thrust (to the inside high line)! Via! Hup! On guard!

(Master engages in third) Disengage (to the inside high line)! Via! Hup! On guard!

Engage in third! Glide (to the outside high line)! Via! Hup! On guard!

Engage in third! Parry fourth with a retreat and riposte along the blade (to the inside high line)! Hup!

Engage in third! Parry fourth with a retreat and riposte by flanconade in fourth! Hup!

(Master engages in third) Feint by disengagement and disengage (to the outside high line)! Via! Hup! On guard!

(Master engages in third) Feint by disengagement and deceive (to the inside high line)! Via! Hup! On guard!

(Master places the weapon in line) Simple beat in fourth and straight thrust (to the inside high line)! Via! Hup! On guard!

(Master places the weapon in line) Simple beat in fourth and disengage (to the outside high line)! Via! Hup! On guard!

(Master places the weapon in line) Simple beat in fourth and feint by disengagement and disengage (to the inside high line)! Via! Hup! On guard!

(Master places the weapon in line) Simple beat in fourth and feint by disengagement and deceive (to the outside high line)! Via! Hup! On guard!

(Master invites in third) Straight thrust (to the inside high line); as the attack is parried in retreat, and the riposte delayed, recover forward with a renewed attack; feint by disengagement and disengage (to the inside high line)! Via! Hup! On guard!

(Master invites in third) Straight thrust (to the inside high line); as the attack is parried in retreat, and the riposte delayed, recover forward with a renewed attack; feint by disengagement and deceive (to the outside high line)! Via! Hup! On guard!

(Master invites in third) Straight thrust (to the inside high line)! Via! Hup! On guard!

(Master invites in third) Straight thrust (to the inside high line)! More slowly! Via! Hup! On guard!

(Master invites in third) Straight thrust (to the inside high line)! Even more slowly! Via! Hup! On guard! First position! Mask off! Salute! Shake hands!

Observation: The beat must be performed with a flexed sword arm; it should be tightly controlled and sharp, striking the opposing steel at one point only, strong against medium. In the renewed attack with a recovery forward, the student, after his first lunge, must return to a correct guard position, with his feet properly spaced, and his rear arm elevated, before making the second lunge.

FOIL LESSON 13 (ADVANCED) – MASTER'S COMMANDS

First position! Salute! Mask on! On! Guard!

(Master invites in third) Blade in line! Straight thrust (to the inside high line)! Via! Hup! On guard! Now in one motion!

(Master invites in third) Straight thrust (to the inside high line)! Via! Hup! On guard!

(Master engages in third) Disengage (to the inside high line)! Via! Hup! On guard!

Engage in third! Glide (to the outside high line)! Via! Hup! On guard!

Engage in third! Parry fourth with a retreat and riposte along the blade (to the inside high line)! Hup!

Engage in third! Parry counter of third with a retreat and riposte along the blade (to the outside high line)! Hup! Retreat!

(Master places the weapon in line) Blade seizure in fourth with an advance and glide (to the inside high line)! Via! Hup! On guard! Retreat!

Weapon in line! As I attempt to engage your blade in fourth with an advance, disengage in time! Hup! On guard! Retreat!

(Master places the weapon in line) Attempt to engage my blade in fourth with an advance, as I disengage in time, parry counter of fourth in countertime and riposte along the blade (to the inside high line)! Via! Hup! Retreat!

Weapon in line! As I attempt to engage your blade in fourth with an advance, feint by disengagement in time and deceive (to the outside high line)! Hup! On guard!

(Master invites in third) Straight thrust (to the inside high line)! Via! Hup! On guard!

(Master invites in third) Straight thrust (to the inside high line)! More slowly! Via! Hup! On guard!

(Master invites in third) Straight thrust (to the inside high line)! Even more slowly! Via! Hup! On guard! Mask off! Salute! Shake hands!

Observation: It should be noted that the disengagement in time and feint by disengagement in time are executed with a lunge, while the parry in countertime is performed from the guard position. Mention must also be made here of contraries, so that the student understands that countertime is the contrary of the counterattack, and that the feint in time is the contrary of countertime.

Foil Lesson 14 (advanced) – Master's Commands

First position! Salute! Mask on! On! Guard!

(Master invites in third) Blade in line! Straight thrust (to the inside high line)! Via! Hup! On guard! Now in one motion!

(Master invites in third) Straight thrust (to the inside high line)! Via! Hup! On guard!

In time, as I move from engagement in fourth to invitation in third, the instant that you sense a break in blade contact, execute a straight thrust (to the inside high line)! Hup! On guard!

In time, as I attempt to engage your blade in fourth, disengage (to the outside high line)! Hup! On guard! Retreat!

Weapon in line! In time, as I attempt to engage your blade in fourth with an advance, feint by disengagement and disengage (to the inside high line)! Hup! On guard! Retreat!

Weapon in line! In time, as I attempt to engage your blade in fourth with an advance, feint by disengagement and deceive (to the outside high line)! Hup! On guard! Retreat!

Weapon in line! In time, as I attempt to engage your blade in fourth with an advance, feint by disengagement and disengage (to the inside high line) if I execute a simple parry, or deceive (to the outside high line) if I perform a circular parry! Hold the feint long enough to determine whether I oppose the feint with a simple or circular parry! Hup! On guard! Retreat!

Weapon in line! In time, as I attempt to engage your blade in fourth with an advance, feint by disengagement and disengage (to the inside high line); when I parry and riposte, remain in the lunge, and counterparry riposte: fourth, direct, fourth, and disengage (to the outside high line)! Hup! On guard!

(Master invites in third) Straight thrust (to the inside high line)! Via! Hup! On guard!

(Master invites in third) Straight thrust (to the inside high line)! More slowly! Via! Hup! On guard!

(Master invites in third) Straight thrust (to the inside high line)! Even more slowly! Via! Hup! On guard! First position! Mask off! Salute! Shake hands!

Observation: The same compound attacks in time can be performed with mobility. This is accomplished by advancing and retreating until the master attempts to engage. Movement on the fencing strip must be unhurried and smooth.

FOIL LESSON 15 (ADVANCED) – MASTER'S COMMANDS

First position! Salute! Mask on! On! Guard!

(Master invites in third) Blade in line! Straight thrust (to the inside high line)! Via! Hup! On guard! Now in one motion!

(Master invites in third) Straight thrust (to the inside high line)! Via! Hup! On guard!

In time, as I move from engagement in fourth to invitation in third, execute a straight thrust (to the inside high line)! Hup! On guard!

In time, as I attempt to engage your blade in fourth, disengage (to the outside high line)! Hup! On guard!

In time, simple beat in fourth and straight thrust (to the inside high line)! Hup! On guard! Retreat!

In time, simple beat in fourth and straight thrust (to the inside high line) with an advance lunge! Hup! On guard! Retreat!

In time, simple beat in fourth and straight thrust (to the inside high line) with a jump lunge! Short jump! Hup! On guard! Retreat!

In time, and with mobility, simple beat in fourth and straight thrust (to the inside high line) with a jump lunge! Hup! On guard! Retreat!

In time, and with mobility, simple beat in fourth and straight thrust (to the inside high line) with a jump lunge; as the attack is parried in retreat, and the riposte delayed, recover forward with a renewed attack; feint by disengagement and disengage (to the inside high line)! Hup! On guard! Retreat!

In time, and with mobility, simple beat in fourth and straight thrust (to the inside high line) with a jump lunge; as the attack is parried in retreat, and the riposte delayed, recover forward with a renewed attack; feint by disengagement and deceive (to the outside high line)! Hup! On guard! Retreat!

In time, and with mobility, simple beat in fourth and straight thrust (to the inside high line) with a jump lunge; as the attack is parried in retreat, and the riposte delayed, recover forward with a renewed attack; feint by disengagement and disengage (to the inside high line) if I execute a simple parry, or deceive (to the outside high line) if I perform a circular parry. Hup! On guard!

Engage in third! Parry counter of third with a retreat and riposte along the blade (to the outside high line)! Hup!

Engage in third! Parry double counter of third with a retreat and riposte along the blade (to the outside high line)! Hup!

Engage in third! Parry double counter of third with a retreat, change engagement to fourth and riposte by glide (to the inside high line). Hup!

Engage in third! Parry double counter of third with a retreat, change engagement to fourth and riposte by flanconade in fourth. Hup! On guard!

Engage in third! Parry double counter of third with a retreat, change engagement in fourth and riposte by flanconade in fourth; when I counterparry and riposte, remain in the lunge, and counterparry riposte: fourth, direct, fourth, and disengage (to the outside high line)! Hup! On guard!

(Master invites in third) Straight thrust (to the inside high line)! Via! Hup! On guard!

(Master invites in third) Straight thrust (to the inside high line)! More slowly! Via! Hup! On guard!

(Master invites in third) Straight thrust (to the inside high line)! Even more slowly! Via! Hup! On guard! First position! Mask off! Salute! Shake hands!

FOIL LESSON 16 (ADVANCED) – MASTER'S COMMANDS

First position! Salute! Mask on! On! Guard!

(Master invites in third) Blade in line! Straight thrust (to the inside high line)! Via! Hup! On guard! Now in one motion!

(Master invites in third) Straight thrust (to the inside high line)! Via! Hup! On guard!

(Master engages in fourth) Without commands, execute the appropriate counteractions! (As he shifts from engagement in fourth to invitation in third – in time, straight thrust to the inside high line) Hup! On guard!

(Master invites in third; as he attempts to engage in fourth – in time, disengagement to the outside high line) Hup! On guard! (Master signals a retreat with his hand)

(Master invites in third; as he attempts to engage in fourth with an advance – in time, feint by disengagement and disengagement to the inside high line) Hup! On guard! (Master signals a retreat with his hand)

(Master invites in third; as he attempts to engage in fourth with an advance – in time, feint by disengagement and deceive to the outside high line) Hup! On guard! (Master signals a retreat with his hand)

(Master invites in third; as he attempts to engage in fourth with an advance – in time, feint by disengagement and disengagement or deceive, depending upon the teacher's parry) Hup! On guard! (Master signals a retreat with his hand)

(Master invites in third; as he attempts to engage in fourth with an advance – in time, feint by disengagement and disengagement or deceive, depending upon the teacher's parry; periodically, the student's final action is parried so that he is forced to counterparry riposte from the lunge) Hup! On guard!

(Master invites in third) Straight thrust (to the inside high line)! Via! Hup! On guard!

(Master invites in third) Straight thrust (to the inside high line)! More slowly! Via! Hup! On guard!

(Master invites in third) Straight thrust (to the inside high line)! Even more slowly! Via! Hup! On guard! First position! Mask off! Salute! Shake hands!

Sabre Lessons

After several years of serious preparation with the foil, the fencer may be permitted to commence work with the sabre. Again, his preliminary lessons must be concerned with basic elements, such as holding the weapon properly, hand positions, and placement of the cut. From the beginning, emphasis should be placed on mobility and control of fencing measure.

It is important to encourage the fencer who wishes to specialize in sabre to continue his foil lessons.

Sabre Lesson 1 (beginning) – Master's Commands

First position! Salute! Mask on! On! Guard!

(Master invites in third) Blade in line! Direct point thrust (to the inside chest)! Hand in first in second position, opposition to the right, arm and blade forming an obtuse angle! Via! Hup! On guard! Now in one motion!

(Master invites in third) Direct point thrust (to the inside chest)! Via! Hup! On guard!

(Master engages in third) Disengage with the point (to the inside chest)! Make the disengagement as small as possible, using the fingers alone! Via! Hup! On guard!

Engage in third! Glide with the point (to the outside chest)! Via! Hup! On guard!

(Master invites in second) Direct cut to the head! Hand in third position, in line with the shoulder, and shoulder high! Snap the wrist downward and push the cut lightly across the top of the head! The cut must be executed with the first third of the blade! Via! Hup! On guard!

(Master invites in second) Direct cut to the right or outside cheek! Hand in second position, and to the right! Push the cut forward! Via! Hup! On guard!

(Master invites in third) Direct cut to the left or inside cheek! Hand in fourth position! Pull the cut backward, and, in a continuous motion, return to the guard in third! Do not permit your hand to drift toward the inside so that the arm is exposed! Via! Hup! On guard!

(Master invites in third) Direct cut to the chest! Hand in third in fourth position! Draw the cut diagonally across the chest, and, in a continuous movement, return to the guard in third! Reach out for the cut! Do not exaggerate the hand motion, and keep the cut short! Via! Hup! On guard!

(Master invites in third) Direct cut to the abdomen! Hand in fourth position! Reach out and pull the cut backward, returning, in a continuous motion, to the guard in third! Via! Hup! On guard!

(Master invites in fifth) Direct cut to the flank! Hand in second position, and to the right! Push the cut forward! Via! Hup! On guard!

Invite in third! Parry first and riposte by direct cut to the flank! Keep the point forward as you parry, and the hand to the right as you riposte! The point must travel a semicircular path from the invitation in third to the parry in first! Hup!

Invite in first! Parry second and riposte by direct cut to the right cheek! Remember, sink with the parry and lean into the riposte! Hup!

Invite in fourth! Parry third and riposte by direct cut to the head! Hup!

Invite in third! Parry fourth and riposte by direct cut to the right cheek! Hup!

Invite in third! Parry fifth and riposte by direct cut to the flank! Keep the point forward in the parry! Again, the point must follow a semicircular route from the invitation in third to the parry of fifth! Hup!

Invite in third! Parry sixth and riposte by direct cut to the abdomen! Hup!

(Master invites in third) Direct point thrust (to the inside chest)! Via! Hup! On guard!

(Master invites in third) Direct point thrust (to the inside chest)! More slowly! Via! Hup! On guard!

(Master invites in third) Direct point thrust (to the inside chest)! Even more slowly! Via! Hup! On guard! First position! Mask off! Salute! Shake hands!

Observation: When the student is on guard the master should check to see that the sabre is gripped correctly. Stress must be placed on precedence of point and cut; the sword arm should be fully extended before the leading foot is permitted to move. The rear hand must remain closed in a fist, and rest on the left hip, both in the guard and lunge.

SABRE LESSON 2 (BEGINNING) – MASTER'S COMMANDS

First position! Salute! Mask on! On! Guard!

(Master invites in third) Blade in line! Direct point thrust (to the inside chest)! Via! Hup! On guard! Now in one motion!

(Master invites in third) Direct point thrust (to the inside chest)! Via! Hup! On guard!

(Master engages in third) Disengage with the point (to the inside chest)! Via! Hup! On guard!

Engage in third! Glide with the point (to the outside chest)! Via! Hup! On guard!

(Master invites in second) Direct cut to the head! Via! Hup! On guard!

(Master invites in fifth) Direct cut to the flank! Via! Hup! On guard!

(Master invites in third) Direct cut to the abdomen! Via! Hup! On guard!

(Master invites in third) Cuts to the arm may be executed from the guard, without a lunge. Direct cut with the cut to the internal arm! Hand in third in fourth position! Via! Hup!

(Master invites in third) Direct cut with the counter-cut to the internal arm! Hand in second in third! Reach out, and then draw the hand back! Via! Hup!

(Master invites in fourth) Direct cut with the cut to the external arm! Hand in first in second position! Via! Hup!

(Master invites in fourth) Direct cut with the cut to the top of the arm! Hand in third position! Via! Hup!

(Master invites in fifth) Direct cut with the cut to the bottom of the arm! Hand in first in second position! Via! Hup!

(Master invites in fifth) Direct cut with the counter-cut to the bottom of the arm! Hand in second in third position! Again, reach out, and then draw the hand back! Via! Hup!

Invite in second! Parry first with a retreat and riposte by direct cut to the flank! Hup!

Invite in first! Parry second with a retreat and riposte by direct cut to the right cheek! Hup!

Invite in second! Parry fifth with a retreat and riposte by direct cut to the flank! Hup!

(Master invites in third) Feint direct point thrust and disengage with the point (to the outside chest)! Hand in second position for the feint direct point thrust, and rotated to first in second position for the disengagement with the point! The hand must be kept to the right, and the arm fully extended for the feint direct point thrust and disengagement with the point! Via! Hup! On guard!

(Master invites in third) Double feint direct point thrust and disengage with the point (to the inside chest)! Hand in second position for the feint direct point thrust and feint by disengagement with the point, and turned to first in second position for the disengagement with the point! There should be a little reserve in the arm during the feint direct point thrust, and complete extension for the feint by disengagement with the point and disengagement with the point! Via! Hup! On guard!

Invite in third! Parry fourth and third with a retreat and riposte by direct cut to the head! Hup!

Invite in third! Parry fourth, third, and fourth with a retreat and riposte by direct cut to the right cheek! Hup!

(Master invites in third) Direct point thrust (to the inside chest)! Via! Hup! On guard!

(Master invites in third) Direct point thrust (to the inside chest)! More slowly! Via! Hup! On guard!

(Master invites in third) Direct point thrust (to the inside chest)! Even more slowly! Via! Hup! On guard! First position! Mask off! Salute! Shake hands!

Observation: Periodically, the master must parry the student's attack, so that he will be forced to counterparry riposte from the lunge. Particular emphasis should be placed on developing the parry combination of first, second, and fifth. In each of these parries the arm must be only slightly flexed, with the point of the weapon directed forward, and in a threatening position.

SABRE LESSON 3 (BEGINNING)

Lesson 2 is repeated with an advance added to the compound attacks with single and double feints. In sabre, as in foil, the teacher must stress the importance of a short step and long lunge.

SABRE LESSON 4 (INTERMEDIATE) – MASTER'S COMMANDS

First position! Salute! Mask on! On! Guard!

(Master invites in third) Blade in line! Direct point thrust (to the inside chest)! Via! Hup! On guard! Now in one motion!

(Master invites in third) Direct point thrust (to the inside chest)! Via! Hup! On guard!

(Master engages in third) Disengage with the point (to the inside chest)! Via! Hup! On guard!

Engage in third! Glide with the point (to the outside chest)! Via! Hup! On guard!

(Master invites in second) Direct cut to the head! Via! Hup! On guard!

(Master invites in fifth) Direct cut to the flank! Via! Hup! On guard!

(Master invites in third) Direct cut to the abdomen! Via! Hup! On guard!

Engage in first! Circular cut to the head (from the left)! Movement should be centered at the elbow! Weapon, hand, and forearm must function as one unit, with the fingers tightening progressively as the action nears completion! Lunge late! Via! Hup! On guard!

Engage in second! Circular cut to the head (from the right)! Again, the elbow is the point of rotation! Concentrate on keeping the elbow high throughout the action! Via! Hup! On guard!

(Master engages in third) Descending cut to the head (inside)! Lunge late! Via! Hup! On guard!

(Master engages in fourth) Descending cut to the head (outside)! Via! Hup! On guard!

Invite in first! Parry counter of first with a retreat and riposte by circular cut to the head! The circular parry is effected with the hand and forearm! Parry and riposte must be combined in a continuous motion! Hup!

Invite in second! Parry counter of second with a retreat and riposte along the blade with the point (to the flank)! Hup!

Invite in third! Parry counter of third with a retreat and riposte along the blade with the point (to the outside chest)! Hup!

Invite in fourth! Parry counter of fourth with a retreat and riposte by direct cut to the right cheek! Hup!

Invite in fifth! Parry counter of fifth with a retreat and riposte by direct cut to the flank! Hup!

(Master invites in third) Feint direct point thrust and disengage with the point (to the outside chest)! Via! Hup! On guard!

(Master invites in third) Feint direct point thrust and deceive with the point (to the inside chest)! Via! Hup! On guard!

Invite in third! Parry fourth and counter of fourth and riposte by direct cut to the right cheek! Hup!

Invite in third! Parry counter of third and fourth and riposte by direct cut to the right cheek! Hup!

(Master invites in third) Feint direct point thrust and circular cut to the head (from the right)! Via! Hup! On guard!

(Master invites in third) Feint direct point thrust and descending cut to the head (outside)! Via! Hup! On guard!

(Master invites in third) Direct point thrust (to the inside chest)! Via! Hup! On guard!

(Master invites in third) Direct point thrust (to the inside chest)! More slowly! Via! Hup! On guard!

(Master invites in third) Direct point thrust (to the inside chest)! Even more slowly! Via! Hup! On guard! First position! Mask off! Salute! Shake hands!

SABRE LESSON 5 (INTERMEDIATE)

Lesson 4 is repeated with an advance added to the compound attacks.

SABRE LESSON 6 (INTERMEDIATE) – MASTER'S COMMANDS

First position! Salute! Mask on! On! Guard!

(Master invites in third) Blade in line! Direct point thrust (to the inside chest)! Via! Hup! On guard! Now in one motion!

(Master invites in third) Direct point thrust (to the inside chest)! Via! Hup! On guard!

(Master engages in third) Disengage with the point (to the inside chest)! Via! Hup! On guard!

Engage in third! Glide with the point (to the outside chest)! Via! Hup! On guard!

(Master invites in second) Direct cut to the head! Via! Hup! On guard!

(Master invites in fifth) Direct cut to the flank! Via! Hup! On guard!

(Master invites in third) Direct cut to the abdomen! Via! Hup! On guard!

Engage in first! Circular cut to the head (from the left)! Via! Hup! On guard!

Engage in second! Circular cut to the head (from the right)! Via! Hup! On guard!

Engage in third! Circular cut to the abdomen! Via! Hup! On guard!

Engage in fourth! Circular cut to the flank! Via! Hup! On guard!

Invite in third! Parry fourth with a retreat and riposte with the point (to the inside chest)! Hup!

Invite in third! Parry fourth with a retreat and riposte by direct cut to the right cheek! Hup!

Invite in third! Parry fourth with a retreat and riposte by direct cut to the head! Hup!

Invite in third! Parry fourth with a retreat and riposte by direct cut to the left cheek! Hup!

Invite in third! Parry fourth with a retreat and riposte by direct cut to the chest! Hup!

Invite in third! Parry fourth with a retreat and riposte by direct cut to the abdomen! Hup!

Invite in third! Parry fourth with a retreat and riposte by circular cut to the flank! Hup!

(Master invites in second) Feint head cut, cut flank! Arm fully extended for the feint head cut, and hand shoulder high! Rotate the hand from third to second position, shifting it to the right for the flank cut! Via! Hup! On guard!

(Master invites in fifth) Feint flank cut, cut head! Via! Hup! On guard!

(Master invites in second) Double feint head cut, flank cut, cut head! There should be a little reserve in the arm for the feint head cut, and full extension for the feint flank cut and the head cut! Via! Hup! On guard!

(Master invites in fifth) Double feint flank cut, head cut, cut flank! Via! Hup! On guard!

Invite in second! Parry fifth and second with a retreat and riposte by feint right cheek cut, cut flank! Hup!

Invite in fifth! Parry second and fifth with a retreat and riposte by feint flank cut, cut right cheek! Hup!

Invite in second! Parry fifth, second, and fifth with a retreat and riposte by feint flank cut, cut right cheek! Hup!

Invite in fifth! Parry second, fifth, and second with a retreat and riposte by feint right cheek cut, cut flank! Hup!

(Master invites in third) Direct point thrust (to the inside chest)! Via! Hup! On guard!

(Master invites in third) Direct point thrust (to the inside chest)! More slowly! Via! Hup! On guard!

(Master invites in third) Direct point thrust (to the inside chest)! Even more slowly! Via! Hup! On guard! First position! Mask off! Salute! Shake hands!

SABRE LESSON 7 (INTERMEDIATE)

Lesson 6 is repeated with an advance added to the compound attacks.

SABRE LESSON 8 (INTERMEDIATE) – MASTER'S COMMANDS

First position! Salute! Mask on! On! Guard!

(Master invites in third) Blade in line! Direct point thrust (to the inside chest)! Via! Hup! On guard! Now in one motion!

(Master invites in third) Direct point thrust (to the inside chest)! Via! Hup! On guard!

(Master engages in third) Disengage with the point (to the inside chest)! Via! Hup! On guard!

Engage in third! Glide with the point (to the outside chest)! Via! Hup! On guard!

(Master invites in second) Direct cut to the head! Via! Hup! On guard!

(Master invites in fifth) Direct cut to the flank! Via! Hup! On guard!

(Master invites in third) Direct cut to the abdomen! Via! Hup! On guard!

Engage in first! Circular cut to the head (from the left)! Via! Hup! On guard!

(Master engages in third) Descending cut to the head (inside)! Via! Hup! On guard!

(Master engages in third) Parry ceding parry of first with a retreat and riposte by circular cut to the head (inside)! Hup!

(Master engages in second) Parry ceding parry of fourth with a retreat and riposte by direct cut to the right cheek! Hup!

Engage in second! Change engagement to third and glide with the point (to the outside chest)! Via! Hup! On guard!

Engage in third! Change engagement to second and glide with the point (to the flank)! Via! Hup! On guard!

Engage in third! Transport to first and circular cut to the head (from the left)! Via! Hup! On guard!

Engage in second! Transport to fourth and direct cut to the right cheek! Via! Hup! On guard!

(Master invites in third) Direct point thrust (to the inside chest)! Via! Hup! On guard!

(Master invites in third) Direct point thrust (to the inside chest)! More slowly! Via! Hup! On guard!

(Master invites in third) Direct point thrust (to the inside chest)! Even more slowly! Via! Hup! On guard! First position! Mask off! Salute! Shake hands!

SABRE LESSON 9 (INTERMEDIATE) – MASTER'S COMMANDS

First position! Salute! Mask on! On! Guard!

(Master invites in third) Blade in line! Direct point thrust (to the inside chest)! Via! Hup! On guard! Now in one motion!

(Master invites in third) Direct point thrust (to the inside chest)! Via! Hup! On guard!

(Master engages in third) Disengage with the point (to the inside chest)! Via! Hup! On guard!

Engage in third! Glide with the point (to the outside chest)! Via! Hup! On guard!

(Master invites in second) Direct cut to the head! Via! Hup! On guard!

(Master invites in fifth) Direct cut to the flank! Via! Hup! On guard!

(Master invites in third) Direct cut to the abdomen! Via! Hup! On guard!

Engage in first! Circular cut to the head (from the left)! Via! Hup! On guard!

(Master engages in third) Descending cut to the head (inside)! Via! Hup! On guard!

Invite in fourth! Parry third with a retreat and riposte by circular cut to the abdomen! Hup!

Invite in third! Parry fourth with a retreat and riposte by circular cut to the flank! Hup!

(Master places the weapon in line) Simple beat in fourth with the cut and direct cut to the right cheek! Via! Hup! On guard!

(Master places the weapon in line) Simple beat in fourth with the back edge of the blade and direct cut to the right cheek! Via! Hup! On guard! Retreat!

(Master places the weapon in line) Simple beat in fourth with the back edge of the blade and direct cut to the right cheek with an advance lunge! Via! Hup! On guard! Retreat!

(Master places the weapon in line) Simple beat in fourth with the back edge of the blade and direct cut to the right cheek with a jump lunge! Via! Hup! On guard!

(Master places the weapon in line) Grazing beat in fourth with the back edge of the blade and cut to the flank! Via! Hup! On guard!

Engage in third! Expulsion in third and direct cut to the head! Via! Hup! On guard!

(Master invites in third) Direct point thrust (to the inside chest); as the attack is parried in retreat, and the riposte delayed, recover forward with a renewed attack; feint by disengagement with the point (to the outside chest) and disengage with the point (to the inside chest)! Via! Hup! On guard!

(Master invites in third) Direct point thrust (to the inside chest); as the attack is parried in retreat, and the riposte delayed, recover forward with a renewed attack; feint by disengagement with the point (to the outside chest) and descending cut to the head (inside)! Via! Hup! On guard!

(Master invites in third) Direct point thrust (to the inside chest)! Via! Hup! On guard!

(Master invites in third) Direct point thrust (to the inside chest)! More slowly! Via! Hup! On guard!

(Master invites in third) Direct point thrust (to the inside chest)! Even more slowly! Via! Hup! On guard! First position! Mask off! Salute! Shake hands!

Observation: When the student has mastered the renewed attack with two lunges, he should be directed to substitute a running attack for the second lunge. It is important to note that he must pass on the teacher's inside.

SABRE LESSON 10 (ADVANCED) – MASTER'S COMMANDS

First position! Salute! Mask on! On! Guard!

(Master invites in third) Blade in line! Direct point thrust (to the inside chest)! Via! Hup! On guard! Now in one motion!

(Master invites in third) Direct point thrust (to the inside chest)! Via! Hup! On guard!

(Master engages in third) Disengage with the point (to the inside chest)! Via! Hup! On guard!

Engage in third! Glide with the point (to the outside chest)! Via! Hup! On guard!

(Master invites in second) Direct cut to the head! Via! Hup! On guard!

(Master invites in fifth) Direct cut to the flank! Via! Hup! On guard!

(Master invites in third) Direct cut to the abdomen! Via! Hup! On guard!

Engage in first! Circular cut to the head (from the left)! Via! Hup! On guard!

(Master engages in third) Descending cut to the head (inside)! Via! Hup! On guard!

Invite in fourth! Parry third with a retreat and riposte by circular cut to the abdomen! Hup!

Invite in third! Parry fourth with a retreat and riposte by circular cut to the flank! Hup! Retreat!

(Master places the weapon in line) Blade seizure in fourth with an advance and direct cut to the right cheek! The opposing steel is engaged with the cut, strong against weak. Via! Hup! On guard! Retreat!

Weapon in line! As I attempt to engage your blade in fourth with an advance, disengage in time with the point! Hup! On guard! Retreat!

On my feint head cut, exposing the lower arm, with an advance, time cut to the bottom of the arm with the cut, hand in first in second position, and jump back, assuming the parry position of third. Reach out for the time cut! Hup! Retreat!

(Master places the weapon in line) Attempt to engage my blade in fourth with an advance, as I disengage in time with the point, parry third in countertime and riposte by direct cut to the head! Via! Hup! Retreat!

(Master places the weapon in line) Attempt to engage my blade in fourth with an advance, as I disengage in time with the point, parry counter of fourth in countertime and riposte by direct cut to the right cheek! Via! Hup!

Invite in second! Parry fifth with a retreat and riposte by direct cut to the flank! Hup!

Invite in second! Parry fifth with a retreat and riposte by direct cut to the flank; and on my counterparry riposte, counterparry fifth with a retreat and riposte by circular cut to the abdomen! Hup!

Invite in second! Parry fifth with a retreat and riposte by direct cut to the flank; on my counterparry riposte, counterparry fifth with a retreat and riposte by circular cut to the abdomen; and on my counterparry riposte, counterparry fifth with a retreat and riposte by direct cut to the flank! Hup!

Repeat the preceding counterparry riposte exercise, adding a lunge to the final riposte to the flank! Hup!

Repeat the preceding counterparry riposte exercise, adding a running attack to the final riposte! Hup!

(Master invites in third) Direct point thrust (to the inside chest)! Via! Hup! On guard!

(Master invites in third) Direct point thrust (to the inside chest)! More slowly! Via! Hup! On guard!

(Master invites in third) Direct point thrust (to the inside chest)! Even more slowly! Via! Hup! On guard! First position! Mask off! Salute! Shake hands!

Observation: When the running attack is added to the parry-riposte, counterparry riposte exercise, the student must pass to the teacher's outside.

SABRE LESSON 11 (ADVANCED) – MASTER'S COMMANDS

First position! Salute! Mask on! On! Guard!

(Master invites in third) Blade in line! Direct point thrust (to the inside chest)! Via! Hup! On guard! Now in one motion!

(Master invites in third) Direct point thrust (to the inside chest)! Via! Hup! On guard!

In time, as I move from engagement in fourth to invitation in third, perform a direct point thrust (to the inside chest)! Hup! On guard!

In time, as I attempt to engage your blade in fourth, disengage with the cut to the right cheek! Hup! On guard!

In time, as I shift from engagement in third to invitation in second, execute a direct cut to the head! Hup! On guard! Retreat!

In time, as I change from invitation in fifth to invitation in second, feint head cut, cut flank with an advance! Hup! On guard! Retreat!

In time, as I shift from invitation in second to invitation in fifth, feint flank cut, cut head with an advance! Hup! On guard! Retreat!

In time, as I change from invitation in fifth to invitation in second, double feint head cut, flank cut, cut head with an advance! Hup! On guard! Retreat!

In time, as I shift from invitation in second to invitation in fifth, double feint flank cut, head cut, cut flank with an advance! Hup! On guard!

In time, simple beat in fourth with the back edge of the blade and direct cut to the right cheek! Hup! On guard! Retreat!

In time, simple beat in fourth with the back edge of the blade and direct cut to the right cheek with an advance! Hup! On guard! Retreat!

In time, simple beat in fourth with the back edge of the blade and direct cut to the right cheek with a jump lunge! Hup! On guard! Retreat!

In time, simple beat in fourth with the back edge of the blade and direct cut to the right cheek with a jump lunge; when I parry and riposte by direct cut to the head, remain in the lunge, and counterparry riposte: fifth, direct cut to the flank, fifth, and circular cut to the abdomen! Hup! On guard!

(Master invites in third) Direct point thrust (to the inside chest)! Via! Hup! On guard!

(Master invites in third) Direct point thrust (to the inside chest)! More slowly! Via! Hup! On guard!

(Master invites in third) Direct point thrust (to the inside chest)! Even more slowly! Via! Hup! On guard! First position! Mask off! Salute! Shake hands!

Observation: The same compound attacks should be executed with mobility; periodically, the teacher must parry the pupil's final action, so that he will be forced to counterparry riposte from the lunge.

SABRE LESSON 12 (ADVANCED) – MASTER'S COMMANDS

First position! Salute! Mask on! On! Guard!

(Master invites in third) Blade in line! Direct point thrust (to the inside chest)! Via! Hup! On guard! Now in one motion!

(Master invites in third) Direct point thrust (to the inside chest)! Via! Hup! On guard!

(Master engages in fourth) Without commands, execute the appropriate counteractions! (As he shifts from engagement in fourth to invitation in third – in time, point thrust to the inside chest) Hup! On guard!

(Master invites in third; as he attempts to engage in fourth – in time, disengagement with the point to the outside chest) Hup! On guard!

(Master invites in fifth; as he shifts from invitation in fifth to invitation in second – in time, direct cut to the head) Hup! On guard!

(Master invites in second; as he changes from invitation in second to invitation in fifth – in time, direct cut to the flank) Hup! On guard!

(Master invites in fourth; as he moves from invitation in fourth to invitation in third – in time, direct cut to the abdomen) Hup! On guard!

(Master invites in third; as he attempts to engage in fourth – in time, descending cut to the head) Hup! On guard! (Master signals a retreat with his hand)

In time, feint abdomen cut, cut flank with an advance! Hup! On guard! Retreat!

In time, and with mobility, feint abdomen cut, cut flank with an advance! Hup! On guard! Retreat!

In time, double feint abdomen cut, flank cut, and cut head with an advance! Hup! On guard! Retreat!

In time, and with mobility, double feint abdomen cut, flank cut, and cut head with an advance! Hup! On guard! Retreat!

Invite in second! Parry first and second with a retreat and riposte by direct cut to the right cheek! If I retreat, you must riposte with a lunge! Hup!

Invite in second! Parry first, second, and fifth with a retreat and riposte by direct cut to the flank! If I retreat, you must riposte with a running attack! Hup!

(Master invites in third) Direct point thrust (to the inside chest)! Via! Hup! On guard!

(Master invites in third) Direct point thrust (to the inside chest)! More slowly! Via! Hup! On guard!

(Master invites in third) Direct point thrust (to the inside chest)! Even more slowly! Via! Hup! On guard! First position! Mask off! Salute! Shake hands!

Observation: To develop dexterity, exercises with multiple cuts may be included in the advanced sabre lesson. For example, during the sequence of actions with beats, the student can be directed to execute a beat in fourth with the back edge of the blade and direct cut to the right cheek; during recovery from the lunge he should be told to perform a direct cut to the arm and, on regaining the guard position, to deliver an immediate circular cut (from the left) to the head with a second lunge. The three cuts should be placed with precision and follow one another as rapidly as possible. When the pupil has mastered this combination of actions, the teacher may parry the final cut to the head and riposte, thus forcing the student to counterparry and riposte from the lunge.

ÉPÉE LESSONS

Like sabre, épée should only be taught after the fencer has received some years of foil instruction. The preliminary lessons must again be devoted to the fundamentals of fencing. Given that the foilsman will know how to attack the torso, his work with the épée should be centered principally on the advanced target, with exercises that begin with single hits and gradually include multiple hits, moving from the body to the arm, that is, from the largest to the smallest target areas, and then in reverse, from the arm to the body. The fencer must learn to keep his sword arm well extended, with the point of the weapon threatening the adversary's advanced target. Emphasis should be placed on the counterattack, rather than the parry-riposte.

Even if a fencer dedicates himself exclusively to the épée, he must still be encouraged to continue taking foil lessons.

ÉPÉE LESSON 1 (BEGINNING) – MASTER'S COMMANDS

First position! Salute! Mask on! On! Guard! Your arm must be well extended and relaxed, with the point of the weapon aimed at my wrist, and your blade and forearm forming a straight line parallel with the floor!

(Master invites in third) Blade in line! Straight thrust to the body (inside high line)! Keep the shoulders relaxed, and extend the arm smoothly, bringing the hand gradually up to shoulder level! Via! Hup! On guard! Now in one motion!

(Master invites in third) Straight thrust to the body (inside high line)! Via! Hup! On guard! Retreat!

(Master places the weapon in line, top of the arm exposed) Straight thrust to the top (crook) of the arm! Via! Hup! On guard! Retreat!

(Master places the weapon in line, top of the arm exposed) Straight thrust to the top (wrist) of the arm! Via! Hup! On guard! Advance! Advance again!

(Master engages in fourth) Disengage to the body (outside high line)! Tight point motion! Via! Hup! On guard! Retreat!

(Master engages in fourth) Disengage to the external arm! Via! Hup! On guard! Advance!

Engage in third! Glide to the body (outside high line)! Via! Hup! On guard!

Engage in third! Parry second with a retreat and riposte by detaching the blade to the top of the arm! Sink with the parry! Hup!

Engage in third! Parry second with a retreat and riposte along the blade to the body (outside low line)! Hup!

Engage in second! Parry third with a retreat and riposte by detaching the blade to the bottom of the arm! Hup!

Engage in second! Parry third with a retreat and riposte along the blade to the body (outside high line)! Hup!

(Master invites in third) Straight thrust to the body (inside high line)! Via! Hup! On guard!

(Master invites in third) Straight thrust to the body (inside high line)! More slowly! Via! Hup! On guard!

(Master invites in third) Straight thrust to the body (inside high line)! Even more slowly! Via! Hup! On guard! First position! Mask off! Salute! Shake hands!

Épée Lesson 2 (beginning) – Master's Commands

First position! Salute! Mask on! On! Guard!

(Master invites in third) Blade in line! Straight thrust to the body (inside high line)! Via! Hup! On guard! Now in one motion!

(Master invites in third) Straight thrust to the body (inside high line)! Via! Hup! On guard! Retreat!

(Master places the weapon in line, top of the arm exposed) Straight thrust to the top (crook) of the arm! Via! Hup! On guard! Retreat!

(Master places the weapon in line, top of the arm exposed) Straight thrust to the top (wrist) of the arm! Via! Hup! On guard! Advance! Advance again!

Engage in third! Glide to the body (outside high line)! Via! Hup! On guard! Retreat! Retreat again!

(Master places the weapon in line) Angulation to the top of the arm! Keeping the hand in fourth position, raise it progressively to form an angle by breaking at the wrist! Via! Hup! On guard!

(Master places the weapon in line) Angulation to the bottom of the arm! Drop the hand, rotating it to second position, and break at the wrist! Via! Hup! On guard!

(Master places the weapon in line) Angulation to the internal arm! Maintain the hand in fourth position, and move it to the right! Via! Hup! On guard!

(Master places the weapon in line) Angulation to the external arm! Keep the hand in fourth position, and move it to the left! Via! Hup! On guard! Advance! Advance again!

Engage in third! Parry second with a retreat and riposte along the blade to body (outside low line)! Hup!

Engage in second! Parry third with a retreat and riposte along the blade to the top (crook) of the arm! Hup! Retreat! Retreat again!

(Master invites in third) Feint direct and disengage to the external arm! Via! Hup! On guard! Advance! Advance again!

Engage in second! Parry third with a retreat and riposte by feint direct to the bottom of the arm, and disengage to the top of the arm! Direct the feint just below the wrist! Keep the point motion tight! Hup!

(Master invites in third) Straight thrust to the body (inside high line)! Via! Hup! On guard!

(Master invites in third) Straight thrust to the body (inside high line)! More slowly! Via! Hup! On guard!

(Master invites in third) Straight thrust to the body (inside high line)! Even more slowly! Via! Hup! On guard! First position! Mask off! Salute! Shake hands!

ÉPÉE LESSON 3 (BEGINNING) – MASTER'S COMMANDS

First position! Salute! Mask on! On! Guard!

(Master invites in third) Blade in line! Straight thrust to the body (inside high line)! Via! Hup! On guard! Now in one motion!

(Master invites in third) Straight thrust to the body (inside high line)! Via! Hup! On guard! Retreat!

(Master places the weapon in line, top of the arm exposed) Straight thrust to the top (crook) of the arm! Via! Hup! On guard! Retreat!

(Master places the weapon in line, top of the arm exposed) Straight thrust to the top (wrist) of the arm! Via! Hup! On guard! Advance! Advance again!

Engage in third! Glide to the body (outside high line)! Via! Hup! On guard! Retreat! Retreat again!

(Master places the weapon in line) Angulation to the top of the arm with an advance! No lunge! Weapon and arm move first! Via! Hup! Retreat!

(Master places the weapon in line) Angulation to the bottom of the arm with an advance! Via! Hup! Retreat!

(Master places the weapon in line) Angulation to the internal arm with an advance! Via! Hup! Retreat!

(Master places the weapon in line) Angulation to the external arm with an advance! Via! Hup! Retreat!

(Master places the weapon in line) Angulations to the top and bottom of the arm, internal and external arm, advancing with each thrust! Via! Hup! Hup! Hup! Hup!

(Master places the weapon in line) Angulations to the top and bottom of the arm, internal and external arm, retreating after each thrust! Score the hit, then retreat! Via! Hup! Hup! Hup! Hup! Advance! Advance again!

Engage in third! Parry second with a retreat and riposte by detaching the blade to the top of the arm! Hup!

Engage in second! Parry third with a retreat and riposte by detaching the blade to the bottom of the arm! Hup!

(Master invites in third) Straight thrust to the body (inside high line)! Via! Hup! On guard!

(Master invites in third) Straight thrust to the body (inside high line)! More slowly! Via! Hup! On guard!

(Master invites in third) Straight thrust to the body (inside high line)! Even more slowly! Via! Hup! On guard! First position! Mask off! Salute! Shake hands!

ÉPÉE LESSON 4 (BEGINNING) – MASTER'S COMMANDS

First position! Salute! Mask on! On! Guard!

(Master invites in third) Blade in line! Straight thrust to the body (inside high line)! Via! Hup! On guard! Now in one motion!

(Master invites in third) Straight thrust to the body (inside high line)! Via! Hup! On guard!

Engage in third! Glide to the body (outside high line)! Via! Hup! On guard! Retreat! Retreat again!

(Master places the weapon in line) Angulation to the top of the arm! Via! Hup! On guard!

(Master places the weapon in line) Angulation to the bottom of the arm! Via! Hup! On guard! Advance! Advance again!

Engage in second! Parry counter of second with a retreat and riposte along the blade to the body (outside low line)! Hup!

Engage in third! Parry counter of third with a retreat and riposte along the blade to the top (crook) of the arm! Hup! Retreat! Retreat again!

(Master invites in fourth) Feint direct and deceive to the external arm! Via! Hup! On guard!

(Master invites in fourth) Feint direct and deceive to the external arm; as the attack is parried, and the riposte delayed, remain in the lunge and direct an angulation to the bottom of the arm! With the angulation, execute an appel! Via! Hup! On guard! Advance! Advance again!

Engage in third! Parry double counter of third with a retreat and riposte along the blade to the top (crook) of the arm! Hup!

(Master invites in third) Straight thrust to the body (inside high line)! Via! Hup! On guard!

(Master invites in third) Straight thrust to the body (inside high line)! More slowly! Via! Hup! On guard!

(Master invites in third) Straight thrust to the body (inside high line)! Even more slowly! Via! Hup! On guard! First position! Mask off! Salute! Shake hands!

ÉPÉE LESSON 5 (INTERMEDIATE) – MASTER'S COMMANDS

First position! Salute! Mask on! On! Guard!

(Master invites in third) Blade in line! Straight thrust to the body (inside high line)! Via! Hup! On guard! Now in one motion!

(Master invites in third) Straight thrust to the body (inside high line)! Via! Hup! On guard!

Engage in third! Glide to the body (outside high line)! Via! Hup! On guard! Retreat! Retreat again!

(Master places the weapon in line) Angulation to the top of the arm! Via! Hup! On guard!

(Master places the weapon in line) Angulation to the bottom of the arm! Via! Hup! On guard! Advance! Advance again!

Engage in third! Change engagement to fourth and transport to second and glide to the body (outside low line)! Via! Hup! On guard!

Engage in third! Change engagement to fourth and transport to second and glide to the body (outside low line) with a running attack! Pass on the outside! Via! Hup! On guard!

(Master places the weapon in line) Simple beat in fourth and straight thrust to the body (inside high line)! Via! Hup! On guard!

(Master places the weapon in line) Simple beat in fourth and disengage to the body (outside high line)! Via! Hup! On guard! Retreat!

(Master places the weapon in line) Simple beat in fourth and disengage to the external arm! Via! Hup! On guard!

(Master places the weapon in line) Simple beat in fourth and disengage to the external arm; as I parry and riposte to the thigh, reassemble backward and arrest to the top of the arm! After the attack is parried, keep your arm extended, with the point in line! Via! Hup! On guard! Advance!

(Master engages in second) Parry ceding parry of fourth and riposte to the body (inside high line)! Hup!

(Master invites in third) Straight thrust to the body (inside high line)! Via! Hup! On guard!

(Master invites in third) Straight thrust to the body (inside high line)! More slowly! Via! Hup! On guard!

(Master invites in third) Straight thrust to the body (inside high line)! Even more slowly! Via! Hup! On guard! First position! Mask off! Salute! Shake hands!

Observation: The student's change of engagement from third to fourth, preceding the transport to second, must be tight; and the point, during the transport and glide, should be close to the opposing steel.

Épée Lesson 6 (advanced) – Master's Commands

First position! Salute! Mask on! On! Guard!

(Master invites in third) Blade in line! Straight thrust to the body (inside high line)! Via! On guard! Now in one motion!

(Master invites in third) Straight thrust to the body (inside high line)! Via! Hup! On guard!

(Master engages in fourth) Disengage to the body (outside high line)! Via! Hup! On guard! Retreat!

(Master engages in fourth) Disengage to the external arm! Via! Hup! On guard! Advance!

Engage in third! Glide to the body (outside high line)! Via! Hup! On guard! Retreat! Retreat again!

(Master places the weapon in line) Angulation to the top of the arm! Via! Hup! On guard!

(Master places the weapon in line) Angulation to the bottom of the arm! Via! Hup! On guard! Advance! Advance again!

Engage in second! Parry counter of second with a retreat and riposte by detaching the blade to the top of the arm! Hup!

Engage in third! Parry counter of third with a retreat and riposte by detaching the blade to the bottom of the arm! Hup! Retreat!

(Master invites in fourth) Feint direct and deceive to the external arm! Via! Hup! On guard!

(Master invites in fourth) Feint direct and deceive to the external arm; remain in the lunge and direct an angulation to the bottom of the arm! You score two rapid hits! Via! Hup! Hup! On guard!

(Master invites in fourth) Feint direct and deceive to the external arm; remain in the lunge and direct an angulation to the bottom of the arm; then reassemble backward with an arrest to the top of the arm!

You score three hits! Do not search for my arm to execute the arrest, simply place the point in line so that I will impale myself! Reassemble quickly! Via! Hup! Hup! Hup! On guard!

Invite in third! Parry second and counter of second with a retreat and riposte by detaching the blade to the top of the arm! Hup!

Invite in second! Parry third and counter of third with a retreat and riposte by detaching the blade to the bottom of the arm! Hup!

(Master invites in third) Straight thrust to the body (inside high line)! Via! Hup! On guard!

(Master invites in third) Straight thrust to the body (inside high line)! More slowly! Via! Hup! On guard!

(Master invites in third) Straight thrust to the body (inside high line)! Even more slowly! Via! Hup! On guard! First position! Mask off! Salute! Shake hands!

Observation: The speed of the double and triple hits must be progressively increased.

ÉPÉE LESSON 7 (ADVANCED) – MASTER'S COMMANDS

First position! Salute! Mask on! On! Guard!

(Master invites in third) Blade in line! Straight thrust to the body (inside high line)! Via! Hup! On guard! Now in one motion!

(Master invites in third) Straight thrust to the body (inside high line)! Via! Hup! On guard!

Engage in third! Glide to the body (outside high line)! Via! Hup! On guard!

Invite in second! Parry third with a retreat and riposte along the blade to the top (crook) of the arm! Hup! Retreat! Retreat again!

(Master invites in third) Feint direct to the bottom of the arm and disengage to the top of the arm with an advance! Via! Hup! On guard! Retreat!

(Master places the weapon in line) Blade seizure in fourth with an advance and glide to the body (inside high line)! Via! Hup! On guard! Retreat!

Invite in third! As I feint direct to the bottom of the arm with an advance, execute an arrest to the top of the arm! No lunge! Hup! Retreat!

(Master places the weapon in line, bottom of the arm exposed) Feint direct to the bottom of the arm with an advance; as I attempt to arrest to the top of the arm, parry third in countertime and riposte to the top of the arm! Place the feint just under the wrist! Via! Hup! Retreat!

Invite in third! As I feint direct to the bottom of the arm with an advance, feint direct in time to the top of the arm, and elude the parry in countertime with a disengagement to the bottom of the arm! No lunge! Hup! Retreat!

Weapon in line! In time, as I attempt to engage the blade in fourth with an advance, disengage to the external arm! No lunge! Hup! Retreat!

(Master places the weapon in line) Attempt to engage the blade in fourth with an advance; as I disengage in time, parry third in countertime and riposte to the top (crook) of the arm! Via! Hup! Retreat!

Weapon in line! In time, as I attempt to engage the blade in fourth with an advance, feint by disengagement in time and elude my parry in countertime with a disengagement to the internal arm! No lunge! Hup!

(Master invites in third) Straight thrust to the body (inside high line)! Via! Hup! On guard!

(Master invites in third) Straight thrust to the body (inside high line)! More slowly! Via! Hup! On guard!

(Master invites in third) Straight thrust to the body (inside high line)! Even more slowly! Via! Hup! On guard! First position! Mask off! Salute! Shake hands!

Épée Lesson 8 (advanced) – Master's Commands

First position! Salute! Mask on! On! Guard!

(Master invites in third) Blade in line! Straight thrust to the body (inside high line)! Via! Hup! On guard! Now in one motion!

(Master invites in third) Straight thrust to the body (inside high line)! Via! Hup! On guard!

In time, as I move from engagement in fourth to invitation in third, execute a straight thrust to the body (inside high line)! Hup! On guard!

In time, as I attempt to engage your blade in third, disengage to the body (inside high line)! Hup! On guard! Retreat!

In time, as I attempt to engage your blade in third, disengage to the internal arm! Hup! On guard! Advance!

In time, as I attempt to engage your blade in fourth, disengage to the body (outside high line)! Hup! On guard! Retreat!

In time, as I attempt to engage your blade in fourth, disengage to the external (crook) arm! Hup! On guard! Retreat!

Weapon in line! In time, as I attempt to engage your blade in third, disengage to the internal arm with an advance! No lunge! Hand motion first, then foot movement! Hup! Retreat!

Weapon in line! In time, as I attempt to engage your blade in fourth, disengage to the external arm with an advance! No lunge! Hup! Retreat!

Weapon in line! In time, as I attempt to engage your blade in third, disengage to the internal arm with an advance; and as I attempt to engage your blade in fourth, disengage to the external arm with an advance! No lunge! Two hits! Hup! Hup! Retreat!

Weapon in line! In time, as I attempt to engage your blade in third with an advance, disengage to the internal arm and retreat! Touch first, and then retreat! Hup! Retreat!

Weapon in line! In time, as I attempt to engage your blade in fourth with an advance, disengage to the external arm and retreat! Hup! Retreat!

Weapon in line! In time, as I attempt to engage your blade in third with an advance, disengage to the internal arm and retreat; and as I attempt to engage your blade in fourth with an advance, disengage to the external arm and retreat! Hup! Hup! Advance!

Engage in third! Parry counter of third with a retreat and riposte along the blade to the top (crook) of the arm! Hup!

Engage in third! Parry double counter of third with a retreat, change engagement to fourth, and riposte by flanconade in fourth! Make the change of engagement as tight as possible, and do not lunge with the riposte by flanconade in fourth! Hup!

(Master invites in third) Straight thrust to the body (inside high line)! Via! Hup! On guard!

(Master invites in third) Straight thrust to the body (inside high line)! More slowly! Via! Hup! On guard!

(Master invites in third) Straight thrust to the body (inside high line)! Even more slowly! Via! Hup! On guard! First position! Mask off! Salute! Shake hands!

ÉPÉE LESSON 9 (ADVANCED) – MASTER'S COMMANDS

First position! Salute! Mask on! On! Guard!

(Master invites in third) Blade in line! Straight thrust to the body (inside high line)! Via! On guard! Now in one motion!

(Master invites in third) Straight thrust to the body (inside high line)! Via! Hup! On guard!

In time, as I shift from engagement in fourth to invitation in third, perform a straight thrust to the body (inside high line)! Hup! On guard! Retreat! Retreat again!

Weapon in line! In time, as I attempt to engage your blade in third, disengage to the internal arm with an advance! No lunge! Hup! Retreat!

Weapon in line! In time, as I attempt to engage your blade in fourth, disengage to the external arm with an advance! No lunge! Hup! Retreat!

Weapon in line! In time, as I attempt to engage your blade in third, disengage to the internal arm with an advance; and as I attempt to engage your blade in fourth, disengage to the external arm with an advance! No lunge! Two hits! Hup! Hup! Retreat!

Weapon in line! In time, as I attempt to engage your blade in third, disengage to the internal arm with an advance; as I attempt to engage your blade in fourth, disengage to the external arm with an advance; parry third and riposte along the blade to the body (outside high line) with a lunge; reassemble backward and arrest to the top of the arm! There are four hits! Hup! Hup! Hup! Hup! Retreat!

Weapon in line! In time, as I attempt to engage your blade in third, disengage to the internal arm with an advance; as I attempt to engage your blade in fourth, disengage to the external arm with an advance; parry third and counter of third and riposte along the blade to the body (outside high line) with a lunge; reassemble backward and arrest to the top of the arm! Hup! Hup! Hup! Hup! Advance!

(Master invites in third) Straight thrust to the body (inside high line)! Via! Hup! On guard!

(Master invites in third) Straight thrust to the body (inside high line)! More slowly! Via! Hup! On guard!

(Master invites in third) Straight thrust to the body (inside high line)! Even more slowly! Via! Hup! On guard! First position! Mask off! Salute! Shake hands!

Épée Lesson 10 (advanced) – Master's Commands

First position! Salute! Mask on! On! Guard!

(Master invites in third) Blade in line! Straight thrust to the body (inside high line)! Via! On guard! Now in one motion!

(Master invites in third) Straight thrust to the body (inside high line)! Via! Hup! On guard! Retreat!

(Master places the weapon in line, top of the arm exposed) Without commands, execute the appropriate counteractions! (Straight thrust to the crook of the arm) Hup! On guard! (Master signals a retreat with his hand)

(Master places the weapon in line, top of the arm exposed – straight thrust to the wrist) Hup! On guard!

(Master invites in fourth; he attempts to engage in third with an advance – in time, disengagement to the internal arm; no lunge) Hup! (Master signals a retreat with his hand)

(Master invites in third; he attempts to engage in fourth with an advance – in time, disengagement to the external arm; no lunge) Hup! (Master signals a retreat with his hand)

(Master invites in fourth; he attempts to engage in third with an advance, and then parries fourth – in time, feint by disengagement and disengagement to the external arm; no lunge) Hup! (Master signals a retreat with his hand)

(Master invites in third; he attempts to engage in fourth with an advance, and then parries third – in time, feint by disengagement and disengagement to the internal arm; no lunge) Hup! (Master signals a retreat with his hand)

(Master invites in fourth; he attempts to engage in third with an advance, and then parries counter of third – in time, feint by disengagement and deceive to the internal arm; no lunge) Hup! (Master signals a retreat with his hand)

(Master invites in third; he attempts to engage in fourth with an advance, and then parries counter of fourth – in time, feint by disengagement and deceive to the external arm; no lunge) Hup! (Master signals a retreat with his hand)

(Master invites in fourth; he attempts to engage in third with an advance, and then parries either fourth or counter of third – in time, feint by disengagement and disengagement to the external arm, or deceive to the internal arm, depending upon the teacher's parry; no lunge) Hup! (Master signals a retreat with his hand)

(Master invites in third; he attempts to engage in fourth with an advance, and then parries either third or counter of fourth – in time, feint by disengagement and disengagement to the internal arm, or deceive to the external arm, depending upon the teacher's parry; no lunge) Hup! (Master signals a retreat with his hand)

(Master invites in third; he attempts to engage in fourth with an advance, and then parries counter of fourth with a retreat – in time, feint by disengagement and deceive to the external arm with lunge; the teacher allows the hit to arrive, and then directs a thrust to the student's thigh, forcing him to reassemble and arrest to the top of the arm)

Engage in third! Parry fourth and riposte direct to the internal arm, or fourth, direct, fourth, and disengagement to the external arm, depending upon my response! Hup!

(Master invites in third) Straight thrust (to the inside high line)! Via! Hup! On guard!

(Master invites in third) Straight thrust (to the inside high line)! More slowly! Via! Hup! On guard!

(Master invites in third) Straight thrust (to the inside high line)! Even more slowly! Via! Hup! On guard! First position! Mask off! Salute! Shake hands!

Observation: The same compound attacks in time can be performed with mobility; but special care must be taken to maintain proper fencing measure.

Fencing Teacher Diploma Examinations

In diploma examinations the most prudent course of action is to present the commission of fencing masters with relatively simple demonstration lessons. The more complicated the actions, the greater the possibility for error, either on the part of the teacher or pupil. In particular, the tendency to move quickly into actions in time must be curbed; instead, the candidate should impart to his student lessons at the intermediate level, such as Foil Lessons 5 or 12, Sabre Lesson 9, and Épée Lesson 5. In these, and all other demonstration lessons, emphasis should be placed on a correct guard position, smooth lunge, small blade motions, proper timing, progressive increase of speed, and correct fencing measure. Throughout the lessons every fault must be drawn to the pupil's attention and corrected.

And if the members of the commission should ask for advanced lessons, then lessons with actions in time, such as Foil Lesson 14, Sabre Lesson 11, and Épée Lesson 9 would be appropriate. With these lessons, special care must be taken that the student is not pushed forward too rapidly; he should be given sufficient time to develop the self-confidence necessary to execute his actions with speed and precision.

APPENDIX B

QUESTIONS FOR REVIEW

PART I – THE FOIL

1. Name three early seventeenth-century Italian authors of fencing treatises.
2. What are the principal parts of the foil?
3. How many elements comprise the Italian foil guard, and what are their names?
4. Of how many elements does the Italian foil blade consist, and what are they?
5. By regulation what is the maximum length that a foil blade may be?
6. How many different degrees of strength are there in the blade, and what are they?
7. How do we know whether or not a foil is correctly balanced?
8. By regulation what is the maximum weight that a foil may be?
9. By regulation what is the maximum length that a foil may be?
10. How is the Italian foil properly gripped?
11. How many hand positions are there in foil, and what are their names?
12. Describe first position.
13. What is the position of the weapon when it is in line?
14. Describe the movements of the salute.
15. What is the line of direction?
16. What is the purpose of the guard position?
17. Describe the guard position in foil.
18. What is the line of offense?
19. What is the lunge?
20. Describe the execution of a lunge.
21. What are the prerequisites for an efficient lunge?
22. Describe the execution of an advance, a retreat, and a jump back.
23. What is an appel, and how is it used?
24. What is fencing measure, and how many measures are there?
25. How is the advance lunge performed?
26. Describe the execution of the jump lunge.
27. What is gaining on the lunge?
28. Describe the execution of a running attack.
29. How many placements of the weapon are there, and what are they?
30. Describe the limits of the foil target.

31. How many lines of attack are there, and how are they designated?
32. What are invitations, how many are there in foil, and what are their names?
33. How do the Italian and the French numbering systems for invitations correspond?
34. What are engagements, how many are there in foil, and what are their names?
35. Describe single and double changes of engagement.
36. What are transports, and how are they designated?
37. What are envelopments, and how are they named?
38. Define offense.
39. What is a simple attack, how many are there, and what are their names?
40. Describe in detail the execution of each of the simple attacks.
41. By what other name is the flanconade in fourth known?
42. What are forced glides?
43. When is the thrust to low fourth used?
44. Define defense.
45. What are parries, how many kinds are there, and what are they called?
46. How do opposition parries differ from beating parries?
47. What are simple parries, how many are there in foil, what are their names, and which target areas do they defend?
48. What are ceding parries, how many are there, what are their names, and against which attacks are they employed?
49. What is the riposte?
50. Specify where the simple riposte can be directed after each parry.
51. What are compound attacks, and into which groups may they be divided?
52. What is the feint?
53. How many parries does a single feint elude?
54. Describe the execution of the feint direct and disengagement in opposition to the invitation in first, indicating both the master's and pupil's movements.
55. Describe the execution of the feint by disengagement and disengagement in opposition to the engagement in second, indicating both the teacher's and student's movements.
56. Describe the execution of the feint by glide and disengagement from engagement in third, indicating both the master's and pupil's movements.
57. Describe the execution of the feint by flanconade in fourth and disengagement from engagement in fourth, indicating both the teacher's and student's movements.

58. What are compound ripostes, and how are they used?
59. How many parries does a double feint elude?
60. How is an advance coordinated with a double feint?
61. Describe the execution of the double feint direct and disengagement in opposition to the invitation in first, indicating both the master's and pupil's movements.
62. Describe the execution of the double feint by disengagement and disengagement in opposition to the engagement in second, indicating both the teacher's and student's movements.
63. Describe the execution of the double feint by glide and disengagement from engagement in third, indicating both the master's and pupil's movements.
64. Describe the double feint by flanconade in fourth and disengagement from engagement in fourth, indicating both the teacher's and student's movements.
65. What are conventional exercises, and what is their purpose?
66. What are circular parries, how many are there in foil, what are their names, and which target areas do they protect?
67. What are half circular parries, and how are they executed in foil?
68. How are circular parries opposed?
69. Describe the execution of the feint direct and deceive in opposition to the invitation in third, indicating both the master's and pupil's movements.
70. How are one circular and one simple parry eluded?
71. How are one simple and one circular parry eluded?
72. How are two circular parries eluded?
73. How are one simple, one circular, and one simple parry eluded?
74. How are one circular, one simple, and one circular parry eluded?
75. When are circular ripostes used?
76. What is the cut-over, and how is it used?
77. Describe the execution of the feint direct and cut-over in opposition to the invitation in third, indicating both the teacher's and student's movements.
78. Describe the execution of the feint by cut-over and disengagement in opposition to the engagement in fourth, indicating both the master's and pupil's movements.
79. Define actions on the blade, and list those that are used in foil.
80. From which engagements may blade seizure be effected?
81. How are the internal flanconade and flanconade in second executed?
82. Why should the internal flanconade and the flanconade in second not be employed as ripostes?

83. What are beats, and how are they identified?
84. What are false beats?
85. Describe the execution of the simple beat, change beat, and circular beat in fourth followed by a straight thrust.
86. What is a grazing beat?
87. What are expulsions, and how are they performed?
88. What advantage do expulsions have over beats?
89. What are pressures, and how are they executed?
90. What is blade cover, and how is it accomplished?
91. What are disarmaments, and how are they effected?
92. What are renewed attacks, and how are they executed?
93. Define time, velocity, and measure.
94. What is fencing time?
95. List the counterattacks used by the Italian school, and indicate how each is employed.
96. What is countertime, and how is it used?
97. How may countertime be opposed?
98. When is the arrest in countertime employed?
99. What are probing actions, and actions of concealment?
100. What are attacks in time?
101. When does a straight thrust become an action in time?
102. How is the counter-disengagement executed?
103. What is the distinction between second intention and countertime?
104. What is the basic principle of fencing?
105. What is *tempo comune?*
106. When a right-handed fencer executes the inquartata against a left-handed adversary, where does he direct his thrust?

Part II – Sabre

1. How many elements comprise the sabre guard, and what are their names?
2. Of how many elements does the sabre blade consist, and what are they called?
3. By regulation what is the maximum length that a sabre blade may be?
4. How many different degrees of strength are there in the blade, and what are they?
5. How do we know whether or not a sabre is correctly balanced?
6. By regulation what is the maximum weight that a sabre may be?
7. By regulation what is the maximum length that a sabre may be?
8. How is the sabre correctly held?
9. How many hand positions are there in sabre, and what are their names?
10. Describe the movements of the salute.
11. Describe the sabre guard in third.

12. What is done with the left hand in sabre during the lunge?
13. Is fencing measure the same in sabre as in foil?
14. Describe the limits of the sabre target.
15. Identify the lines of attack and specify the target areas in sabre.
16. How many invitations are there in sabre, and what are their names?
17. How many engagements are there in sabre, and what are their names?
18. Which engagements in sabre are preferred today, and why?
19. List the changes of engagement that can be effected in sabre.
20. In making changes of engagement, where should movement be centered, at the elbow or wrist?
21. List the transports that can be made in sabre?
22. Indicate the function of the six preliminary sabre exercises, and describe their execution.
23. State the purpose of the exercises with circular cuts, and describe their execution.
24. Which parts of the sabre blade may be employed in offense?
25. In sabre, how many simple attacks with the point are there, and what are their names?
26. In sabre, how many simple attacks with the cut are there, and what are their names?
27. Which hand position is adopted for the direct point thrust in sabre?
28. Why should the sword arm and blade form an obtuse angle in sabre?
29. How many glides with the point are there in sabre, and what are their names?
30. Describe the execution of the direct cut to the head.
31. Is the direct cut to the head pushed or pulled?
32. Describe the execution of the direct cut to the flank.
33. Describe the execution of the direct cut to the abdomen.
34. Is the direct cut to the abdomen pushed or pulled?
35. How do circular cuts differ from descending cuts?
36. To which target areas are ascending circular cuts directed?
37. From which engagements are descending cuts performed?
38. Identify the target areas on the arm, indicating the part of the blade that may be used in the cutting action, and the hand position employed for each cut.
39. How many simple parries are there in sabre, what are their names, and which target areas do they defend?
40. How many ceding parries are there in sabre, what are their names, and against which attacks are they used?
41. What is the function of the three parry exercises in sabre, and how are they executed?

42. Specify the target areas where simple ripostes in sabre may be directed after each parry.
43. Describe the execution of the feint with the direct point thrust or direct cut in opposition to the invitation in first, indicating both the master's and pupil's movements.
44. Describe the execution of the feint by glide with the point from engagement in second, indicating both the teacher's and student's movements.
45. Describe the execution of the double feint with the direct point thrust or direct cut in opposition to the invitation in fifth, indicating both the master's and pupil's movements.
46. Describe the execution of the double feint by glide with the point from engagement in third, indicating both the teacher's and student's movements.
47. How many circular parries are there in sabre, what are their names, and which target areas do they protect?
48. How are half circular parries executed in sabre?
49. Describe the execution of the feint with the direct point thrust and deceive in opposition to the invitation in first, indicating both the master's and pupil's movements.
50. List the actions on the blade employed in sabre.
51. Describe the execution of blade seizure in fourth and direct cut to the right cheek.
52. Describe the execution of the simple beat in fourth with the back edge of the blade and direct cut to the right cheek.
53. To which target areas is the point thrust or cut directed after the grazing beat in fourth?
54. List the counterattacks employed in sabre by the Italian school.

PART III – ÉPÉE

1. How many elements comprise the Italian épée guard, and what are their names?
2. By regulation what is the maximum length that an épée blade may be?
3. How does the épée blade differ from the foil blade?
4. How many different degrees of strength are there in the blade, and what are they?
5. How do we know whether or not an épée is correctly balanced?
6. By regulation what is the maximum weight that an épée may be?
7. By regulation what is the maximum length that an épée may be?
8. How is the Italian épée properly gripped?
9. How does the épée guard differ from the foil guard?

10. Is fencing measure the same in épée as in foil?
11. How much of the body is valid target area in épée?
12. How many simple attacks are there in épée, and what are their names?
13. To which target areas are angulations generally directed?
14. Which parries expose the external arm?
15. To which target area is the riposte in épée usually directed in the lesson?
16. Why should double feints be avoided in épée?
17. Which of the renewed attacks is most commonly used in épée?
18. Are there conventions in épée concerning priority of hits?
19. Which counterattack is most frequently employed in épée?
20. Regarding tactics, where should emphasis be placed in épée?

Answers to the Questions

Part I – Foil

1.	Preface	37.	No. 28	73.	No. 79
2.	No. 1	38.	No. 29	74.	No. 83
3.	No. 1	39.	No. 30	75.	No. 88
4.	No. 1	40.	Nos. 31, 32, 33	76.	No. 89
5.	No. 1	41.	No. 33	77.	No. 91
6.	No. 1	42.	No. 33	78.	No. 94
7.	No. 2	43.	No. 33	79.	No. 96
8.	No. 2	44.	No. 34	80.	No. 97
9.	No. 2	45.	No. 35	81.	No. 99
10.	No. 3	46.	No. 35	82.	No. 99
11.	No. 4	47.	No. 36	83.	No. 101
12.	No. 5	48.	No. 38	84.	No. 102
13.	No. 6	49.	No. 39	85.	Nos. 103, 106, 108
14.	No. 7	50.	No. 40	86.	No. 109
15.	No. 8	51.	No. 41	87.	No. 110
16.	No. 9	52.	No. 42	88.	No. 110
17.	No. 9	53.	No. 43	89.	No. 111
18.	No. 10	54.	No. 46	90.	No. 112
19.	No. 11	55.	No. 48	91.	No. 113
20.	No. 11	56.	No. 50	92.	No. 124
21.	No. 11	57.	No. 50	93.	No. 125
22.	Nos. 13, 14, 15	58.	No. 51	94.	No. 126
23.	No. 16	59.	No. 53	95.	Nos. 127-134
24.	No. 17	60.	No. 53	96.	No. 135
25.	No. 18	61.	No. 55	97.	No. 136
26.	No. 19	62.	No. 56	98.	No. 137
27.	No. 20	63.	No. 57	99.	Nos. 138, 139
28.	No. 21	64.	No. 57	100.	No. 141
29.	No. 22	65.	No. 58	101.	No. 141
30.	No. 23	66.	No. 59	102.	No. 142
31.	No. 23	67.	No. 60	103.	No. 143
32.	No. 24	68.	No. 61	104.	No. 150
33.	No. 24	69.	No. 63	105.	No. 150
34.	No. 25	70.	No. 66	106.	No. 151
35.	No. 26	71.	No. 70		
36.	No. 27	72.	No. 74		

PART II – SABRE

1. No. 1	19. No. 19	37. No. 30
2. No. 1	20. No. 19	38. No. 31
3. No. 1	21. No. 20	39. No. 34
4. No. 1	22. No. 21	40. No. 36
5. No. 2	23. No. 22	41. No. 37
6. No. 2	24. No. 24	42. No. 39
7. No. 2	25. No. 24	43. No. 43
8. No. 3	26. No. 24	44. No. 45
9. No. 4	27. No. 25	45. No. 49
10. No. 7	28. No. 25	46. No. 51
11. No. 9	29. No. 27	47. No. 53
12. No. 11	30. No. 28	48. No. 54
13. No. 14	31. No. 28	49. No. 56
14. No. 16	32. No. 28	50. No. 67
15. No. 16	33. No. 28	51. No. 69
16. No. 17	34. No. 28	52. No. 74
17. No. 18	35. Nos. 29, 30	53. No. 78
18. No. 18	36. No. 22	54. No. 87

PART III – EPEE

1. No. 1	8. No. 3	15. No. 31
2. No. 1	9. No. 9	16. No. 37
3. No. 1	10. No. 14	17. No. 45
4. No. 1	11. No. 16	18. No. 47
5. No. 2	12. No. 23	19. No. 48
6. No. 2	13. No. 24	20. No. 65
7. No. 2	14. Nos. 27, 39	

ORGANIZATIONS & EQUIPMENT

For information concerning fencing instruction, location of fencing schools, schedules of national and international competitions, and international regulations governing fencing competitions, contact either the United States Fencing Association or in Great Britain, British Fencing.

United States Fencing Assoc.
One Olympic Plaza
Colorado Springs, CO 80909
Phone: (719) 578-4511
Fax: (719) 632-5737

British Fencing
1 Barons Gate
33-35 Rothschild Road
London W4 5HT
Phone: (0181) 742-3032

FENCING EQUIPMENT

American Fencers Supply Co.
1180 Folsom Street
San Francisco, CA 94103
Phone: (415) 863-7911
Fax: (415) 431-4931

George Santelli, Inc.
465 South Dean Street
Englewood, NJ 07631
Phone: (201) 871-3105
Fax: (201) 871-8718

Blade Fencing Equipment, Inc.
212 West 15th Street
New York, NY 10011
Phone: 1-800-828-5661
NY/NJ/CT: (212) 620-0114
Fax: (212) 620-0116

Triplette Competition Arms
101 East Main Street
Elkin, NC 28621
Phone: (910) 835-7774
Fax: (910) 835-4099

Leon Paul
Units 1 & 2, Cedar Way
Camley St., London NW1 0JQ
Phone: (0171) 388-8132
Fax: (0171) 388-8134

Blades
35 Edinburgh Drive
Staines, Middlesex TW18 1PJ
Phone: (01784) 255-522
Fax: (01784) 245-942

TABLE OF FENCING TERMINOLOGY

ENGLISH	ITALIAN	FRENCH	GERMAN
Actions of Concealment	Traccheggio	Préparations D'Attaques	Verbergungsaktionen
Advance	Passo Avanti	Marche	Schritt vorwärts
Angulation	Colpo Angolato	Attaque en Cavant	Winkelstoß
Appel	Appello	Appel	Appell
Appuntata	Appuntata	Remise	Appuntata (Sperrstoß in die Fintriposte)
Arrest	Colpo D'Arresto	Coup D'Arrêt	Aufhaltstoß
Arrest in Countertime	Colpo D'Arresto in Controtempo	Coup D'Arrêt en Contre-temps	Aufhaltstoß ins Controtempo
Attack	Attacco	Attaque	Angriff
Attack in Time	Attacco in Tempo	Attaque en Temps	Angriff ins Tempo
Beat	Battuta	Battement	Battutaangriff (Klingenschlagangriff)
Blade Cover	Copertino	Copertino	Sicherheits-oder-Druckbindung
Blade Seizure	Presa di Ferro	Opposition	Bindungsangriff
Ceding Parry	Parata di Ceduta	Parade en Cédant	Zedierungsparade (Nachgebeparade)
Change Beat	Intrecciata	Battement en Changeant de Ligne	Wechselbattuta
Circular Cut	Molinello	Moulinet	Schwingungshieb
Circular Parry	Parata di Contro	Parade par le Contre	Kreisparade
Compound Attack	Attacco Composto	Attaque Composée	Zusammengesetzer Angriff
Conventional Exercises	Esercizi Convenzionali	Exercices Conventionnels	Konventionelle Übungen
Counterattack	Uscita in Tempo	Contre-attaque	Gegenangriff
Counter-disengagement	Controcavazione	Contre-dégagement	Kreisstoß ins Tempo
Countertime	Controtempo	Contre-temps	Controtempo
Cut	Sciabolata	Coup de Tranchant	Hieb
Cut-over	Cavazione Angolata	Coupé	Wurfstoß
Deceive	Circolazione	Contre-dégagement	Kreisstoß
Defense	Difesa	Défensive	Verteidigung
Descending Cut	Fendente	Coupé	Wurfhieb
Disarmament	Disarmo	Desarmement	Entwaffnung
Disengagement	Cavazione	Dégagement	Cavation (Umgehung)
Disengagement in Time	Cavazione in Tempo	Derobement	Cavation ins Tempo (Ausweichstoß)
Double Feint	Doppia Finta	Double Feinte	Doppelfinte
Double Feint by Disengagement	Doppia Finta di Cavazione	Double Feinte de Dégagement	Doppelcavationsfinte
Double Feint by Glide	Doppia Finta del Filo	Double Feinte de Coulé	Doppelfilofinte
Double Feint Direct	Doppia Finta Dritta	Double Feinte de Coup Droit	Doppelstoßfinte
Double Hit	Colpo Doppio	Coup Double	Doppeltreffer
Engagement	Legamento	Engagement	Bindung
Envelopment	Riporto	Enveloppement	Kreisbindung
Épée	Spada	Épée	Degen
Expulsion	Storzo	Froissement	Schleif-oder-Streichbattuta
Feint	Finta	Feinte	Finte
Feint by Disengagement	Finta di Cavazione	Feinte de Dégagement	Cavationsfinte
Feint by Glide	Finta del Filo	Feinte de Coulé	Filofinte
Feint Direct	Finta Semplice	Feinte de Coup Droit	Stoßfinte
Feint in Time	Finta in Tempo	Feinte en Cavant en Temps	Finte ins Tempo
Fencer	Schermitore	Escrimeur	Fechter
Fencing	Scherma	Escrime	Fechten
Fencing Measure	Misura	Mesure	Mensur (Fechtabstand)
Fencing Strip	Pedana	Piste	Kampfbahn
Fifth	Quinta	Quinte	Quint
First	Prima (Mezzocerchio)	Septime (Demi-cercle)	Prim
First and Second Intention	Prima e Seconda Intenzione	Premiere et Deuxieme Intention	Erste und Zweite Absicht

ENGLISH	ITALIAN	FRENCH	GERMAN
First Position	Prima Posizione	Premiere Position	Grundstellung
Foil	Floretto	Fleuret	Florett
Forced Glide	Filo Sottomesso	Coulé	Gezwungener Filo
Fourth	Quarta	Quarte	Quart
Free Fencing	Assalto	Assaut	Freies Fechten
Gaining on the Lunge	Raddoppio	Redoublement	Wiederholung des Ausfalles
Glide	Filo	Coulé	Filo (Gleitstoß)
Grazing Beat	Battuta di Passagio	Battement en Passant	Abstreichbuttuta
Guard	Guardia	Garde	Fechtstellung
Half Circular Parry	Parata di Mezza Contro	Parade de Demi-contre	Halbkreisparade
Hand Position	Posizione di Pugno	Position de la Main	Faustlagen
Imbroccata	Imbroccata	Imbroccata	Imbroccata (Sperrgleitstoß)
Inquartata	Inquartata	Esquive (Inquartata)	Inquartata (Meidegegenangritt mit Abdrehen)
Invitation	Invito	Invite	Einladung
Jump Backward	Salto Indietro	Saut en Arrière	Sprung rückwärts
Line of Direction	Linea Direttrice	Ligne de Direction	Gefechtslinie
Line of Offense	Linea di Offesa	Ligne	Angriffslinie
Lunge	Affondo	Fente	Ausfall
Mask	Maschera	Masque	Maske
Parry	Parata	Parade	Parade
Passata Sotto	Passata Sotto	Esquive (Passata Sotto)	Passata Sotto (Meidegegenangriff mit Abducken)
Point Thrust	Puntata	Coup de Pointe	Stich
Pressure	Deviamento	Pression	Druckangriff
Probing Actions	Scandaglio	Fausse-attaque	Prüfende Aktionen
Renewed Attack	Ripresa di Attacco	Reprise D'Attaque	Angriffswiederholung
Retreat	Passo Indietro	Pas en Arriere	Schritt rückwärts
Return on Guard	Ritorno in Guardia	Remise en Garde	Rückkehr aus dem Ausfall in die Fechtstellung
Riposte	Risposta	Riposte	Riposte (Nachstoß)
Running Attack	Frecciata	Flèche	Sturzangriff
Sabre	Sciabola	Sabre	Säbel
Salute	Saluto	Salut	Fechtgruß
Second	Seconda	Seconde	Second
Simple Attack	Attacco Semplice	Attaque Simple	Einfacher Angriff
Simple Beat	Battuta Semplice	Battement Simple	Direkte Battuta
Simple Parry	Parata Semplice	Parade Simple	Direkte Parade
Simple Riposte	Risposta Semplice	Riposte Simple	Einfache Riposte
Single Feint (Simple Feint)	Finta Semplice	Feinte Simple	Einfache Finte
Sixth	Sesta	Sixte	Sixt
Straight Thrust	Botta Dritta (Colpo Dritto)	Coup Droit	Gerader Stoß
Target	Bersaglio	Cible	Blöße
Third	Terza	Tierce	Terz
Time	Tempo	Temps	Zeit
Time Thrust	Contrazione	Coup de Temps	Sperrstoß (Contraktion)
Time Thrust or Cut to the Arm	Tempo al Braccio	Coup de Manchette	Tempostich oder Hieb zum Arm
Touch (Hit)	Stoccata (Colpo)	Touche	Treffer
Transport	Trasporto	Liement	Übertragung
Velocity	Velocità	Vitesse	Geschwindigkeit
Weapon in Line	Arma in Linea	Arme en Ligne	Klinge in Linie

GLOSSARY

GLOSSARY

The glossary of fencing terms that follows includes not only the most commonly used contemporary fencing terminology, but also archaic words and phrases encountered in older treatises on swordplay. This additional material should be helpful to scholars interested in the history of fencing theory.

Action. An operation in its entirety, whether offensive or defensive.

Actions of concealment. Movements used to confuse the adversary and hide one's own intentions. These consist of changes in placement of the weapon, transports, envelopments, pressures, and tight disengagements that move rapidly around the opposing steel, combined with small forward and backward steps.

Actions on the blade. Movements that deviate or deflect the opposing steel during the attack; these are glides (*fili*), blade seizure (*presa di ferro*), changes of engagement (*cambiamenti di legamento*), transports (*trasporti*), envelopments (*riporti*), beats (*battute*), expulsions (*sforzi*), pressures (*deviamenti*), blade cover (*copertino*), and disarmaments (*disarmi*). Only the glides are performed in one motion.

Advance. A step forward to decrease measure between oneself and the opponent. This movement is also referred to as gaining ground.

Angulation. In épée fencing, a thrust, effected with a flexed wrist, that passes over, under, or on either side of the antagonist's bell guard to the advanced target. It may be directed to the top of the arm, bottom of the arm, internal arm, and external arm.

Appel. A foot stamp that may be employed to give impetus to the thrust in a renewed attack, or to accent the feint. It can also be used in the lesson as an instructional device to retard the impulse to lunge early.

Appuntata. A counterattack in opposition to the compound riposte. It is employed against the adversary who habitually follows his parry with one or more feints.

Arrest. A counterattack that interrupts completion of a compound attack with feints. Attacks with a single feint are arrested on the first movement; attacks with a double feint, on either the first or second movement.

Arrest in countertime. An action opposed to a single or double feint in time. It is executed in the same manner as an arrest against a compound attack.

Arrest with reassemblement. An épée action in which the arrest to the advanced target or body is performed while withdrawing the right foot until it touches the left heel, straightening the legs, and throwing back the left arm.

Ascending cut. A circular cut to the flank or abdomen delivered in an ascending motion. Its function is to pass under the opponent's elbow.

Assault. A simulated duel.

Attacks in time. Offensive actions effected while the antagonist is in the act of changing the placement of his weapon. In other words, the attack is executed just as the opposing steel is moved from an invitation to an engagement or vice versa, or put in line.

Auxiliary actions. Actions that the Roman-Neapolitan school does not consider fundamental: thrust in low fourth (French *septime*), forced glides, false beats, expulsions, blade cover, change beats, beat in false fourth (French *septime*), disarmaments, and renewed attacks.

Azioni volanti. In old Italian fencing terminology, all offensive actions accomplished without maintaining blade contact. Among these are the straight thrust *(botta dritta)*, disengagement *(cavazione)*, and cut-over *(cavazione angolata)*.

Balestra. An attack effected with a jump and lunge.

Beat. A blow of measured violence delivered with the strong of the blade against the medium of the adversary's steel to dislodge it from engagement or its position in line. The line in which the attacking blade encounters the opposing steel identifies the beat: we therefore speak of beats in first, second, third, and fourth.

Beat in false fourth. An auxiliary action executed when the opponent's weapon is held in the low line. The beat is performed in a horizontal direction from right to left.

Beats (kinds). Simple, change, circular, and grazing.

Bell guard. A small metal shield that protects the fencer's hand.

Blade seizure *(presa di ferro)*. An action on the blade opposed to the antagonist's weapon in line performed by first engaging the hostile steel and then adding the thrust or feint.

Botta. In Italian fencing terminology the thrust is called both *la botta* and *il colpo*.

Cappotto. An old term employed when one of two fencers is hit repeatedly without ever touching his adversary.

Cavatione (see disengagement). The old Italian spelling of *cavazione* or disengagement. Marcelli (1686) states that there are four kinds of disengagements: 1) the half disengagement *(mezza cavatione)*, in which the point is disengaged under the opposing steel, but does not pass completely around it to the other side (e.g., from the opponent's engagement in the outside high line the point is directed in a half semicircle to the outside low line or flank rather than completing the semicircle by continuing around to the inside high line); 2) the disengagement *(cavatione)*, in which the point is disengaged from one side of the opposing steel to the other (e.g., from the antagonist's engagement in the outside high line the point makes a complete semicircle and is aimed at the inside high line); 3) the counter-disengagement *(contracavatione)*, in which the point follows the opposing steel, as the adversary frees his blade, and returns to the original line of engagement (e.g., from one's own engagement in the outside high line the point makes a complete circle and is directed to the outside high line); and 4) the redisengagement (*ricavatione*), in which the counter-disengagement is opposed with an additional disengagement (e.g., from the opponent's engagement in the outside high line, the point is disengaged to the inside high line, and as the counter-disengagement is set in motion, a second disengagement is aimed at the inside high line).

Cavazione angolata (see cut-over). Mentioned already by Capo Ferro (1610), who states that the disengagement can be made both over and under the enemy's sword.

Ceding or yielding parries. Used in opposition to gliding actions in the low lines. There are two ceding parries in foil and épée fencing: the ceding parry of third, and the ceding parry of fourth. The ceding parry of third is employed against the glide in first and the internal flanconade; the ceding parry of fourth, in opposition to the glide in second, flanconade in second, and flanconade in fourth. There are also two ceding parries in sabre fencing: the ceding parry of first, and the ceding parry of fourth. These are used respectively, in opposition to the glide in third, and the glide in second.

Change beat. Made from one's own or the adversary's engagement by carrying the point over or under the opposing steel, and striking it on the opposite side.

Changes of engagement. Used to shift from one engagement to another. These movements are accomplished by passing the point over or under the opposing steel and carrying it to an opposite line of engagement. If the engagement is in the low line, the point passes over the hostile blade; if it is in the high line, it passes under.

Circular beat. Executed in precisely the same manner as a circular parry: the hand remains fixed in its position of invitation or engagement, while the point, set in motion by the fingers and wrist, describes a tight, complete circle around the opponent's extended blade, beating it in the direction of the invitation or engagement.

Circular cut. Made in one movement and reaches the target via a circular route.

Circular parry (also see counter-parry). A defensive blade movement in which the point describes a tight, complete circle around the incoming steel, intercepting and transferring it to the opposite line. At the completion of the action the point is in exactly the same position it was before the parry was performed.

Compound attacks. Offensive actions consisting of two or more blade movements. According to Italian fencing theory, compound attacks may be divided into three groups: feints, actions on the blade, and renewed attacks.

Compound ripostes. Ripostes consisting of two or more blade motions; their function is to elude one or more counterparries, that is, parries opposed to the riposte.

Contraries. Counteractions.

Contracavare (see contro-cavazione). The old Italian expression to counter-disengage.

Contro-cavazione. Florio (1844), following the oldest Italian tradition, states that the contro-cavazione is a circle made in the same direction as that of the antagonist, but he prefers to call this action a concavazione. Pessina and Pignotti (1970) designate a feint by disengagement and deceive (finta di cavazione circolata) a controcavazione.

Conventional exercises. Pre-established actions accomplished by two fencers alternately assuming the role of attacker and defender. The purpose of the exercises is to perfect the various offensive and defensive movements studied in the lesson, and to develop, through practice, a sense of fencing measure and time.

Counter-cut. A third of the back edge of the sabre blade, beginning at the tip and extending to the grooves.

Counter-disengagement (see contro-cavazione). An action in time used in opposition to the adversary who repeatedly frees his blade from engagement, or disengages in time to avoid contact.

Counter-parry (see circular parry).

Counterparry riposte. The parry and riposte that follow the initial parry and riposte; in other words, after the attack has been parried the riposte may be opposed with the counterparry riposte.

Countertime. A movement used in opposition to counterattacks. It is a simulated attack designed to provoke the opponent's counterthrust, thus exposing him to a parry and riposte, or to the counterattack into the counterattack.

Cut. The thin edge of the sabre blade that begins at the point and comprises about two-thirds of the blade.

Cut-over. A disengagement over the blade; it is an indirect attack executed in one movement, and may be used when the antagonist engages in third or fourth. It can be directed to the inside and outside high lines, and to the outside low line.

Deceive. The counter-disengagement preceded by a feint. The two terms, "counter-disengagement" and "deceive," are interchangeable in English fencing terminology.

Defense. Blade motions that deviate the adversary's point before it reaches the target, or foot movements that remove the body from the range of attack. The first of these is designated the defense of steel, the second, the defense of measure.

Degrees or strength of the blade. Division of the blade into three equal sections: strong, medium, and weak. The strong is the third closest to the bell guard, the medium is the middle third, and the weak is the third nearest the point.

Demi-volte (see inquartata). Angelo (1787) defines the demi-volte as the half round, or bounding turn of the body.

Descending cut (see *fendente*). A cut made in one motion that reaches the target by passing over the point of the opposing steel. From the opponent's engagement in third and fourth the hand is rotated to third position, elbow flexed, and the point passed over the hostile blade; the arm is extended, and a vertical cut delivered to the top of the head.

Direct cut. A cut made in one motion that reaches the target via the shortest route. There are direct cuts to the head, right cheek, left cheek, chest, abdomen, and flank. Cuts to the head, right cheek, and flank are pushed forward across the target in a slicing action. Cuts to the left cheek, chest, and abdomen are pulled back across the target.

Direct point thrust. An action, without blade contact, in which the point of the sabre follows a straight line to the exposed target; it is a direct attack in one movement, and may be used in opposition to the antagonist's invitations. During execution of the direct point thrust the arm and blade form an obtuse angle, so that the external arm is well protected.

Disarmaments. Violent attacks on the opposing steel to disarm the adversary, or to make him lose control of his weapon, so that he is no longer able to defend himself. There are three disarmaments, one vertical; and two spiral, one to the left, and one to the right.

Disengagement. An action in foil and épée in which the blade, with a spiral motion of the point, is detached from the opponent's engagement, and directed to the exposed target; it is an indirect attack in one movement, and may be used when the antagonist engages blades.

Disengagement with the point. An action in sabre in which the blade, with a spiral motion of the point, is detached from the adversary's engagement, and directed to the exposed target; it is an indirect attack in one movement, and may be employed when the opponent engages blades.

Disordinata. The Italian fencing term for multiple feints.

Dominating the blade (*dominare o guadagnare i gradi*). Placing the strong of one's own blade on the weak of the antagonist's steel.

Double changes of engagement. The adversary's steel is carried to an opposite line, and then back again to the original line of engagement. In foil and épée double changes may be effected from first to second to first, second to first to second, third to fourth to third, and fourth to third to fourth. Double changes of engagement are designated by the line of engagement in which they begin and end.

Double feint. Eludes two parries; it is employed in opposition to the invitation and engagement. Each feint is named after its initial movement: we therefore speak of the double feint direct, double feint by disengagement, and double feint by glide. When the double feint is coordinated with an advance, the two feints are completed with the step forward. The first feint should coincide with the motion of the right foot, the second with the movement of the left foot, and the final thrust with the lunge.

Dritto filo. The old Italian term for the cutting edge of the sword.

Engagement. A contact invitation in which the opposing steel is dominated and deviated from the line of offense. There are four engagements in foil and épée: first, second, third, and fourth. In these the hand and weapon assume exactly the same position they did in invitations. Engagements are effected with the strong against the weak, if taken at correct or lunging distance; and with the medium against the weak, if made from out of distance. In sabre there are five engagements: first, second, third, fourth, and fifth. In modern sabre fencing, engagements are generally made only in second and third.

Envelopments. Movements that encircle the opposing steel, so that the blade, in continous motion and without a loss of contact, returns to the original line of engagement. Envelopments in foil and épée may be accomplished in all lines, and are designated by the line of engagement in which they begin and end.

Expulsions. Powerful sliding beats in which the strong of the attacking weapon is forced along the opposing steel, expelling it from its position in engagement or line. Expulsions can be effected in any of the four lines, but they are most commonly used in third and fourth.

External flanconade. A glide in foil and épée to the adversary's flank, with the hand in fourth position, and opposition to the inside.

False beat. When the opponent has engaged blades and a beat is executed.

Falso filo. The old Italian designation for the false edge of the sword.

Feint in time. A movement opposed to actions in countertime. It is a feigned arrest or disengagement in time intended to provoke the antagonist's action in countertime, so that this may be opposed with a disengagement or deceive in time.

Feints. Simulated thrusts or menaces that resemble so closely a genuine assault that the adversary is forced to parry. In contrast to a real attack, feints do not end in a lunge or running attack.

Fendente **(see descending cut).** The Italian term for a cut-over or descending cut in sabre.

Ferire. The old Italian term for attacking or wounding.

Ferire à piede fermo **(see lunge).** According to Fabris (1606), means to deliver the thrust by advancing the right foot.

Ferro. In Italian simply means "iron," but in fencing terminology it signifies "sword or blade," as in the expression, *deviare il ferro dalla linea*, that is, "to deviate the blade from the line."

Filo **(see glide).** Italian for the edge of the blade.

Filo sottomesso **(see forced glide).**

First intention. A given movement is executed with the intent of reaching the target directly through the action itself.

First position. The posture assumed by the fencer with his body and weapon before the salute and during periods of rest. In first position the body is held erect, head up, eyes fixed on the opponent, shoulders down and level, legs together, feet at right angles, heels touching, and right toe pointing at the antagonist; the armed right hand is placed against the body, a little below the belt, with the blade directed diagonally toward the ground, as though ready to be drawn from its sheath, while the left hand rests on the hip, fingers in front, and thumb behind.

Flanconade in fourth (see external flanconade).

Flanconade in second. The transport to second (from engagement in fourth) and glide to the outside low line.

Flanconades. In the Italian school there are three flanconades: the flanconade in fourth or external flanconade, which is executed with one blade motion, and the internal flanconade, and flanconade in second, which are performed with two blade movements.

Forced glide. A glide in opposition to the adversary's imperfect or weak engagement. Its purpose is to regain opposition.

Forconare. Bending the arm, and with the hand low, thrusting upward. Enrichetti (1871) says that this is an action used by inexpert fencers who do not know how to execute the straight thrust correctly.

Frecciata (see running attack). The Italian term for the running attack.

Fundamental elements of fencing. Time, velocity, and measure.

Gaining on the lunge. A movement in which the left foot is drawn forward until the left heel touches the right heel followed immediately by a lunge. The ground covered may be equal to, or even greater, than that obtained by means of the advance lunge.

Glide (see filo). A foil and épée action in which the blade, with opposition, slides along the opposing steel to the exposed target; it is an attack in one movement that may be used when the opponent's blade is engaged.

Glide with the point. A sabre action analogous to the glide in foil and épée.

Grazing beat. A sliding beat in which the point is withdrawn, and the line changed by passing over the opposing steel.

Grip. A hollow wooden or plastic handle through which the tang of the blade passes.

Grooves. Channels that run the length of the sabre blade, commencing a third of the way back from the tip, and terminating at the heel.

Guard position. The position taken by the fencer with his body and weapon to be ready for the offense, defense, or counteroffense.

Hand positions. In foil fencing there are six hand positions. Four of these are designated principal positions, and two, intermediate positions. The principal positions are first, second, third, and fourth; and the intermediate positions, second in third, and third in fourth. With the weapon in hand, the positions are obtained by rotating the hand one quarter turn for the principal positions, and one eighth turn for the intermediate positions. And in sabre fencing there are seven hand positions. Four of these are termed principal positions, and three, intermediate positions. The principal positions are first, second, third, and fourth; and the intermediate positions, first in second, second in third, and third in fourth. Again, with the weapon in hand, positions are effected by rotating the hand one quarter turn for the principal positions, and one eighth turn for the intermediate positions.

Hand positions for parries. In the foil and épée parry of first or half-circle the hand is in third in fourth position; in the parry of second the hand is in fourth or second position; in the parry of third the hand is in fourth or second in third position; and in the parry of fourth the hand is in third in fourth position. And in the sabre parry of first the hand is in first position; in the parry of second the hand is in first in second position; in the parry of third the hand is in second in third position; in the parry of fourth the hand is in third in fourth position; and in the parries of fifth and sixth the hand is in first position.

Imbroccata. A counterattack against gliding attacks and ripostes that end in the outside low line, that is, the external flanconade, and the flanconade in second. The action is effected from the guard position with the hand in fourth or second position. As the antagonist is in the act of completing his attack or riposte, a counterthrust, with opposition to the right, is directed along the incoming steel to the outside low line.

In-fighting. Scoring a touch at close range before the director calls a halt to the action. In this mode of combat the fencer generally maintains a low guard position and concentrates on offensive actions.

Initiative for the attack. Attacks may be executed on one's own initiative, or on the adversary's. In the first instance it is one's own selection of time that determines the moment of the assault; in the second, it is the opponent's movement of his weapon that prompts the attack.

Inquartata. A counterattack in opposition to both simple and compound attacks terminating in the inside high line. In foil and épée, from an invitation or engagement in third, the attack with a straight thrust or disengagement to the inside high line is opposed with the counterthrust to the same line, hand in fourth position, opposition to the left, left leg extended backward, as in a lunge, and left foot shifted approximately forty-five degrees to the right of the line of direction. In opposition to a compound attack, the counterattack follows a parry. And in sabre, from an invitation or engagement in third, the attack with a point thrust to the inside chest, or cut to the head, or left cheek, is opposed with a point thrust to the chest or a cut to the left cheek, while simultaneously extending the left leg, and shifting the left foot to the right of the line of direction.

Intagliata. Enrichetti (1871) describes the *intagliata* as the inverse of the inquartata. In opposition to the antagonist's thrust to the outside high line, the left foot remains fixed on the line of direction, and the right foot is carried to the left of the line of direction, and the thrust delivered to the adversary's flank.

Internal flanconade. The transport to first (from engagement in third) and glide to the inside low line.

Invitations. Positions taken with the weapon, exposing a specific line, to induce the opponent to attack. There are four invitations in foil and épée: first, second, third, and fourth. The invitation in first uncovers the flank or outside low line; the invitation in second, the chest or high line; the invitation in third, the chest or inside high line; and the invitation in fourth, the chest or outside high line. And there are five invitations in sabre: first, second, third, fourth, and fifth. The invitation in first exposes the flank; the invitation in second, the right or outside cheek; the invitation in third, the abdomen and left or inside cheek; the invitation in fourth, the right or outside cheek; and the invitation in fifth, the flank and abdomen.

Jump lunge (see *balestra*).

Knuckle guard or bow. The curved metal portion of the sabre bell guard which protects the fencer from cuts to the hand.

Line of direction. The imaginary line connecting two fencers, beginning at the left heel of one, passing through the axis of his right foot, and continuing until it encounters the same points in his antagonist's feet. This is the normal route the feet must travel in the lesson, in exercise, and in combat.

Line of offense. When the point of the weapon, with the arm naturally extended, menaces some part of the adversary's target.

Lines. To describe the lines of attack in foil and épée the opponent's body is divided into four quarters: inside, outside, high, and low. When the antagonist is in the correct guard position all assaults will pass to the right or left of his sword arm, or above or below it. An attack to the right of the arm is said to enter the outside line; to the left of the arm, the inside line; above the arm, the high line; and below the arm, the low line.

Lunge. The position the fencer assumes with his body at the end of an offensive action executed from the guard. The passage from guard to lunge must be effected in a single movement.

Mandritto. The old Italian term for cuts delivered from the right side. Marcelli (1686) says that the *mandritto fendente* is a vertical cut that travels from the top of the adversary's head downward; that the *mandritto obliquo* or *squalembro* is a circular cut that passes diagonally from the opponent's left shoulder downward to the left; that the *mandritto tondo* is a circular cut that moves horizontally from the antagonist's left flank to his right flank; and that the *mandritto* to the right leg travels diagonally downward from right to left.

Measure. The distance that separates two fencers placed on guard. There are three measures: out of distance, correct distance, and close distance. In foil from out of distance the adversary's chest can be touched by taking a step forward and lunging; from correct distance it can be hit by lunging; and from close distance it can be reached without lunging. In sabre and épée from out of distance the opponent's trunk can be touched by taking a step forward and lunging, and his arm by lunging directly; from correct distance his torso can be hit by lunging, and his arm by remaining in the guard position; and from close distance his trunk or arm can be reached without lunging.

Mezzo-cerchio. The old Italian parry of half-circle now called first. However, it should be noted that many contemporary Italian masters still use the term *mezzocerchio*.

Molinello (see circular cut). The Italian name for the circular cut.

Molinello montante (see ascending circular cut). The Italian term for the ascending circular cut.

Montante. Marcelli (1686) tells us that an ascending cut that travels at a slight angle diagonally upward from right to left is designated *montante*.

Nut. A metal fastening device that holds the threaded end of the tang on a sabre blade.

Opposition. With the thrust the hand is shifted progressively to the right or left, depending upon the line of entry. These displacements of the hand are called oppositions, and their function is to provide protection by closing the line.

Parry. Defensive movement of the blade that deflects the incoming steel. Parries can be simple, circular, half circular, or ceding. Simple, circular, and half circular parries may be executed either as opposition or beating motions; ceding parries can only be performed through opposition. In the one instance the antagonist's steel is deviated merely by closing the line; in the other it is deflected by striking it to one side.

Parts of the weapon. The foil is divided into two principal parts: the guard and the blade. The Italian guard is composed of six elements: bell guard, cushion, crossbar, arches, grip, and pommel. And the blade consists of three elements: button, ricasso, and tang. The épée is also divided into two major parts: the guard and the blade. The Italian guard, however, has only five elements: bell guard, cushion, crossbar, grip, and pommel. Again, the blade is comprised of three elements: button, ricasso, and tang. And like the foil and épée, the sabre is divided into two main parts: the guard, and the blade. The guard is composed of four elements: guard, cushion, grip, and nut. And the blade consists of seven elements: blunted end, counter-cut, back, cut, grooves, heel, and tang.

Passata sotto. A counterattack against both simple and compound attacks ending in the outside high line. In foil and épée, from an invitation or engagement in second or fourth, the attack with a straight thrust or disengagement to the high line, or outside high line, is opposed with the counterthrust to the low line, hand in second position, opposition to the right, left leg extended along the line of direction, and body lowered, with the chest close to the right thigh, and left hand resting on the floor near the right foot. Against a compound attack, the counterattack follows a parry.

Placement of the weapon. The position the fencer on guard adopts with his armed hand in relation to his adversary. There are three placements of the weapon: invitation, engagement, and blade in line.

Pommel. A cylindrical counterbalance that receives the threaded end of the tang on a foil or épée blade.

Pressure. A gradual application of force with the strong or medium of the blade against the opponent's weak to deviate it from its position in line. Like a beat, the pressure is identified by the line in which it encounters the opposing steel: first or half-circle, second, third, and fourth.

Probing actions. Feigned attacks that test the antagonist's defensive and counteroffensive responses. His reactions to simulated assaults with feints and beats will indicate whether he defends himself with simple or circular parries, or, instead, has a tendency to counterattack.

Punta. The old Italian word for a point thrust.

Raddoppio (see gaining on the lunge).

Reassemblement (see arrest with reassemblement and *riunita*).

Renewed attacks *(ripigliata* or *ripresa di attacco)*. Second offensive actions launched against an adversary who, having parried the initial assault, either hesitates or fails to respond. The second thrust is executed in opposition to the placement of the opponent's weapon at the completion of the parry. Depending upon fencing measure, renewed attacks may be effected from the lunge, with a second lunge, or with a step forward and lunge. When the second thrust is executed from the lunge it is called a replacement.

Retreat. A step backward to increase measure between oneself and the adversary. This motion is also called breaking ground.

Ricasso. A portion of the foil and épée blade between the bell guard and the crossbar.

Riposte. The thrust delivered immediately after the antagonist's attack has been parried. Ripostes may be simple or compound. Opposition parries can be followed by ripostes in which the blade is detached (straight thrust), or kept in contact (glide).

Riunita (see arrest with reassemblement).

Riverso. An old Italian term designating cuts delivered from the left side. Marcelli (1686) observes that the *riverso fendente* is a vertical cut that travels from the adversary's head downward, that the *riverso obliquo* or *squalembro* is a circular cut that passes diagonally from the opponent's right shoulder downward to the right, and that the *riverso* to the right leg moves diagonally downward from left to right.

Roverso or *rovescio* (see *riverso*).

Rubare la misura (see stealing fencing measure).

Running attack. A rapid advance with the left foot passing the right.

Salute. A traditional act of courtesy directed to the antagonist and spectators, and must always be observed at the beginning and end of the lesson and combat.

Sbasso (see passata sotto). Enrichetti (1871) indicates that *sbasso* is another name for passata sotto.

Scandaglio (see probing actions).

Second intention. A given movement performed with the express purpose of provoking defensive responses against which counteractions can be applied. Second intention is especially useful in opposition to the adversary who, following a particular parry, always ripostes in the same line. The distinction between second intention and countertime is that second intention prompts a parry and riposte which is opposed with the counterparry and riposte, while countertime provokes a counterattack which is countered with the parry and riposte, or with another counterattack.

Sforzi (see expulsions).

Simple attacks. Offensive actions consisting of a single blade movement. In foil fencing there are four simple attacks: the straight thrust, the disengagement, the glide and flanconade in fourth, and the cut-over. In sabre fencing simple attacks can be accomplished with the point, the cut, and the counter-cut. Point thrusts may be direct, by disengagement, and by glide; and cuts may be direct, circular, and descending. In épée fencing there are four simple attacks: the straight thrust, the disengagement, the glide, and the angulation.

Simple beat. A beat effected by moving the blade the shortest distance necessary to encounter the opposing steel. It may be executed from an invitation or engagement; the engagement can be one's own, or the opponent's.

Simple parries. Protective displacements of the blade that cover exposed target areas by traveling the shortest route from one invitation or engagement to another. In foil and épée fencing there are four simple parries, each defending a certain portion or portions of the valid target: thus, the parry of first or half-circle protects the inside high and low lines, the parry of second, the outside low line, the parry of third, the outside high line, and the parry of fourth, the inside high line. And in sabre fencing there are six simple parries, each covering certain parts of the valid target: thus, the parry of first protects the left cheek, inside chest, abdomen, and internal arm; the parry of second, the flank, and bottom of arm; the parry of third, the right cheek, outside chest, flank, and external arm; the parry of fourth, the left cheek, inside chest, abdomen, and internal arm; the parry of fifth, the head, and top of arm; and the parry of sixth, the head, and top of arm. In the past there were also parries of low third and low fourth. These are nothing more than lowered parries of third and fourth which serve as alternate parries for second and first to defend, respectively, the flank and abdomen.

Simple ripostes. Ripostes in one movement.

Smarra. The heavy foil used in the past by Italian fencers when taking a lesson.

Sottobotta (see passata sotto). Marcelli (1686) uses the word *sottobotta* for the action we know today as the passata sotto.

Sottomano. Marcelli (1686) indicates that an ascending cut that passes at a slight angle diagonally upward from left to right is designated *sottomano*.

Spada nera. The old Italian name for the practice rapier.

Spade di marra. Practice rapiers were also known as *spade di marra*.

Stealing fencing measure. Closing distance on the antagonist without his knowing it.

Stoccata. The old Italian word for a thrust.

Stoccata in tempo. Marcelli (1686) says that the feint can be opposed with the arrest, which he calls *stoccata in tempo*, known in modern Italian fencing terminology as the *colpo d'arresto*.

Stoccata replicata (see renewed attack). Marcelli (1686) notes that if the adversary opposes the attack with a wide parry, a disengagement can be directed from the lunge to the opponent's open target on the opposite side.

Straight thrust. An action, without blade contact, in which the point of the foil and épée follows a straight line to the exposed target; it is a direct attack in one movement, and may be used when the antagonist makes an invitation, or from one's own invitation or engagement.

Tang. A part of the foil, épée, or sabre blade that passes through the grip and screws into the pommel or nut.

Thrust in low fourth. In the Italian school the thrust in low fourth (*quarta bassa*) is an auxiliary action. It is a simple attack executed in one motion against the adversary who exposes his low line by habitually keeping his hand high in the invitation, engagement, or parry of fourth. Instead of directing the thrust to the outside high line, it is aimed at the low line, with the hand in fourth position.

Time. The favorable moment at which an offensive action will catch the opponent off guard.

Time thrust. A counterattack that precedes the final movement of the attack. It is directed in the same line as the assault, with exactly enough opposition to deviate the incoming steel.

Toccate di spada. Marcelli (1686) calls beats *toccate di spada*.

Tocco. Masiello (1887) employs the word *tocco* for beat.

Traccheggio (see actions of concealment).

Tramazzone. An old Italian word for a circular cut to the antagonist's torso. Marcelli (1686) notes that it is executed with wrist action.

Transports. The opposing steel is carried, strong against weak, without a break in blade contact, from one line of engagement to another. In foil and épée, transports may be executed from first to third and vice versa, or from second to fourth and vice versa. And in sabre they may be performed from first to third and vice versa, from second to fourth and vice versa, or from third to fifth.

Triple feint. Eludes three parries; it is opposed to the invitation and engagement. The feints may be coordinated with an advance. Pini (1903) says that the first feint is made with the motion of the right foot, the second with the movement of the left foot, the third from immobility, and the final thrust with the lunge.

Velocity. The minimum time necessary to complete an offensive, defensive, or counteroffensive movement.

Warde (see guard position and parry). In Di Grassi his true Arte of Defence (1594), used to designate a guard or parry position.

SELECT BIBLIOGRAPHY

GENERAL

Arsène Vigeant, *La bibliographie de l'escrime ancienne et moderne* (Paris, 1882).

Emile Mérignac, *Histoire de l'escrime dans tous les temps et dans tous les pays* (Paris, 1883).

Jacopo Gelli, *Bibliografia generale della scherma* (Firenze, 1890).

Egerton Castle, *Schools and Masters of Fence* (London, 1892).

Carl Thimm, *A Complete Bibliography of Fencing and Duelling* (London, 1896).

Jacopo Gelli, *L'arte dell'armi in Italia* (Bergamo, 1906).

Eduardo De Simone, *La scuola magistrale militare di scherma* (Roma, 1921).

Cravache, *I trent'anni di Agesilao Greco* (Roma, 1926).

Antonino Tarsia in Curia, *Lotte e vittorie d'armi di Agesilao Greco* (Napoli, 1936).

Roma Ferralasco Nadi, *Nedo Nadi l'alfiere dello sport delle tre armi nel mondo* (Genova, 1969).

Lauriano Gonzales, *"Greco" uomini e maestri d'armi* (Roma, 1983).

Aldo Santini, *Nedo Nadi* (Livorno, 1989).

Pierre Lacaze, *En garde: du duel à l'escrime* (Paris, 1991).

Nick Evangelista, *The Encyclopedia of the Sword* (London, 1995).

Aldo Nadi, *The Living Sword: A Fencer's Autobiography* (Sunrise, 1995).

Antonio Spallino, *Una frase d'armi* (Milano, 1997).

THEORY AND PRACTICE

Achille Marozzo, *Opera nova* (Venetia, 1536).

Giacomo Di Grassi, *Ragione di addoprar sicuramente l'arme si da offesa come da difesa* (Venetia, 1570).

Angelo Viggiani, *Lo schermo* (Vinetia, 1575).

Salvator Fabris, *Scienza e pratica d'arme* (Copenhaven, 1606).

Nicoletto Giganti, *Scola e ovvero teatro* (Venetia, 1606).

Ridolfo Capo Ferro, *Gran simulacro dell'arte e dell'uso della scherma* (Siena, 1610).

Francesco Alfieri, *La scherma* (Padova, 1640).

Francesco Marcelli, *Regole della scherma* (Roma, 1686).

Alessandro Di Marco, *Ragionamenti accademici intorno all'arte della scherma* (Napoli, 1758).

Rosaroll Scorza e Pietro Grisetti, *La scienza della scherma* (Milano, 1803)

Blasco Florio, *La scienza della scherma* (Catania, 1844).

Alberto Marchionni, *Trattato di scherma sopra un nuovo sistema di giuoco misto di scuola italiana e francese* (Firenze, 1847).

Giuseppe Radaelli, *Istruzione pel maneggio della sciabola* (Firenze, 1868).

Vittorio Lambertini, *Trattato di scherma* (Bologna, 1870).

Cesare Enrichetti, *Trattato elementare teorico-pratico di scherma* (Parma, 1871).

Giuseppe Radaelli, *Istruzione per la scherma di sciabola e di spada* (Milano, 1876).

Masaniello Parise, *Trattato teorico-pratico della scherma di spada e sciabola* (Roma, 1884).

Giordano Rossi, *Manuale teorico-pratico per la scherma di spada e sciabola* (Milano, 1885).

Ferdinando Masiello, *La scherma italiana di spada e di sciabola* (Firenze, 1887).

————, *La scherma di sciabola* (Firenze, 1893).

Luigi Barbasetti, *Das Säbelfechten* (Wien, 1899).

————, *Das Stoßfechten* (Wien, 1900).

————, *La scherma di spada* (Milano, 1902).

Ferdinando Masiello, *La scherma di fioretto* (Firenze, 1902).

————, *La scherma di sciabola* (Firenze, 1902).

Poggio Vannucchi, *I fondamenti della scherma italiana* (Bologna, n.d.).

Eugenio Pini, *Trattato pratico e teorico sulla scherma di spada* (Livorno, 1903).

Masaniello Parise, *Trattato teorico-pratico della scherma di spada e sciabola* (Torino-Roma, 1904).

Aurelio Greco, *La spada e la sua applicazione* (Roma, 1907).

Salvatore Pecoraro e Carlo Pessina, *La scherma di sciabola* (Roma, 1910).

Agesilao Greco, *La spada e la sua disciplina d'arte* (Roma, 1912).

Luigi Barbasetti, *L'escime à travers les siècles et ma méthode* (Paris, 1928).

Agesilao Greco, *La spada e la sua realtà* (Roma, 1930).

Luigi Barbasetti, *The Art of the Foil* (New York, 1932).

Michele Alajmo, *Come si diventa spadisti* (Rodi, 1936).

Luigi Barbasetti, *The Art of the Sabre and Épée* (New York, 1936).

Giorgio Rastelli, *La scherma* (Milano, 1942).

Aldo Nadi, *On Fencing* (New York, 1943).

Giulio Rusconi, *Elementi di scherma* (Firenze, 1948).

Edoardo Mangiarotti e Aldo Cerchiari, *La vera scherma* (Milano, 1966).

Giorgio Pessina e Ugo Pignotti, *Il fioretto* (Roma, 1970).

Giuseppe Mangiarotti, *La spada* (Milano, 1971).

Giorgio Pessina e Ugo Pignotti, *La sciabola* (Roma, 1972).

Arturo Volpini, *La sciabola: manuale practico* (Milano, 1975).

————, *La spada: manuale practico* (Milano, 1975).

Giuseppe Necchi, *La scherma di fioretto: tecnica e arte* (Milano, 1976).

Renzo Nostini, *Scherma di fioretto* (Roma, 1979).

————, *Die Kunst des Florettfechtens* (Berlin, 1982).

William Gaugler, *Fechten* (München, 1983).

————, *Fechten* (München, 1986)

————, *Fencing Everyone* (Winston-Salem, 1987).

Antonio Lomele, *La scherma col fioretto* (Bari, 1989).

William Gaugler, *La scienza della scherma* (Bologna, 1992).

Aldo Nadi, *On Fencing* (Sunrise, 1994).

Marcello e Giovanni Lodetti, *La scherma* (Milano, 1995).

Giancarlo Toran, *Introduzione alla tattica schermistica* (Roma, 1996).

INDEX